"*The Grieving Student* is an essential resou... provides crucial and factual information with anecdotal examples that will enable school personnel to support students facing mental, emotional, and bereavement or grief issues, which have been magnified during the COVID-19 pandemic."

—Vincent Giordano, M.S.Ed., SDA
New York City Department of Education, Executive Director,
Student Support Services (Retired)

"Unfortunately, all educators and health care providers are faced with the challenges of helping many young people cope with the death of a loved one. This guide is the best and most informative resource available to help teachers, administrators, and school mental health staff understand and support grieving students with practical, beneficial strategies."

—Roger P. Weissberg, Ph.D.
Distinguished Professor Emeritus of Psychology,
University of Illinois at Chicago;
Chief Knowledge Officer, Collaborative for Academic, Social, and
Emotional Learning (CASEL)

"Likely the most practical, accessible, and comprehensive resource for educators on grief and bereavement, *The Grieving Student* should be a fixture on the bookshelves of all school personnel."

—Eric Rossen, Ph.D., NCSP
Director, Professional Development and Standards,
National Association of School Psychologists

"This unparalleled book is a veritable gold mine of how-to interventions for all who encounter bereaved students. There is literally *no better* resource to explain to educators, student support personnel, and administrators how children understand and respond to death, as well as what specifically should be done to help them best cope. I cannot recommend this book highly enough!"

—Therese A. Rando, Ph.D., BCETS, BCBT
Author, *Coping With the Sudden Death of Your Loved One* and
Treatment of Complicated Mourning

To my daughters, Kim and Sara,
who taught me to respect the capacity of children
to understand even difficult issues
and the value of taking the effort to help them comprehend
and cope with challenges in their lives

And to teachers everywhere,
who have the unequaled privilege to play this critical role
in the lives of so many children

The Grieving Student

A Guide for Schools

Second Edition

by

David J. Schonfeld, M.D., FAAP
Director, National Center for School Crisis and Bereavement,
Children's Hospital Los Angeles
Professor of Clinical Pediatrics, Keck School of Medicine,
University of Southern California
Los Angeles

and

Marcia Quackenbush, M.S., MFT, MCHES
Advisor, National Center for School Crisis and Bereavement
Los Angeles, California

·P A U L·H·
BROOKES
PUBLISHING CO ®

Baltimore • London • Sydney

Paul H. Brookes Publishing Co.
Post Office Box 10624
Baltimore, Maryland 21285-0624
USA

www.brookespublishing.com

Typeset by Absolute Services Inc., Towson, Maryland.
Manufactured in the United States of America by
Sheridan Books, Chelsea, Michigan.

The information provided in this book is in no way meant to substitute for a medical or mental health practitioner's advice or expert opinion. Readers should consult a health or mental health professional if they are interested in more information. This book is sold without warranties of any kind, express or implied, and the publisher and authors disclaim any liability, loss, or damage caused by the contents of this book.

The individuals described in this book are composites or real people whose situations are masked and are based on the authors' experiences. In all instances, names and identifying details have been changed to protect confidentiality.

Library of Congress Cataloging-in-Publication Data

Names: Schonfeld, David J., 1959- author. | Quackenbush, Marcia, author.
Title: The grieving student : a guide for schools / by David J. Schonfeld
 and Marcia Quackenbush.
Other titles: Grieving student
Description: Second edition. | Baltimore : Paul H. Brookes Publishing Co.,
 2021. | Includes bibliographical references and index.
Identifiers: LCCN 2020048280 (print) | LCCN 2020048281 (ebook) | ISBN
 9781681254579 (paperback) | ISBN 9781681254586 (pdf) | ISBN
 9781681254593 (epub)
Subjects: LCSH: Grief in adolescence. | Grief in children. |
 Teacher-student relationships.
Classification: LCC BF724.3.G73 S37 2021 (print) | LCC BF724.3.G73
 (ebook) | DDC 155.4/124--dc23
LC record available at https://lccn.loc.gov/2020048280
LC ebook record available at https://lccn.loc.gov/2020048281

British Library Cataloguing in Publication data are available from the British Library.

2026   2025   2024   2023   2022   2021

10   9   8   7   6   5   4   3   2   1

Contents

About the Downloads

The Grieving Student: A Guide for Schools, Second Edition offers online companion materials to supplement and expand the knowledge and strategies provided in this text. All purchasers of the book may access, download, and print the Study Guide for professional and/or educational purposes.

To access the materials that come with this book:

1. Go to the Brookes Publishing Download Hub: http://downloads.brookespublishing.com.
2. Register to create an account or log in with an existing account.
3. Redeem the case-sensitive code **wEjLhDozh** to access locked materials.

The Study Guide was created to help you process and then put into action the information provided throughout this book to better support grieving students. It has been designed so you can print the study guide and use the space provided to answer personal reflection prompts and other questions to check your knowledge or take notes during group discussion.

About the Authors

David J. Schonfeld, M.D., FAAP, Director of the National Center for School Crisis and Bereavement (NCSCB) at Children's Hospital Los Angeles and Professor of Clinical Pediatrics at Keck School of Medicine of the University of Southern California, has provided consultation, technical assistance, and training in the areas of pediatric bereavement and school crisis preparedness and response for more than 3 decades. He has provided more than 1,000 presentations on the topics of crisis and loss, including presentations at national and international meetings throughout the United States and abroad (including Europe, the United Kingdom, Asia, the Middle East, Scandinavia, Latin America, and Africa). In 1991, Dr. Schonfeld established the School Crisis Response Program at Yale University School of Medicine, where he provided training to tens of thousands of school-based personnel throughout the country and technical assistance in hundreds of school crisis events. Dr. Schonfeld has consulted with schools during the aftermath of numerous school and national crisis events. From 2001 to 2004, he consulted with the New York City Department of Education and coordinated training for school crisis teams in the wake of the September 11, 2001, terrorist attacks and provided training to more than 1,000 district- and school-level crisis teams within the system. In 2005, Dr. Schonfeld was awarded funding by the September 11th Children's Fund and the National Philanthropic Trust to establish the NCSCB. Dr. Schonfeld has worked with schools and communities coping with large-scale natural disasters, including flooding from hurricanes Maria in San Juan, Sandy in New York and New Jersey, Katrina in New Orleans, and Ike in Galveston, Texas; tornadoes in Joplin, Missouri, and Alabama; wildfires in Butte County, California, Sonoma County, California, and the Great Smoky Mountains in Sevierville, Tennessee; and the 2008 earthquake in Sichuan, China. He has assisted schools and communities as they recover from episodes of violence, including school and community shootings in Santa Clarita, California; Parkland, Florida; Newtown, Connecticut; Benton, Kentucky; Las Vegas, Nevada; Thousand Oaks, California; Spokane, Washington; Marysville, Washington; Osaka, Japan; Corning, California; Aurora, Colorado; Platte Canyon, Colorado; Chardon, Ohio; and Townville, South Carolina. Dr. Schonfeld also served as a member of the National Commission on Children and Disasters and the Sandy Hook Advisory Commission; he is a member of the

National Biodefense Science Board and the Executive Committee of the American Academy of Pediatrics Council on Children and Disasters. He is a developmental-behavioral pediatrician and a former president of the Society for Developmental and Behavioral Pediatrics. Dr. Schonfeld has authored more than 150 scholarly articles, book chapters, and books and has conducted school-based research (funded by the National Institute of Child Health and Human Development, the National Institute of Mental Health, the National Institute on Drug Abuse, the Maternal and Child Health Bureau, William T. Grant Foundation, and other foundations) involving children's understanding of and adjustment to serious illness and death and school-based interventions to promote adjustment and risk prevention.

Marcia Quackenbush, M.S., MFT, MCHES, is a licensed family therapist and certified Master Health Education Specialist. She has more than 20 years of clinical mental health experience, much of which has been focused on children, adolescents, and families of people living with life-changing conditions or people coping with terminal illness in themselves or family members. Ms. Quackenbush has written extensively in the health education field, publishing numerous articles, curricula, and books.

About the National Center for School Crisis and Bereavement

The NCSCB was founded in 2005 with generous support from the September 11th Children's Fund and the National Philanthropic Trust and currently receives generous support from the New York Life Foundation. The Center has provided support to schools and communities across the country and abroad. The goals of the NCSCB are to promote an appreciation of the role schools can serve to support students, staff, and families at times of crisis and loss; to link efforts to provide trauma-related and bereavement support services within school settings; to collaborate with professional organizations, governmental and nongovernmental agencies, and community groups to further these goals; and to serve as a resource for information, training materials, consultation, and technical assistance. Learn more at www.schoolcrisiscenter.org.

Foreword

I have spent more than 16 years working in America's urban school districts. For almost half of that time, I served in a variety of roles in the Chicago Public Schools and am now in my ninth year as superintendent of Broward County Public Schools, Florida—the nation's sixth largest school district. When I was in Chicago, gang activity and shootings occurred far too often in high-poverty ZIP codes that have been historically deprived of investment and opportunity. Although we had no in-school shootings, we witnessed more than 300 students shot each year outside of school within certain neighborhoods. In any given year, we may have seen as many as 30 to 40 of our kids under the age of 18 die from gun violence.

In Broward County, we've had a host of other crises affecting our schools, from hurricanes to the global COVID-19 pandemic. In 2018, we also suffered the tragic shooting at Marjory Stoneman Douglas High School in Parkland, Florida. Seventeen people were killed and another 17 injured. This created an indescribable level of pain, grief, and heartache that still echoes through our community today.

Arne Duncan (who later became U.S. Secretary of Education) was one of my mentors in Chicago. Watching him taught me that leadership is not about what you do when things are going well. It's about how you respond, stay strong, and lead during times of challenge and crisis. Always do the right thing even when it's not popular or politically expedient.

The Parkland shooting certainly gave me the ultimate challenge to put these convictions to the test. As painful and difficult as it has been, I know that true leaders don't walk away from such a crisis. So, I have worked tirelessly with district staff to provide support and hope in the midst of fear and anger—to find our way forward and heal as much as possible, while realizing that there will always be broken pieces that can never be mended.

There is something else noticeable about the Parkland tragedy. Although the nation gave tremendous attention and focus to the pain and grief of Parkland, it doesn't seem to give the same level of attention and weight to similar kinds of losses that are just as tragic when they happen in communities of color in places like Chicago, Detroit, Baltimore, and elsewhere—home to our most vulnerable and marginalized populations. Places where it seems the country has normalized violence and hopelessness.

As Dr. Schonfeld and Ms. Quackenbush affirm in their well-researched book, I can assure you that wherever your community is and whoever your students are, there are some who have experienced the death of a loved one or some other traumatic event. Wherever you have community violence, domestic violence, parents divorcing, poverty and homelessness, or social media bullying, you will have grieving students in your schools.

My own family came to this country from Jamaica when I was six. We settled in Poughkeepsie, New York, in a working-class neighborhood of apartments and duplexes. Many of these units were occupied by immigrant families like ours. We lived a quiet and basic life. My parents were hard-working, blue-collar, and prayerful people who taught us to live by the Golden Rule: "Do unto others as you would have them do unto you."

One summer afternoon when I was eight, my mother was on the porch reading her Bible as she always did. I was moving about the house with my brother and sister. It was a beautiful, peaceful day. Then in a moment, a neighbor from one of the apartment units walked across the street carrying a shotgun. Suddenly he started shooting at us. I watched all of this unfold before me. My mother was shot in the face. She nearly died and was in the hospital for almost a month. When the police apprehended the man and asked him why he had done this, he told them he was tired of immigrants coming over here and taking away American jobs.

What I have taken away from that tragedy is how my parents dealt with it. They did not prolong this painful experience with us. Instead, they taught us the power of forgiveness in lifting the pain and burden of hate and anger. That gave me and my siblings the psychological freedom to focus on the future and pursue our hopes and dreams.

Over the years, I have grown to understand that there is no successful individual in history who hasn't gone through some sort of painful struggle to get to where they are. Success depends on our capacity to grow through our pain and disappointments, to become a stronger person, and to develop a greater sense of purpose in life.

Talking with students and educators about their own lives and challenges has shaped my perspective on public education. I am absolutely convinced that we must do more than prepare our students with the academic and technical skills that will allow them to contribute to our complex society. That's only half our job.

We must also give them "true life skills"—the social-emotional learning and mental health skills that are essential for anyone to succeed and become a good person and citizen of the world. Our young people need to learn how to face challenges, cope with stress, manage grief, and find healing and meaning after a traumatic experience. We must help them transcend hardship and use what they learn from these difficult experiences to become well-adjusted people who lean toward hope and love rather than fear and hate.

The majority of our nation's students are impacted by some form of adverse childhood experience. These students can learn, and learn well, but only when we address their emotional needs. Coping with issues such as death and bereavement is a vital part of this. Educators must acquire a solid foundation in supporting students who have experienced violence or the loss of a family member or friend. This is a fundamental step in preparing to work effectively with students from all backgrounds and in all communities.

The Grieving Student is an outstanding resource that will help educators and schools formulate real strategies to address student heartache and loss. It offers professional development opportunities for individuals, groups, and even an entire school or district. The guidance in this book has been helpful to Broward County educators at Marjory Stoneman Douglas and at other schools in our district.

I encourage you to read it and put its principles to work in your setting. I believe you will find it as valuable as we have. It may be the greatest gift you ever give to your children.

Robert W. Runcie
Superintendent, Broward County Schools

Preface

In 2019, my coauthor, Marcia Quackenbush, and I decided that it was time to update this book; we were glad that Brookes Publishing readily agreed. We had seen over the previous decade a growing interest among school professionals to understand more about how to support grieving students. This was in large part due to a number of high-visibility school shootings and large-scale natural disasters, including multiple massive wildfires in our home state of California. In response to a growing demand, I had already shifted my career to focus full time on the work of the National Center for School Crisis and Bereavement (NCSCB), which is now located at Children's Hospital Los Angeles.

In January 2020, Marcia and I started working on the second edition of this book. We had no idea of the impending COVID-19 pandemic and the global impact it would have. Just a few weeks later, our lives and work began to change profoundly. Travel restrictions were implemented by my own medical school and hospital in Los Angeles just hours before I was set to board my flight to return to Parkland, Florida, to provide ongoing consultation related to the 2018 shooting at Marjory Stoneman Douglas High School.

At that point, it was becoming clear that the COVID-19 pandemic could dramatically increase the number of grieving children in our nation. The lengthy school closures that quickly followed compromised, as never before, the ability of school professionals to support grieving children. The support educators and school mental health professionals would normally have provided face-to-face to grieving students disappeared. School districts, state departments of education, and school professional organizations stepped up and asked for more training and advice on how to support grieving students in newly configured remote education systems. While writing this preface, I had 10 training webinars scheduled for the next week.

Marcia and I wondered if we needed to dramatically change our book given the current pandemic. Should we be adding new chapters or sections? Did we need to change our recommendations in some way? As we worked quickly to complete the second edition, we realized that the practical strategies and approaches that were present in the first edition were still applicable, even during this unprecedented pandemic. We did make some adaptations and updates. But overall, we have found that what works for supporting grieving students in "normal" times remains the same in extraordinary times—although we sometimes need to be creative and provide that support remotely.

At the time of this writing, it's too early in the pandemic to know what the world and nation will be like when this second edition is released. Whatever may come, it's clear that this book is even more important now than when we published the first edition. While we hope that the pandemic will soon become a historical event, we recognize that there will always be grieving students. And educators can and should be a vital source of support for them, irrespective of the reason they are bereaved. If you are reading this now, chances are you already appreciate that. We thank you for making the effort to become better prepared for this critical role. Your students and their families will be thankful as well.

David J. Schonfeld, M.D.
May 18, 2020

Acknowledgments

The authors would like to acknowledge the generous support of the September 11th Children's Fund and the National Philanthropic Trust, which allowed for the establishment of the National Center for School Crisis and Bereavement (NCSCB) in 2005, as well as the substantial and congoing support of the New York Life Foundation (NYLF). The NYLF has provided the majority of the support for the work of the NCSCB; this book would likely not have been written without their financial and personal support and commitment.

Introduction

YES, THIS MATTERS

If you're reading this book, chances are you're an educator or someone else who works with children and young people. Like most other adults, you've probably experienced the death of a loved one at some point in your life—a friend; a classmate; or perhaps a parent, sibling, spouse, or other family member. You understand that these losses can have powerful and sometimes surprising effects and that the process of grieving takes time and patience.

Children also experience a range of significant losses. How common are these losses? They appear to be virtually universal. Before they reach adulthood, almost all children will experience the death of someone important to them. Approximately 5% will face the death of a parent by age 16 (Schonfeld & Demaria, 2016). Many will confront other deaths that affect them deeply—of siblings, friends, grandparents, beloved aunts or uncles, close family friends, or teachers. We all understand that the death of a parent is a profound loss for most children. It's important to recognize, however, that any of these deaths is likely to be difficult.

> ### We Are Talking About Children of All Ages
>
> In this book, the term *children* refers to children of all ages, including teens, except when we mention a specific age.

A study published in 2005 surveyed more than 8,000 students in grades 4–12 attending New York City public schools (Hoven et al., 2005). The study was conducted 6 months after the terrorist attacks of September 11, 2001, but included questions about experiences of the students before September 11. Thirty-nine percent had seen someone killed or seriously injured prior to the attacks. Almost a third (29%) had experienced the violent or accidental death of a close friend. More than one in four (27%) had experienced the violent or accidental death of a family member.

Of note, a comparable study had looked at these same issues in Kansas back in 1978 (Ewalt & Perkins, 1979). Researchers surveyed students attending two public high schools and found outcomes surprisingly similar to a New York study published in 2005. Ninety percent of students reported having experienced the death of a grandparent, aunt, uncle, sibling, or someone else they cared about. Four in 10 reported the death of a close friend their own age. Twenty percent had witnessed a death directly. These studies make it clear that the death of a friend or relative is a common experience for children.

Naturally, because we care about the welfare of children, we are concerned about the impact of these experiences. How do children make sense of such losses? What effect do these have on their schoolwork? On their personal adjustment? How wide is the arc of these deaths—are friends and classmates affected when a student experiences the death of a friend or relative? What can schools and teachers do to help?

We have discovered answers to these questions through research, the clinical work of health and mental health providers, experiences of teachers and other educators, and work done through the National Center for School Crisis and Bereavement (NCSCB). It is quite clear to us that the effect of a death is felt deeply by children who are close relatives and friends and is often also felt by their classmates and friends. Although the death of a family member or friend is a common and normal event for children, it is also one that has a tremendous impact.

Important Resources for Educators and Schools

These two sites offer a range of resources for educators and schools facing crises or wishing to improve their skills in supporting grieving students.

- **Coalition to Support Grieving Students.** This coalition of more than 100 professional organizations in the education and health fields seeks to create and share resources that empower school communities across America in the ongoing support of grieving students. Its web site offers an extensive library of free video-based training modules and written materials addressing the role of educators and other school professionals in this important effort, as well as downloadable mini-articles that can be used on web sites or in newsletters. For information about the Grief-Sensitive Schools Initiative and how to join, visit https://grievingstudents.org/.

- **National Center for School Crisis and Bereavement (NCSCB).** This organization offers confidential, on-site and remote technical assistance and consultation for K–12 school leadership and educators facing school crises. It hosts a toll-free 24/7 phone number. They can provide support in the immediate aftermath of a crisis and ongoing guidance throughout the long-term recovery. Trainings for school staff and professional development for a range of professionals within and beyond the educational setting are also available. NCSCB coordinates the work of the Coalition to Support Grieving Students. Visit www.schoolcrisiscenter.org to learn more.

THE IMPACT OF DEATH ON CHILDREN

What follows are some of the ways children are typically affected when they experience the death of a parent or other relative or friend:

- **Academics.** Children experiencing grief often find it difficult to concentrate. They may not be able to focus on reading, writing projects, or class discussions. They are easily distracted. Their academic performance and grades may suffer.

- **Confusion.** The fact of the death and what it means often confuse children. The reactions of others can be upsetting or puzzling. What's expected of them from their teachers may be unclear. Their own powerful feelings can be surprising and disconcerting.

- **Feelings and physical complaints.** Depressed mood is common. Children may feel sad or anxious. They may have trouble with sleep, feel tired, or experience outbursts of frustration or anger. They may become clingy or start to act younger and more childish. They may complain of headaches or stomachaches.

- **Guilt and shame.** Children often experience feelings of guilt or shame about the death.

- **Isolation.** Children usually feel isolated by these powerful experiences. They may not know how to communicate their thoughts and feelings to friends, educators, or others.

- **Worsening of preexisting challenges.** Some children are already struggling with learning, social skills, or mental health challenges. The extra burden of grief usually worsens such preexisting conditions.

Friends and classmates may be confused about how to respond to a peer who has lost a relative or friend. What should they say or do? Who can they turn to for guidance? The death may bring up memories of an earlier loss they experienced themselves. Some children may even feel resentful about or frustrated by the changes a friend goes through. Their own anxiety about the health and safety of their parents and family often increases—if this could happen to a friend, could it happen to them, too?

IT HELPS WHEN ADULTS AND CHILDREN TALK

Because people simply don't have conversations about death very often, adults may not even realize how common it can be for children to experience loss. Many adults aren't especially comfortable talking about the subject. Most have little experience, and there aren't many models to follow.

When the topic of death comes up around children, several additional factors can complicate the conversation. To begin with, adults and children have different communication styles about the topic. Sometimes, they miss each other's signals. An adult doesn't realize a child is communicating about grief or death. Children may be confused about what adults are trying to say.

Fortunately, there are some straightforward principles and guidelines that allow educators and others to communicate clearly with children and answer the questions they are likely to have. Helping children talk about and understand death and grief helps them cope more successfully.

Constructive conversations between adults and children help. Grieving students feel more connected and supported. They are likely to do better emotionally, socially, and academically. Students' families feel more confident that their children are getting appropriate support. Most often, families appreciate sharing the burden of these matters with educators. Classmates feel more certain about steps they can take to respond to their friend. Educators themselves are gratified that they can do something to help. This is empowering for everyone and helps educators feel less anxious about their student's welfare.

Common Barriers to Communication

Through our work at the NCSCB, one of the things we have learned most profoundly is that grieving children need the unique kind of information and support educators can give. Communicating about death and grief helps children understand what has happened. They can get answers to their questions about why the person died, how the death might change their lives, or even what death means. Communication also helps them understand what will happen for them in the coming days, weeks, months, and years. This understanding is the first step in coping with these complex events.

Common barriers to communication between adults and children include the following:

- **Adults and children have different communication styles.** Adults tend to use words to communicate. Children often use play. Adults may speak indirectly or abstractly about death. Young children are more concrete and often don't understand analogies or symbolism. Adults have ideas about socially acceptable behaviors to communicate feelings of sadness and grief. Children may not yet have learned these rules or may follow rules accepted by their peers; their behaviors and responses can be confusing or distressing to adults.

- **Death is often a taboo subject.** This is especially true for families in some cultures. Sometimes, for example, it is improper to speak the name of the dead or talk about the details of a death. However, almost everyone feels a special weight in discussions of death. Most people don't have much experience talking about death. These barriers make it a difficult topic to address with anyone, including children.

- **Adults don't want to create fear or anxiety in children or make children upset.** Educators and other caregivers naturally wonder if bringing up a death simply makes the feelings and consequences worse. As we will see, however, it is the death itself—not the conversation—that is upsetting to children.

- **Adults may worry that such discussions will increase their own anxiety.** Because we have limited experiences talking about death, we are not always certain what our own reactions will be as we talk to children.

- **Adults feel unprepared.** Most of us lack practice talking about death. We imagine children might feel just as unprepared as we are. We worry that we'll get ourselves into something we can't manage in a meaningful way.

- **It's difficult to keep trying.** It's not at all uncommon for first or second attempts at such discussions with children to feel "unsuccessful." Children may not respond as we expect or may become upset. Children may brush off an attempt at communication. Adults don't want to keep trying if their efforts aren't really helping the situation.

- **Children worry about creating anxiety in adults.** Children know that these topics make adults uncomfortable. They may have seen powerful expressions of grief among family members that confused them. In the same way that adults hesitate to open up conversations that might cause distress in children, children act to protect the adults in their lives.

- **It's not the right time.** Another reason that both adults and children may avoid these conversations is because it may never quite feel like the right time. Children often worry that their teachers or other school staff are too busy. They're not sure when it would be appropriate to bring up their concerns. Educators may sense that grieving children simply want to apply themselves to the school tasks that await—just to be a regular kid in school.

Educators may have other practical concerns, such as how to find the time to do this given busy classroom schedules, whether families will object, or what to do if children appear to need more support than the teacher can offer.

EDUCATORS CAN HELP STUDENTS

In this book, we provide guidelines that help educators judge how and when to bring up the topic of death with grieving children. We give specific examples of things an educator can say. We address other common concerns, such as what to do if religious topics come up. We also suggest ways to integrate conversations about death into everyday classroom experiences using teachable moments and planned activities.

You'll see that these steps:

- Don't need to take a lot of time
- Are not difficult to take
- Do make an important difference in children's lives
- Make students' learning more efficient and successful

These efforts can give all students the language and tools to talk about death and strong feelings. Everyone should have the benefit of these basic skills that allow them to turn to others for support and understanding in times of need.

EDUCATORS CAN HELP FAMILIES

This book also provides advice on ways educators can advise parents. (For simplicity, we are using the term *parents* throughout this book to refer to parents as well as legal or informal guardians—whatever adults are entrusted with the child's care.) Parents look to educators as trusted authorities and as caring professionals who know a great deal about their children. Many parents are not sure what to do to help their children after the death of a family member or friend. Educators often have opportunities to offer suggestions as they talk to parents about how a child is doing academically and socially in the school setting. This can be some of the most important advice families receive.

We Are Including Parents and Guardians

In this book, the term *parent* refers to parents, legal guardians, and informal guardians who may be caring for children.

The book also includes access to an online Study Guide that can be used as a resource for trainings, workshops, in-services, small study groups, or self-study. It includes summaries of Key Concepts for each chapter; self-check questions addressing knowledge; personal reflection questions that explore the emotions, opinions, and experiences educators have concerning bereavement; discussion questions that help groups share perspectives and ideas; and a practical application section that suggests action steps all educators can take to enhance the likelihood that grieving children in their setting will receive helpful support.

The Key Concepts are also listed at the end of each chapter. Some readers may wish to review these before or after reading the chapter.

IS THIS A TRAUMA-INFORMED APPROACH?

We are often asked if the suggestions in this book are consistent with the principles of trauma-informed care. There are two answers to this question. First, when a child has suffered a trauma in relation to the death of a loved one, the guidelines in this book will be appropriate. They will complement any trauma-informed practices or policies that are currently in use.

But the second answer is a reminder: Bereavement is not a subcategory of trauma. The loss of a family member or other loved one is distressing, but it is not necessarily traumatic. Although major trauma can result in posttraumatic symptoms or disorders, bereavement is not considered a mental illness and doesn't have symptoms or cause illness requiring treatment. Yet, grief and bereavement are challenging—often even more than traumatic experiences. It is important that we not overapply a trauma lens to children's experiences of grief.

The grief children feel over the loss of a loved one may last a lifetime. But it will typically change over time. Most grieving children (and adults, for that matter) will experience the first few days after a death differently than the sixth month. The second year is usually different from the first. Five years after a death, powerful feelings may arise suddenly, but they will typically emerge less often than they did in the first year.

Chapter 7 addresses special concerns for bereaved children. This is where we discuss complicated mourning—a phenomenon that is more likely when there is trauma associated with a death. Trauma might result when children see a family member murdered, when a family member dies by suicide, when children's own lives have been threatened in some way, or in other situations that result in threat or harm to children. In these situations, children may not experience that same sense of transition in their grief over time. They are likely to need additional support.

The framework we use is "grief sensitive." Grief-Sensitive Schools commit to help provide a supportive environment for students who have experienced the death of a loved one. These schools take steps to increase awareness of the issue of grief at the school and share information about death, grief, and bereavement with students, staff, and parents. They will review relevant school policies and procedures and provide learning opportunities for staff.

You can find more information about Grief-Sensitive Schools at the web site of the Coalition to Support Grieving Students (https://grievingstudents.org/gssi/). If you wish, you can enroll your institution in the Grief-Sensitive Schools Initiative.

ABOUT THE STORIES

Throughout the book, we have used stories to illustrate experiences students and educators have involving death and bereavement. Although the stories are based on true experiences, we have altered them for a few reasons: 1) to preserve confidentiality, 2) to make them briefer, and 3) to better illustrate a particular point. As a result, some of the specifics have been changed, and some stories are actually composites. All of the individuals' names have been changed.

Some of the stories focus on schools and classrooms, but we have also included some that are more clinical, involving counselors or health care providers. The clinical stories highlight some of the ways death and grief affect children's school and social behaviors that may not be as evident to teachers in their classroom role or other educators in the school. We think educators will find this additional background understanding helpful.

MAKING A DIFFERENCE: THE DEATH OF A FRIEND

The following essay was written by a 15-year-old student who lost a friend to suicide late one summer. It describes her experience returning to school at the start of the new year and powerfully expresses how important a contact from an educator can be at such times. (In Chapters 4 and 5, we describe some specific ways educators can approach students who have experienced the death of someone they care for.)

> Solace or support during grief was something I found very little of at school. Despite school normally being a bustling haven of friends and intellect and business for me, it became a place of exhausting struggle after T took his life. I felt isolated and ignored almost all of the time. Every day I would watch hundreds of other students rush past me as if they were functioning at a much faster and more confusing pace. I became lost amidst maddeningly unaware, light-hearted teenagers and frighteningly speechless adults.
>
> My mother sent me to school that fall with a note explaining that I was "dealing with the loss of a friend." I had one note and seven teachers—seven blank, uncomfortable stares as they read, and seven pairs of adult eyes ashamedly avoiding my gaze as they calmly handed my note back to me. What they didn't realize as they so quickly returned that small paper was that, at the same time, they were handing to me hard, undeniable evidence that someone had been taken from me, something incomprehensible had happened—something devastating and awful, recorded on paper as a mere fact devoid of emotion.

It was hard to let the testimony of my shattered world pass so irreverently from me, to people I hardly knew, and back to me again, with it staring me in the face the way they could not. The day of T's funeral I also ran into a gym teacher who had had a habit of saying to morose-looking students, "Be happy you woke up alive." That day he chose to bark his mantra at me. I have always known him as a kind, thoughtful man—and I still know him as that man—but now, out of habit, I avoid him.

However, I had one teacher, my algebra teacher, make a difference that day. He held out my mother's note to me and, as I tugged it back, he held fast, catching my eye, and said, "I am truly sorry." Mr. H., with just a solid, unwavering glance and a sincere apology, had begun my process back into the reality I had lost. My classmates and the ticking clock and whirring, harsh world were all still spinning at what seemed to be an almost violent speed. But someone had shown that he cared, and that [made] all the difference. A former history teacher also stopped a friend of mine in the hallway—someone who had also known T—and mentioned that he knew she was going through a hard time. He didn't mean to bring up anything upsetting but wanted to let her know that he was thinking of her.

Things like that—being stopped in the hallway and reminded you're in someone's thoughts, or a genuine smile, or especially a sincere condolence—make the distinction between a teacher and a mentor, an adult and a friend. Showing or reminding someone that you care has a profound effect at any time in his or her life. But the same display of care or concern during grief can mean so much. It provides connection and positive interaction when you have felt that there was none, and a reminder that you haven't completely lost what you used to have. There are people who miss your smile and see your pain and truly mourn your loss [with you]. Despite destruction and death and sadness, I am not alone—and I am thankful for the people who helped me realize that.

KEY CONCEPTS

- **Bereavement is common among children.** The experience of grief appears to be nearly universal among students. Before they reach adulthood, almost all children will experience the death of someone important to them.

- **Bereavement has an impact.** Bereavement can affect children's academic performance, mood, and social function.

- **Talking with children helps.** Supportive conversations between children and adults are immensely helpful to children.

- **Barriers to communicating about death and grief are numerous.** Children and adults often communicate differently about death and grief.

- **Children and educators can learn skills to talk about death and grief.** These skills include understanding essential concepts about death, common reactions to bereavement, and effective ways to support bereaved individuals.

1

Why Schools and Educators? Isn't This Someone Else's Job?

INTRODUCTION

The emphasis of this book is to help students who are grieving. One of the most effective ways to do this is to help *all* children understand more about death as part of their ongoing learning about life. Virtually all students will, at some point, deal with the death of a family member or friend. Offering anticipatory guidance provides them with the understanding and resources that will allow them to better cope when such losses occur, whether in their own lives or in those of friends or classmates.

Schools and educators are an important influence in the lives of children. The relationship they have with children is distinct—different from families, neighbors, faith-based organizations, or clubs. As we will point out, teachers and other educators are uniquely qualified to help students understand more about death. They can play an essential role in supporting children who are grieving.

One of the most effective ways to support students is to help all children understand more about death as part of their ongoing learning about life.

Educators are uniquely qualified to help students understand more about death.

What Is a Child? What Is a Parent?

As mentioned in the Introduction, in this book the term *children* refers to children and/or students of all ages, including teens, except when we mention a specific age. The term *parent* refers to parents as well as both legal and informal guardians.

1

SCHOOLS ARE A SUPPORTIVE ENVIRONMENT

Students look to educators for support and guidance with a variety of issues. For example, teachers help children understand the academic elements of their world, such as how to do long division, choose a good topic for a report, or understand the steps in mitosis. School counselors may help students learn about social and emotional skills. Coaches might help students practice goal setting or understand more about personal responsibility. Students might also make special connections with parent volunteers, bus drivers, members of the custodial staff, or lunchroom employees. It is not surprising, then, that all types of educators are a resource to whom children naturally turn when they are trying to cope with a death.

Often, students who have concerns regarding death are more comfortable turning to a trusted teacher or other educator whom they feel they know well than to a community-based provider or clinician. Similarly, families are frequently more comfortable receiving support and services in a school setting, which is more familiar and accessible than a local mental health service.

What Is an Educator?

Throughout this book, we use a broad definition of the term *educator*. Each member of the school staff community plays a unique role in students' education and well-being. However, students may look for support from any adult with whom they feel an authentic connection. Staff and volunteers in any role within the school may observe changes in children's behavior or be asked questions about death or grief. This is why we believe it is essential that every member of the education community within a school or district understand the basic foundations of supporting grieving students.

The following list includes reasons why schools are meaningful settings for children to learn more about death and how to cope with a loss:

- *Schools are familiar.* They provide a safe and known setting, which makes them ideal for learning more about topics that are unknown, even if those topics might evoke confusion or anxiety.

- *Schools offer a variety of trained staff.* For example, classroom teachers can check with other teachers, administrators, or a range of student support personnel—including school counselors, nurses, psychologists, or social workers—or others for guidance in addressing the complex issues of death and grieving. Students can also be assisted directly by a range of these qualified, knowledgeable professionals.

- *Students spend a good deal of time at school.* There are many different opportunities during the school year to address death and related issues.
- *Large numbers of children can be served.* Schools remain the best setting in which to reach the largest number of children.

Who Are "Student Support Personnel"?

A range of school staff may be available to offer guidance to teachers and administrators working with grieving students, as well as to provide support to students themselves. These include school counselors, psychologists, nurses, and social workers. In some schools or districts, there may be others who can play a role in providing support and guidance, including community volunteers with professional training (such as family counselors), staff or volunteers from nonprofit organizations, or representatives of other organizations who play a role in students' lives.

Schools are also a particularly effective environment for supporting children who are grieving; classroom teachers can often monitor these students more easily than counselors or other professionals because they have ongoing contact with them. Teachers spend more time with students on a daily basis in a natural environment and are often more familiar with students.

A student's grief may exhibit itself in a variety of ways that emerge in school settings rather than at home. For example, a child may begin acting out, put less effort into lessons and homework, or have conflicts with classmates. Grieving students who find themselves unable to concentrate may become frustrated or anxious. Educators may be able to compare how a student's behavior differs before and after a loss. They can also evaluate a student's behavior considering the many other students with whom they have worked. This gives educators a strong basis for comparison and helps them determine whether a child needs additional support or services.

Most of the time, families appreciate the additional support that educators and schools can provide. They view teachers and other school staff as reliable sources of information about their children. Grieving families may be too overwhelmed to see or accurately assess the effects of grief on their children. Families respect educators' expertise and look to them for advice during challenging times.

When a family is touched by a death, children also need support beyond the family.

EDUCATORS' DISTANCE FROM THE LOSS CAN BE A BENEFIT

Schools and educators must balance many demands during the school day. Classroom time is committed to required subjects and test preparation, which leaves little time for addressing other needs. Many educators, however, feel that they are also being asked to act as social workers. Some, quite reasonably, might ask, "Shouldn't families be taking on this role of helping children understand death and cope with grief?"

The answer, of course, is that families *do* need to give their children opportunities to understand life and death. When families have experienced a loss, their children will look first to them for emotional support. Families have a unique and essential role in helping children through these experiences. However, when a family is touched by a death, children also need support beyond the family. Children learn quickly that grief places burdens on family members. A child knows, for example, that if he talks with his mother about how much he misses his father, she will feel sad. Some parents, struggling with their own grief, simply cannot give their children full support. Even parents who are able to be emotionally present and supportive with their children cannot fulfill all the needs children have at such times.

Educators, therefore, have something to offer children that their families cannot—a perspective informed by a distance from the loss. In most instances, an educator is not as personally involved in the death, even though the child's questions may bring up sadness and even personal memories of loss. However, children experience an immediate quality of personal grief that is part of their interactions with family after the death of a family member or friend. This personal grief is not part of students' communication with their teacher or a school administrator, for example. It can be an immense relief for children to ask their questions and seek support without feeling that they have to protect the educator's emotions. This distance—in addition to educators' understanding of child development, their familiarity with students' day-to-day behavior, and their experiences responding to children's questions and needs—makes it clear how powerful this support can be.

———

Educators have something to offer that families cannot—a perspective informed by a distance from the loss.

———

UNDERSTANDING WHAT TO DO

The introduction to this book acknowledges that death *is* a challenging topic. Educators may feel apprehensive about having conversations with students concerning death for valid reasons. The same strategies and skills that allow educators to be effective in other areas of teaching, however, work very well when talking with children about death and grief. These strategies include having a basic understanding of the topic and a framework for addressing the subject in ways that make sense to students. This book provides both. The information here allows educators to address issues relevant to children's understanding about death and apply strategies that align with their own approaches to teaching.

Often, these interventions can be quite brief. In most cases, supporting grieving children and helping all students learn more about death provides impressive benefits with a very modest investment of time. To do this well, however, educators need to understand more about how children understand death, how to talk to them about it, and how to determine what to do if a grieving child is having problems.

Why should educators make these efforts? For the same reason they do everything they do—because good educators don't just teach the basics, they make a difference in children's lives.

LAYING THE GROUNDWORK: HELPING ALL STUDENTS

The foundation for helping children understand death begins with all students, not just grieving students. Educators can use three approaches when addressing grief and loss: 1) planned coursework, 2) teachable moments at the class level, and 3) teachable moments with individuals or small groups. These approaches give students opportunities to address misconceptions and gain a greater understanding of the topic. What they learn in these exchanges will help them at any point in the future when they experience the death of a family member or friend. These approaches can also help students make sense of a death they may have already experienced or allow students to be better supports for friends and classmates who are experiencing a loss.

Helping All Students

Educators can use three approaches to help all students understand death.

1. Planned coursework

2. Teachable moments at the class level

3. Teachable moments with individuals or small groups

The vignettes that follow give examples of each of these strategies at work. Although these examples involve elementary and middle school students, similar principles and interventions would also be appropriate with older students.

Planned Coursework

Some classes may have lessons in place that specifically address issues of death and grief. (For a research study demonstrating that school-based lessons can advance young children's understanding of concepts related to death, see Schonfeld and Kappelman [1990].) Some may address emotions, such as sadness, grief, happiness, and anger. This sort of coursework might be a part of a health education program or social development and life skills classes. Older students might address these issues in a psychology or comparative religions class.

A Classmate's Help

A kindergarten class had talked about what it means when someone dies. Students discussed times when they had been sad and shared ideas about things they could do when they had sad feelings. Suggestions included talking with their parents or a friend. Some said that drawing a picture made them feel better. Some liked to play with their pets.

A few days after one of these lessons, the teacher overheard one of her students, Misha, talking with Liza, a child from the other kindergarten class. Liza said she was feeling very sad because her grandmother had recently died. Misha said, "I'm sorry. Maybe you would like to draw a picture of your grandma. We learned that can help you feel better."

Teachable Moments at the Class Level

Teachable moments that address the topic of death will come up in most classes at some point. History and current events often involve issues of death and loss. Local events, such as a natural disaster (e.g., flood, earthquake, fire), or other crises such as a pandemic often involve deaths that students want to talk about. Celebrities known to students may die or become seriously ill or injured, which may increase students' anxiety and concern. In addition, it is common for elementary classes to have a class pet, such as a fish or a hamster, that may die, which will have an effect on the students.

The Hamster Died

One Monday morning, students in a seventh-grade science class were surprised to discover that the hamster in the cage at the back of the classroom had died over the weekend. The animal hadn't really been a pet; in fact, it belonged to one of the other classes. No one in the class expressed any strong feelings of sadness.

One of the boys, however, looked at the curled body and said, "Look! He was going to the bathroom when he died. Yuck!" All of the students crowded around the cage to stare, joke, push each other, and laugh about this strange indignity. Their teacher called for order, got them to their seats, and matter-of-factly began to describe some of the physiological processes of death. He described several features that were evident in the body of the hamster, including the relaxation of the sphincter muscles, which might result in excretion of feces.

After their initial display of anxiety and discomfort, the students settled down, listened to their teacher, and asked honest and thoughtful questions about biology and death. It became an instructive morning for the class.

Teachable Moments With Individual Students or Small Groups

Interactions related to attitudes or understanding of death may occur on the playground, in small groups working on a class project together, or among friends. For example, children may tease one another, challenge beliefs or experiences, or provide misinformation to one another. Educators who observe these exchanges can use the opportunity to provide clarification and guidance.

Unruly in Line

A group of fifth graders stood in line at one of the playground games during recess. Two of the girls began a commotion. "You're dead," said Mariah as she pushed the other.

"No, you're dead," Felicia replied, pushing back.

Both girls were smiling and seemed playful as they did this. They continued to push each other, however, and both the taunts and the pushing became fiercer. The other students, annoyed at being shoved out of place themselves, started pushing and shouting back. From across the playground, their teacher saw her usually well-behaved students in an unruly process of shoving and shouting. She heard one of the boys call, "You guys are so dead."

"You're dead, you're dead," said another.

"No, you're all dead," Mariah called back.

"Stop it. This isn't funny," another student cried.

"Please stop," the teacher called as she approached the group. She waited until they calmed down, and then asked, "What is going on here?"

All the students spoke at once with descriptions, defenses, and accusations. The teacher stopped them and asked them to talk about how they felt about the words that were being used. Several students mentioned being disturbed by the taunting and repetitions about death. The group became more serious, and everyone seemed willing to acknowledge that this kind of play had been hurtful. Mariah and Felicia became quite contrite and apologized to the group.

Later that day, the teacher spoke with the two of them privately. She talked with them about the seriousness of death and mentioned some of the feelings people often have when they lose someone they care about. She asked directly if either of them was going through a loss. Neither indicated anything troubling going on in their own lives. Their teacher knew, however, that their relationship could occasionally become aggressive.

The teacher explained that it was not possible for them to know if people around them had experienced the death of a loved one. Their teasing could be hurtful in ways they probably didn't realize. They agreed that they had not meant to upset their classmates.

The three of them talked about better ways Mariah and Felicia could deal with each other's teasing in the future, and both seemed willing to speak with the teacher if they had problems. Their apologies seemed genuine, and they agreed to avoid future disturbances on the playground.

BEING READY: SETTING THE STAGE

Educators can use the relatively simple steps of planned coursework and teachable moments at the class, small group, or individual level to help children better understand death and cope with the loss of a loved one. These interventions *are* important. Children have questions about death. Taking time to help them understand death and grief clarifies misconceptions and reduces anxiety, which promotes better academic achievement.

When educators and students are able to comfortably have these conversations, educators will find it easier to approach a bereaved child. This can also help prevent or minimize some of the common difficulties grieving children have, such as having trouble concentrating, becoming disruptive in class, or becoming withdrawn or isolated.

When bereaved children receive support outside of their home, they are more likely to navigate the entire grief process with less difficulty. Although each child will experience this support differently, it can help children achieve healthy social-emotional skills such as positive emotional health and the ability to maintain strong social connections and contribute to their community, in addition to the later satisfaction of enjoying a rewarding life as an adult.

Key Concepts

- **Children in general benefit by learning more about death and grief.** Anticipatory guidance, starting at the earliest grades, can help children cope better if they do experience a loss. This also prepares students to support peers who experience the death of a friend or family member.

- **Schools are an excellent setting for this learning.** Many school and classroom features offer unique and powerful support to bereaved children.

- **Educators play a unique role in these matters.** In most cases, educators' distance from the death allows children to discuss their feelings and reactions without feeling a need to protect the educator's emotions.

- **Educators can help all students learn about death** through planned coursework, teachable moments at the class level, and teachable moments with individuals or small groups.

2

How Children Understand Death

When a death occurs, children share many of the same experiences as adults, but their understanding of what those experiences mean may be different. Educators and other adults can help children understand death accurately. This involves more than simply giving them the facts, however. It also means helping them grasp some important concepts.

Adult support allows children to achieve a more complete understanding of death so that children may view death realistically and with less anxiety. It helps grieving children adjust to their loss as they continue to move forward in their lives.

FOUR BASIC CONCEPTS ABOUT DEATH

Some discussions about children's understanding of death draw upon an ages and stages model—the idea that children will achieve certain levels of understanding depending on their age and developmental milestones. However, there is wide variation in the ways children of the same age understand death based on what they have experienced and what they already know about it. In general, most children will learn the four basic concepts discussed here by 5–7 years of age (Schonfeld, 1993; Speece & Brent, 1984); however, when personal experience is supported by thoughtful explanations and knowledge provided by educators, children several years younger can often come to understand these concepts as well (Schonfeld & Kappelman, 1990). Everyone, including children, must understand the Four Concepts About Death to fully grieve and come to terms with a death (see Schonfeld, 1993, 1996; Speece & Brent, 1984; Smilansky, 1987).

Similar to young children, teens and adults often struggle with accepting the reality of a death. Intellectually, they may have a full and rational understanding, but emotionally they find it difficult to accept what they know to be true. Children who do not yet understand these basic concepts are at a

9

marked disadvantage. They cannot begin to accept something they do not yet understand.

It is best not to assume that children know certain things about death based on their age. Instead, educators can ask them to talk about their ideas, thoughts, and feelings. As children explain what they already understand about death, what they still need to learn becomes evident.

***

It is best not to assume that children know certain things about death based on their age.

***

Four Concepts About Death

1.   Death is irreversible.

2.   All life functions end completely at the time of death.

3.   Everything that is alive eventually dies.

4.   Death is caused by physical reasons.

Concept 1: Death Is Irreversible

In cartoons, television shows, and movies, children may see characters "die" and then come back to life. In real life, this obviously does not happen. Children who do not fully understand this concept may view death as a kind of temporary separation. They often think of people who have died as being far away, perhaps on a trip. Sometimes adults reinforce this misunderstanding by talking about the person who died as having "gone on a long journey." Children who have had a family member or friend die may feel angry when the person does not call or return for important occasions.

If children do not think of a death as permanent, they have little reason to begin to mourn. Mourning is a painful process that requires people to adjust their ties to the person who has died. Understanding that the loss is permanent is an essential first step in this process in addition to, at some level, accepting that the loss is permanent.

***

An essential first step in grieving is understanding and, at some level, accepting that the loss is permanent.

***

Concept 2: All Life Functions End Completely at the Time of Death

Very young children view all things as living—their sister, a toy, the mean rock that just "tripped" them. In daily conversations, adults may add to this confusion by talking about the child's doll being hungry or saying they got home late because the car "died." Yet, whereas adults understand that there is a difference between pretending a doll is hungry and believing the doll is hungry, this difference may not be clear to a young child.

Young children are sometimes encouraged to talk to a family member who has died. They may be told that their loved one is "watching over them" from heaven. Sometimes children are asked to draw a picture or write a note to the person who died so that it can be placed in the coffin. These requests and comments can be confusing and even frightening to some children who do not yet understand the finality of death. In a young child's mind, they could be wondering, if the person who has died could read a note, does it mean he or she will be aware of being in the coffin? Will the person realize he or she has been buried?

Children may know that people cannot move after they have died but may believe this is because the coffin is too small. They may know people cannot see after death but may believe this is because it is dark underground. It is possible that these children could become preoccupied with what they perceive as the physical suffering of the deceased.

When children can correctly identify what living functions are, they can also understand that these functions end completely at the time of death. For example, only the living can think, be afraid, feel hunger, or feel pain. Only the living have beating hearts or the need for air to breathe.

Older Children and Adults Wonder, Too

Consider the numerous horror films about zombies, vampires, or other characters that are dead but still retain some life functions. Many are doomed to suffer through eternity. These films are frightening to both children and adults. They are also quite popular. Why? They speak to concerns all of us have experienced about this basic concept of death.

Concept 3: Everything That Is Alive Eventually Dies

Children may believe that they and others close to them will never die. Parents often reassure children that they will always be there to take care of them. They tell their children not to worry about dying themselves. This wish to shield children from death is understandable, but when a death directly affects a child, this reality can no longer be hidden. When a parent or other significant person dies, children usually fear that others close to them—perhaps everyone they care about—will also die.

Children, just like adults, struggle to make sense of a death. If they do not understand that death is an inevitable part of life, they will have misunderstandings while trying to figure out why this particular death occurred. They may assume it happened because of something bad they did or something they failed to do. They may think it happened because of bad thoughts they had. This misunderstanding then leads to guilt. Children may also assume the person who died did or thought bad things or did not do something that should have been done. This misunderstanding leads to shame. These reactions make it difficult for children to adjust to a loss. Many children do not want to talk about the death because it will expose these terrible feelings of guilt and shame.

When educators talk to children about how everyone eventually dies, children may raise concerns about the health and safety of their own family members. If individual children are particularly concerned about the well-being of their parents, educators can ask students if they can talk with their parents. They can also suggest that parents reassure their children that they are doing everything they can to stay healthy and that they hope and expect to live a long life. For example, if a child's father died of a heart attack, the child may benefit from knowing that his or her mother has seen her doctor and had a physical exam. This shows the child that family members are taking steps to stay healthy and safe. This is different from telling children that they or their parents will never die.

Concept 4: Death Is Caused by Physical Reasons

When children experience the death of a family member or friend, they must understand why the person died. If children do not understand the real reason their family member has died, they are more likely to come up with explanations that cause guilt or shame.

The goal is to help children understand what has happened. When explaining a death to children, educators should aim for a brief explanation that uses simple and direct language. They can watch for cues from the children and allow them to ask for further explanations. Graphic details are not necessary and should be avoided, especially if the death was violent.

Although it would be unusual for an educator to be the first to tell an individual child of the death of a family member (for an excellent and thorough discussion of how to conduct death notification, see Leash, 1994), teachers may need to make a class announcement about someone in the school or community who has died, a classmate who has lost a parent or other family member, or another death that affects students in a classroom or school. Parents may also ask educators for guidance about how to tell their child about death.

If children do not understand the real reason their family member has died, they are more likely to come up with explanations that cause guilt or shame.

COMMON PROBLEMS ASSOCIATED WITH EXPLAINING DEATH TO CHILDREN

Children may not react to the news of a death in the way adults would expect. Explanations about death can confuse children in many ways. Often, misunderstandings are related to misconceptions about the Four Concepts About Death. By listening carefully to what children say and watching what they do, educators can reinforce these essential concepts and address areas of confusion.

The following are some examples of common problems children have with understanding death:

- **Explanations and terms may not be clear.** Adults often choose words they feel are gentler or less frightening for children. They might avoid using the words *dead* or *died*, which seem harsh at such an emotional time. However, with less direct terms, children may not understand what the adult is saying. For example, if an adult tells a child that the family member who died is now in a state of "eternal sleep," the child may become afraid to go to sleep. Therefore, it is important to speak gently, but frankly and directly, to children. Use the words *dead* and *died*.

- **Children may only understand part of the explanation.** Even when adults give clear, direct explanations, children may not fully understand. For example, some children who have been told that the body was placed in a casket worry about where the head has been placed. When discussing a death, it is a good idea to check back with children to see what they understand. You might say, "Let me see if I've explained this well. Please tell me what you understand has happened."

- **Religious concepts may be confusing.** It is appropriate for a family to share its religious beliefs with children when a death has occurred; however, religious beliefs are often abstract and difficult for young children to understand. It is helpful to provide the facts about what happens to the physical body while supporting the religious beliefs held by the family. Ideally, the family will tell the children that the person has died and clarify that the person no longer thinks, feels, or sees. They might then explain that the person's entire body was placed in a casket and buried, or that the body, which cannot feel anything, was cremated—or turned into ashes. In some faiths, the family might add that there is a special part of the person that cannot be seen or touched, which some people call the spirit or soul. They can explain that this part continues on in a place that cannot be seen or visited, which some religions refer to as heaven.

    When students are confused about religious beliefs and the physical state of a dead person's body, educators can focus on the second concept, which is that all life functions end completely at the time of death. In public schools or secular private schools, religious discussions are a matter for families and not part of the classroom instruction. However, families might appreciate guidance on how to help their children understand what may appear to be conflicts between religious beliefs and the physical reality of death. These explanations can help children come to a better understanding of both.

When children are learning about death or personally experiencing bereavement, they may mention a belief in heaven. These beliefs can be comforting to children, and it is important to give children opportunities to express them. Educators can then affirm that people have different religious beliefs and that all beliefs are respected in the school setting.

Educators who acquire a clear understanding of the Four Concepts About Death have one of the most effective tools available for supporting students, especially young students, and for responding to their questions or misunderstandings about death.

VERY YOUNG CHILDREN'S CAPACITY FOR UNDERSTANDING DEATH

Even infants and very young children respond to the death of those close to them (Schonfeld, 1993). They miss the familiar person's presence. They are sensitive to the emotions being expressed around them, and if surviving parents are distressed, infants and toddlers notice. They may have trouble eating and sleeping and may even lose weight.

Parents and preschool educators often wonder how much very young children can understand about death. When a death occurs, it is difficult to know what explanations will be most useful to them. There are, however, a number of ways very young children can understand aspects of death, such as the absence of a loved one and the permanence of loss.

During the second half of the first year of life, infants begin to develop object permanence and come to understand that people and things continue to exist even when they cannot be seen or otherwise sensed—out of sight is no longer out of mind. With this, children can start to understand, and worry about, permanent loss of people important to them. It is no coincidence that at this point children in cultures all over the world begin to play the first of many games that help them understand the concepts of death. This game is known as Peekaboo. In this game, infants fix their attention on someone and then experience a brief separation. This is followed by heightened awareness and concern and then by joy at the reunion. This is a game of loss that infants and toddlers will play over and over again as they attempt to understand and cope with loss. Peekaboo translates literally from Old English as "alive or dead."

As they grow older, young children will play Hide and Seek and other similar games. As the games become more sophisticated, so does children's understanding of temporary and permanent loss. When explaining death to children, adults should use simple terms that children have learned and used in games and stories, such as *all gone*. The child may not fully understand all of the concepts at first, but providing the language to talk about these ideas helps children develop the concepts when they are ready and able.

It is important to explain the death of a close family member to young children. They may need to hear the concepts many times before they fully understand them, but in time, they will grasp the concepts and, similar to older children, will strive to make meaning from their experiences and cope with their sense of loss.

All Gone

Eva sensed something was happening. She was 21 months old, and she and her family had just driven to her grandparents' house. This was usually a happy occasion, but this time, everyone was very sad. "Happen, happen?" she asked. Eva's father said her grandmother had just died.

Her grandmother had been ill for as long as Eva had known her, but Eva did not understand what dead meant. Grandma always smiled when she saw her, gave her cookies and other treats, and laughed when Eva sat on her lap. Eva went looking for her grandmother in her room but found it empty. She came back out. "Grandma?" she asked. Then her father said again, "Grandma died."

"Grandma died?" Eva asked, confused by a word she did not understand.

"Grandma is all gone," her father explained.

"All gone?" Eva asked. She ran to get one of her books and brought it back, turning to the page where the baby had turned over her cereal bowl. "All gone!" she exclaimed. Then she turned to her father and asked, "Grandma all gone?"

"Yes," her father said.

Eva ran to her grandfather and grabbed him around the knees. "Grandpa all gone?" she asked.

"No," her grandfather answered. "Grandpa is fine."

From that point on, Eva never went looking for her grandmother again. She demonstrated that she had begun to understand several of the concepts about death, such as irreversibility—her grandmother would not return—and inevitability—one day her grandfather would die as well.

ADOLESCENTS' UNDERSTANDING OF DEATH

Adolescents begin to develop increasingly complex abilities to analyze and understand abstractions. It makes sense that abstractions about death would be easier for teens to master than younger children, and in general, this is true. However, teens who have experienced the death of a friend or family member often find themselves struggling, just as adults do, to accept the Four Concepts About Death as they relate to a personal loss. Teens say a number of things that illustrate this. The following are some examples:

- "I keep imagining I see my brother in a crowd or hear his voice in the next room. I just can't believe I will never see him again."
- "Somehow I still feel like my mother can hear or see me."
- "While I know that anyone can die, I just never realized that could include my own father."
- "I just don't understand why he died and wonder, deep down, if it was because I made him so sad."

As with younger children, teens will benefit from authentic and caring interest and a chance to respond to open-ended questions, which can often reveal questions, concerns, and even persistent questions about the meaning of death. Chapters 4 and 5 offer guidelines for talking to children, including adolescents, about death.

HELPING CHILDREN WITH INTELLECTUAL AND NEURODEVELOPMENTAL DISABILITIES UNDERSTAND DEATH

Like all children, children with intellectual and neurodevelopmental disabilities may experience the death of a loved one. These children often face distinctive challenges at such moments. Here are some points to keep in mind.

Grief Behaviors

Children who cannot communicate well verbally will express their feelings in nonverbal ways. When grieving, they may show a range of behaviors in response to stress and strong emotions, including a reappearance of past behaviors or greater intensity in current ones. They may be more irritable or angrier than usual. They might lose weight or regress to earlier activities, such as being clingy or bedwetting.

These children may begin or increase self-stimulating behaviors such as pacing, flapping arms, or repeating a word or phrase. They might rock, chew on clothes or fingers, or want a lot of bathroom breaks during class. They might also exhibit disruptive behavior, difficulty concentrating, or want more explanations than usual. They may express their grief through rituals or other unusual behaviors that are misinterpreted by others.

These are common expressions of distress among children who have difficulty regulating their emotions. Educators can respond with strategies that have worked with a child previously. That might include verbally acknowledging that the child is experiencing strong feelings to help the child learn better how to label feelings, gently distracting the child or offering a comfort object, encouraging alternative behaviors (such as chewing on an object intended for that purpose rather than on the child's fingers), or providing the child time to be quiet and away from a stimulating environment if the child seems overwhelmed. If the behavior is not disruptive to others or harmful to the child, then the educator can ignore the behavior or simply sit in company with the child as the emotional expression runs its course.

Offer Explanations Matched to Their Level

It is important for any grieving child to understand the Four Concepts About Death. Educators familiar with the communication style of children with intellectual and neurodevelopmental disabilities have a unique opportunity to engage in these exchanges and conversations.

As with other students, talk about these concepts in ways that match a child's intellectual level. Follow up with questions that can highlight any misunderstandings.

For example, imagine you are explaining the concept "All life functions end completely at the time of death" to a child with a developmental age of approximately 5 years. You might say, "When people die, their body stops working forever. They can't see or hear, move, or feel pain. They aren't hungry or scared." If the child then talks about their grandfather's funeral, you might ask, "What was it like for you when your grandpa was being buried?" If the child replies that he thought his grandpa was probably scared, reassure the child again that once people have died, they no longer feel pain or fear.

The Challenge of Coping With Death for Children With Autism Spectrum Disorder

Children with autism spectrum disorder (ASD) or other neurodevelopmental disabilities have distinct styles of social interaction. Although these children may not be able to express their feelings or ask for support as clearly as other children, they do experience grief.

You may be familiar with some common stressors for children with ASD. These include unexpected events, disruptions in routine, changes in the behaviors of family or peers, powerful emotions, trying to communicate thoughts and feelings, and facing new sensory processing demands.

The death of someone close brings challenges in every one of these realms. A loved one is gone. Visitors show up in the home. There may be new people at the dinner table, a memorial service to attend, or new and confusing emotions to manage.

In addition to the actual loss of the loved one, grieving children experience a range of secondary losses that resonate powerfully for those with ASD. (See Chapter 7 for a further discussion of secondary loss.) Their routines are likely to be disrupted, perhaps temporarily, but sometimes permanently. There may be a change in family finances, home location, school, and social connections. A parent or sibling who has been a vital support may be distracted and less available due to their own grief feelings.

Provide Support Matched to Each Child's Intellectual and Neurodevelopmental Abilities

Use strategies that have been effective with the child in other areas. Tell a social story about someone who has experienced the death of a pet or family member. Ask a child to demonstrate body language that expresses sadness. Talk about ideas for regulating the strong emotions that come with grieving. Reassure children that these difficult feelings are common for all people who are grieving, not just for those with ASD or other disabilities.

There is no single approach that is "right" for all children with different intellectual and neurodevelopmental abilities. There are, however, myriad options that educators and providers have used to support their students in both emotional and academic learning. Similar strategies will also allow children the opportunity to engage productively in the processes of grieving as they cope with their loss.

There is no single approach that is "right" for all children with different intellectual and neurodevelopmental abilities.

HELPING ALL CHILDREN LEARN ABOUT DEATH

Educators who take classroom time to address concepts about death, grief, strong emotions, and supporting friends who are grieving are giving all children tools they can use during challenging times in their lives. This sort of preparedness is especially helpful when children do experience a death. They will already understand the basic concepts about death, which helps minimize some of the confusion. These children will also understand that their feelings will probably be powerful, that they may feel guilty or have other confusing feelings, that their feelings will change over time, and that they can receive support from friends and family.

The following are some important points for educators to remember as they think about offering such lessons:

- **Small efforts have important effects.** Students have an amazing range of life experiences. Educators cannot possibly know about all of them, and many will never hear about some of the most powerful events in their students' lives. Yet, virtually every class will have at least one student, and often several, who have experienced the death of a family member or close friend. Simple lessons and concepts about death and grieving can help children master challenges in ways educators do not expect or realize.

An Important Message

David Schonfeld, coauthor of this volume, was invited by a teacher to speak to her class of third and fourth graders. There were 20 children in the class. During their discussions, he learned that more than half of the students had experienced the death of someone close.

David spoke with them for about 45 minutes, covering much of the general information in this book. He talked about some of the things people feel and think after someone they know dies. He said that most people find it helpful to talk about their feelings and about the person who died. He mentioned that people often feel guilty when someone they love dies and wonder if they could have done something to prevent the death. The class discussed ways to support friends who had experienced a loss and how to receive support themselves if needed.

It was a straightforward presentation, and the children were interested, participated actively, and seemed to benefit from the discussion. Although many had been through difficult experiences, nothing disturbing or troubling occurred during the class.

About a week later, David received a collection of handwritten thank-you notes from the class. One of them read, "Dear Dr. Schonfeld, thank you for talking to our class. Now I realize it was not my fault my dad killed himself. Have a happy Valentine's Day. Love, Natalie."

This is a moving example of the way matter-of-fact discussions about death and other challenging topics help children in ways we might not anticipate. Although Natalie certainly has lingering questions and concerns regarding her father's suicide, the discussion seemed to make it easier for her to communicate her feelings of guilt. It is likely she will find other opportunities to share this with caring adults in her life. Talking about her feelings is an important step toward adjusting to this tragedy. Often, very simple comments and interventions have profound effects on children who are struggling with some aspect of grief.

- **Keep discussions positive and productive.** Some educators worry that discussions about death and grief will become negative or upsetting to children. Although it is possible that children may become upset during a discussion, it is always important to remember that it is the feelings of grief and loss—and the death itself—that are upsetting, not the act of discussion. Educators can watch for signs of distress among students. It is appropriate to check with a student who is upset (see the story "Classmates Offer Support" later in this chapter). Students should always be invited to talk with a teacher after class if they have additional questions or concerns.

  In general, these conversations help children recognize and identify their feelings, express them appropriately, and think about ways to receive support when they need it. They give children a better sense of the range of feelings people may have in response to a death and usually reassure them that their own feelings and experiences are normal.

It is always important to remember that it is the feelings of grief and loss—and the death itself—that are upsetting, not the act of discussion.

How Do You Feel Better?

A fifth-grade student died suddenly and unexpectedly. The teacher in the third-grade class shared this information with his students. He talked with them about what it meant when someone died. His students then began to share their stories of loss and sadness. Many of these were unrelated to the death of their schoolmate. As the discussion went on, some of the children became tearful and seemed to be becoming more upset.

The teacher then asked the class if anyone could share an example of something they did, or something that someone did for them, that helped them feel better when they were sad. His students eagerly began to share examples of support and coping. One student played with his dog. Another student's mother talked with her and helped her understand and cope with difficult feelings. One girl liked to ride bikes with her friend next door. A boy's brother took him to a basketball game and told him he was there for him and that they could talk any time. A girl's father cuddled with her as they read a book.

The tone of the classroom discussion became more positive and uplifting as the children focused on ways to deal with distress; however, the conversation did not in any way diminish their expressions of sadness or shift attention away from their own experiences and needs.

- **Offer lessons about death and grief to prepare children to support their peers.** Discussions about death, grief, and sadness give children greater skills in expressing their own feelings and having their needs met. As a result, they will have fewer fears and worries and be less likely to engage in hurtful teasing about death or grief. They will also demonstrate greater empathy for peers.

Classmates Offer Support

A second-grade class was watching a short educational video about death and grief. The narrator made the statement, "You might remember an event such as the death of a pet. This could make you sad." One of the students began crying. The teacher, seeing the boy crying, stopped the video. The other students looked up at her and said, "Hey! Why did you stop the movie?"

The teacher pointed out that the movie seemed to be upsetting one of their classmates. They all turned to the student who was crying. One boy in the class got up from his desk, walked over to the counter, and got some tissues for the crying student. Another went over to the student's desk and put his arm around him.

"What should we do now?" the teacher asked.

The student who had gone to comfort the crying boy said, "It's up to him. If he wants to keep watching, we'll keep watching. If it makes him too sad, we'll do something else." The other students all nodded their heads in agreement.

The crying boy took a big breath and sighed. He seemed calmer. He thought for a moment, and his friends continued to reassure him. "Let's watch the movie," he said.

The students returned to their seats, the movie went forward, and the class had a good discussion about the material afterward.

When the class was over, the teacher spoke alone to the boy who had been upset. "What was going on for you when you started crying?" she asked.

"Oh, I just felt very sad about my dog," the boy answered. "He died."

The teacher asked the boy if he'd like to talk to his mom or dad. Yes, he thought that would be nice. They called the mother, and the teacher briefly explained what had happened. The boy talked to his mom for a couple of minutes. He seemed fine by then, the mother felt comfortable with the situation, and there was no further incident.

The students in this classroom showed a level of understanding, maturity, and compassion that many people would consider unusual for 7-year-old children. What this story demonstrates is that children this age can learn these skills, given the chance, and benefit from these sorts of lessons.

HELPING CHILDREN MAKE SENSE OF THEIR WORLD

Two points are emphasized throughout this book. The first is that every student and situation is unique. No two students will feel loss or show grief the same way or respond to lessons and stories the same. Different students will benefit from different types of support. The second point is that the principles described in this book work well across a range of situations. The stories in this chapter reinforce this point. The following are some of the common themes that emerge:

- Children have deep and powerful feelings about grief and loss.
- Children are capable of considerable empathy for their peers or others who are grieving.
- Children respond well to direct, clear, and truthful communications.
- Children benefit from an understanding of the Four Concepts About Death.
- Children have good ideas about how to receive and give support and how to cope with feelings of sadness and grief. They appreciate the opportunity to share their ideas and learn from others.
- When educators approach children in an open, nonjudgmental fashion about these issues, most are open in return and share their thoughts and feelings.
- Children look to educators and other adults for guidance on these and other challenging issues.

_____

No two students will feel loss or show grief the same way or respond to lessons and stories the same.

_____

Key Concepts

- **Children and adults must understand the Four Concepts About Death to cope effectively with a personal loss.** These four concepts are as follows:
    1. Death is irreversible.
    2. All life functions end completely at the time of death.
    3. Everything that is alive eventually dies.
    4. Death is caused by physical reasons.

- **It is best not to assume what children know based on their age.** Most children understand these concepts by 5–7 years of age, but children who are much younger may also understand some or all of these concepts. Children with intellectual or neurodevelopmental disabilities may find the concepts difficult or confusing and need repeated conversations to fully understand a death. Even adults, though, sometimes have problems accepting these concepts in times of grief.

- **Children often have difficulty understanding adult explanations of death.** If they do not fully understand the concepts, they may misunderstand what an adult is saying. It is always important to check back to see what they do understand.

3

When a Death
Occurs in a Child's Life

Educators may wonder what to expect if one of their students experiences
the death of a family member or someone else close. Although we can make
many generalizations about what children typically go through, it is important
to remember that children grieve in individual ways, just as adults do. The
"appropriate" time line for grief is different for every student and each unique
circumstance.

COMMON REACTIONS THAT CHILDREN MAY HAVE

What we can be certain about is that children's reactions to a death relate to
their thoughts and feelings. Sometimes these reactions make sense to educators, parents, and other adults. At other times, they can be confusing. However,
when adults understand what children are thinking and feeling, things tend to
become much clearer.

The following are some common reactions children may have to death.

Children May Become Upset by Discussions About Their Loved One

As previously mentioned, it is not the conversation that causes distress, but
the very painful loss felt from the death of a loved one. Talking with children
provides a chance for them to show their feelings. When this is understood, it
is easier to help them cope with the experience.

Children May Be Reluctant to Talk About a Recent Death

Often children are uncomfortable talking about a death because they see that
the adults around them are uncomfortable talking about it. Children may
withhold their own comments or questions to avoid upsetting family members, family friends, teachers, or other educators. They may believe it is wrong

to talk about such things. It is common for older children and teens to turn to peers to discuss a death. They sometimes tell adults close to them that they do not want or need to talk about it.

———

Often children are uncomfortable talking about a death because they see that the adults around them are uncomfortable talking about it.

———

Children May Express Their Feelings in Ways Other Than Talking

Children may use play or creative activities, such as drawing or writing, to express their grief. Often, they come to a better understanding of grief through play and creative outlets. These expressions can offer some important clues about what children are thinking, but it is important not to jump to conclusions.

For example, young children who produce very happy drawings after a traumatic death might give the impression that they are not affected by the death. In fact, this is more likely a sign that the child is not yet ready to deal with the grieving process. Similarly, teens who only want to listen to "happy" music or see "happy" movies may be signaling that they are not ready to open up to the profound emotions of grief.

Children Often Feel Guilty After a Death Has Occurred

Young children have a limited understanding of why things happen as they do. They often use magical thinking—they believe their own thoughts, wishes, and actions can make things happen in the greater world beyond their own control. Adults may reinforce this misconception when they suggest that children make a wish for something they want to happen.

Magical thinking is useful at times. Being able to wish for things to be better in their lives and in the world can help young children feel stronger and more in control; however, there is also a downside. When something tragic happens, such as the death of a family member, children may believe it happened because of something they said, did, thought, or wished.

Older children and teens usually wonder if there is something they could have done—or should have done—to prevent the death. For example, the parent would not have had a heart attack if the child had not misbehaved and caused stress in the family. The car crash would not have happened if the child did not need to be picked up after school. The cancer would not have progressed if the child had just made sure the parent had seen a doctor. Children and adults may, at some level (often unconsciously), choose to accept responsibility for a death rather than recognize that the death of someone close to them can happen again at any point, no matter what they do. This allows them the illusion of control. But an illusion of control doesn't help prevent future losses, and the associated guilt can make it more difficult to cope with the loss.

In addition, children often feel guilty for surviving the death of a sibling. They may also feel guilty if they are having fun or not feeling very sad after a family member has died. When talking with children about the death of someone close, it is appropriate to assume that some sense of guilt is likely present. This will usually be the case even if there is no logical reason for the children to feel responsible.

Can People Tell the Future?

The mascot of the basketball team of an all-girl high school spent the night with a friend after a game. She died during the night, and her sudden death was a shock to everyone at the school. After the death, one of her friends, Kara, a senior, was speaking privately to a bereavement counselor at the school. She asked the counselor if he believed people could tell the future.

"Why do you ask?" he replied.

"This seems odd, I know," Kara answered, "but I believe I can sometimes tell the future. When I look at my classmates, I can see what college they're going to attend."

"I'm curious," the counselor said, "what this has to do with your friend's death."

"I looked at her the week prior to her death and didn't see any college, and I knew somehow that she was going to die. But I didn't tell anyone. I keep thinking I should have said something, that maybe I could have stopped it."

The counselor explained to her that after a death, people often wonder if there was something they could have done to prevent the death. They might feel guilty about something they did or didn't do that they think contributed to the death. Something that seems unimportant when it happens may feel more important after a death occurs. Because her friend's death was so unexpected, there were probably a lot of people wondering the same thing she was—whether they could have done anything to change the situation.

As they discussed these issues, Kara was reassured to hear that her concerns were common. She started to see that the belief that she had foreseen her friend's death was a way her mind was trying to understand this sudden and troubling event. She thanked the counselor and said that although she was still upset and sad, she no longer felt she was at fault for her friend's death.

When Guilt Is More Likely

Guilt is common for children after any death. They are most likely to feel guilty when there have been challenges in the relationship with the person who died or in the circumstances of the death. The following are some examples:

- The child was angry with the person just before the death occurred.
- The death occurred after a long illness. During this time, the child may have occasionally wished the person would die to end everyone's suffering.

- Some action of the child seems related to the death. For example, a teen was in a heated argument with his mother shortly before she died in a car crash.

Children Often Express Anger About the Death

Children may focus on someone they feel is responsible for the death. They may feel angry at God. They may feel angry at the person who died for leaving them. Family members sometimes become the focus of this anger because they are near and are "safe" targets.

Older Children and Teens May Engage in Risky Behaviors

Older children may react to a death by driving recklessly, getting into fights, drinking alcohol, smoking cigarettes, or using drugs. They may become involved in sexual activity or delinquency. Sometimes they start to have problems at school or conflicts with friends.

Children May Appear to Think Only About Themselves When Confronted With a Death

During the best of times, children are usually most concerned with the things that affect them personally. During times of stress, such as after the death of someone they care about, they may appear even more self-centered. Yet, after a tragedy, adults often expect children to rise to the occasion and act more grown-up. It is true that children who have coped with difficult events often emerge with greater maturity, but in the moment itself, most children, and even adults, may act less maturely. They may respond to the death in ways that seem cold or selfish.

For example, they may respond by saying, "Does this mean I can't have my birthday party this weekend?" or "Am I still going to be able to go to the college I want?" Children typically think more about themselves when they are grieving, at least at first. Once they feel their needs are being met, they will be able to think more about the needs of others.

Under Stress, Children May Behave as They Did at a Younger Age

Stress may cause some children to regress. For example, young children who have recently mastered toilet training may start to have accidents. Children who have been acting with greater independence may become clingy or have difficulty with separation. Children and teens may also act less mature socially. They can become demanding, refuse to share, or pick fights with family members.

There is quite a range of common reactions among children who are coping with the death of a loved one. It is useful to remember that these reactions—regression, anger, selfishness, fear, reticence to talk about a death, magical thinking, and more—all serve the painful and confusing process of coping with grief. When educators offer support, they help students navigate the unique path of their bereavement. This allows students to bring personal meaning to their loss and do the hard work of preparing themselves for a life without the presence of the person who has died.

The remaining chapters in this book outline how educators can do this.

FACTORS THAT MAY AFFECT BEREAVEMENT

A number of different factors affect the way children respond to a death, in both the short and long term (Osterweis et al., 1984). These include:

- **Age.** Although the death will be felt deeply by all children, the specific challenges that grieving children face often change as they grow older.

- **Personality.** Some children are more resilient. Some have more difficulties with mood or social relationships. Personality factors can both help and hinder the grieving process.

- **Existing coping skills.** Some children have already developed skills for coping with powerful feelings, emotional challenges, or loss.

- **History of prior difficulties.** Students who have had previous difficulties personally or in school may have more difficulty with a loss. Students with a history of disciplinary problems, mental illness, personal trauma, or loss are at greater risk for difficulties with grief.

- **Available support systems.** When children receive strong and steady support from their families, schools, and communities, they are likely to cope more successfully with the loss and move through the grief process in a healthy fashion. Those who have inconsistent or weak support often have more difficulty.

- **Type of death.** Children may respond differently to a death that came after a long illness—for which they were prepared—than a sudden or traumatic death.

- **Relationship with the deceased.** It is always difficult for a child to lose someone he or she loves; however, the specifics of the relationship will have an impact on bereavement. For example, the death of an absent parent who was never very involved with a child might bring up feelings of conflict and confusion. The death of a sole parent who raised the child single-handedly will evoke feelings of anxiety about who will care for the child in the future.

CHILDREN'S TIME LINES FOR GRIEF

A child's time line for grief is a unique and personal matter. The goal of successful coping does not mean pushing or rushing children through their grief. In fact, the loss of a family member or friend is an experience that never fully leaves a person. In many ways, deep losses stay with us throughout our lives.

There are, however, some factors that can affect how much time it takes for children to begin to cope with the death and reach a point where a return to typical functioning in school, family, and social life is possible. These factors include the following:

- **How well the family functions.** Families that have a history of emotional closeness and open communication can usually offer more consistent support to grieving children. When a parent is clinically depressed or has other mental health problems, it may take a child longer to move through grief. When families are troubled by domestic violence, substance abuse, prior experiences of trauma, or the absence of a parent (e.g., working overseas, deployed in the military, in jail or prison), children often receive less support.

- **Parent coping skills.** Most parents do not have experience helping their children cope with the death of a close family member, such as a parent or sibling. Parents are usually just learning how to cope with their own feelings of grief. Those who are also able to provide effective support to their children can help them process the grief experience more successfully.

- **Provision of warmth.** Children who feel connected to and loved by their family have better emotional resources to address their grief.

- **Coping skills of children.** As mentioned previously, some children have better skills for dealing with strong emotions. These children will have greater success coping with bereavement.

- **Nature of the death itself.** Every loss of a family member or friend is difficult. Some deaths, however, are more challenging than others. Deaths by suicide, violence (Schonfeld & Demaria, 2020a, 2020b), or acts of terrorism (see Schonfeld, 2005, for an overview of the impact of terrorism on children), for example, are difficult in ways that death by illness may not be. Children may struggle more if the family feels shame about the cause of a death, such as a drug overdose or a disease such as AIDS. Deaths that receive a good deal of media notice or community attention may also be more difficult for children to process.

These situations are discussed in more detail in Chapter 7.

The goal of successful coping does not mean pushing or rushing children through their grief.

IDENTIFYING DISTRESS IN CHILDREN

Educators and parents often feel they can accurately assess levels of distress in grieving children. They know the children well. They are familiar with the ways a child acts when happy, sad, angry, frustrated, confused, or uncertain. They understand a child's typical expressions and behaviors.

When children are experiencing grief, they may not know how to describe what they are feeling.

Interestingly, close adults, such as educators and parents, are actually more likely to underestimate children's reactions to death and the need for support. The following are some of the reasons:

- **Adults may not expect young children to understand death or grieve a loss.** When adults do not expect children to be grieving, they may fail to see otherwise obvious cues about their distress.

- **Children's behaviors may not communicate a sense of grief to adults.** Adults usually look for and recognize behaviors that indicate grief to them—sad expressions, tears, or perhaps a quieter, more subdued way of speaking. Yet, some grieving children may be silly, impulsive, irritable, or loud. Their behavior may not communicate the distress they are feeling. They may seem "fine" to observers.

- **Children's language may not communicate a sense of grief to adults.** Many adults are used to children asking for what they want and describing what they need. When children are experiencing grief, however, they may not know how to describe what they are feeling, or they may not feel comfortable sharing those feelings with others. They also may not know what kind of support would help them feel better or the words to ask for what they want.

- **Adults want children to be okay, so they tend to see them that way when possible.** When children's behaviors and language seem normal and untroubled, adults feel relieved that the children are doing well.

- **Children are sensitive to adults' feelings and often want to protect them.** Children understand that direct mention of a death can be distressing to a parent, other family members, or teachers. They often choose not to bring up topics that would make these people whom they care about uncomfortable or unhappy.

Educators and parents are more likely to *underestimate* children's reactions to death and the need for support.

SPECIFIC CHALLENGES FOR EDUCATORS

Anyone who is close to children—parents, educators, or health care providers—might miss opportunities to support children because of the difficulties in identifying distress that were discussed in the previous section. Educators, however, face some additional, specific challenges in reaching grieving children. The following are some examples:

- **Children may not realize their teachers or other adults at their school are available for discussions about death.** If children have not had personal conversations with educators before, starting with the topic of death is difficult. If they have a stricter sense of what's "appropriate" to discuss with teachers (e.g., asking questions about math homework or an assignment), they may feel this is not an acceptable topic. If children think of teachers as a resource for intellectual knowledge, but not the practical matters of daily living, they may not think to approach them. In addition, children may feel that the educators in their lives are too busy or have other more important demands.

- **Children may be reluctant to start conversations about death at school.** Children often have a sense of their feelings being "out of control," especially when their grief is new. They do not always know how they will respond. They may worry that if they start to share their feelings, they will become upset and have difficulty maintaining their composure in front of their peers.

- **The conversation may feel too personal.** Adolescents are especially likely to feel that revealing personal thoughts, feelings, and experiences to their teachers is uncomfortable or inappropriate.

Chapter 5 discusses steps educators can take to let students know that they are available to talk about such matters and how to invite students to participate in these discussions.

ATTENDING FUNERALS

Families may look to educators for advice about whether children should participate in funerals. Families sometimes worry that a funeral will be frightening or confusing for children. However, children benefit from attending funerals, and it is helpful when educators can support children's opportunities to attend funerals or memorial services of a family member or close friend. In fact, educators are often the only professionals who can provide such advice to parents prior to the time of the funeral.

When children are not allowed to attend services, they often create fantasies that are far more frightening than what actually occurs at a funeral. They are likely to wonder, "What can they possibly be doing with my mother that is so awful I'm not allowed to see?" They may also feel hurt if they are not included in this important family event. They lose an opportunity to feel the comfort of spiritual and community support provided through services.

The following are some guidelines educators can share with families to help prepare children for services.

- **Explain what will happen.** In simple terms, it is helpful for children to know what to expect. This can include general points, such as where the service will be and who will be there. It is also useful to describe what will occur during the service, such as music, speakers, and prayers, as well as the overall tone of the event. For example, people may be crying, laughing about fond memories, or telling stories about the deceased. It is good to review some of the specific features of the service as well, such as whether there will be a casket, whether the casket will be open, whether there will be a funeral procession or graveside service, and so forth.

- **Answer questions.** Families can encourage children to ask any questions they have before the service. It is a good idea to check in with them more than once on this.

- **Let children decide whether to attend.** Parents can let their children know that they would like them to be there. It is often helpful to let children know that they can leave at any point or just take a break for a few minutes if they would like. If children feel quite certain they do not want to attend, it is generally best to respect this preference.

- **Find an adult to be with each child.** It is especially helpful for young children and preteens to have a specific adult who can stay with them throughout the service. This person can answer questions, provide comfort, and give the child individualized attention. Ideally, this will be someone the child knows and likes who is not as directly affected by the death, such as a babysitter or neighbor. This allows the adult to focus on the child's needs, including leaving the service if the child wishes. In some cases, educators may offer to play this important role for a child who is or has been their student.

- **Allow options.** Younger children might want to play quietly in the back of the room during the service. This can give them a sense of having participated in the ritual in a direct way. Older children or teens may want to invite a close friend to sit with them in the family section.

- **Offer a role in the service.** It may be helpful for children to have a simple task, such as handing out memorial cards or helping to choose flowers or a favorite song for the service. Suggest something that will comfort children but not overwhelm them.

- **Check in afterward.** It is important that family members speak to children after a service and offer comfort and love. In the days following the service, it is useful to check in again and ask the children what they thought of the service. Educators may be able to participate in this check-in as well by speaking privately to students who have attended a service and asking how it went, what they felt, and whether they have any questions.

I Want to Be at My Parents' Funeral

A family took a short drive to attend a family get-together. On the way, they were involved in a crash. Both parents were killed. The 8-year-old daughter, Hana, was seriously injured with many broken bones and internal injuries. She was admitted to the hospital, spent time in intensive care, and was still recovering at the time of her parents' funeral 1 week later. Physically, there was no way Hana could attend the service, but she wanted very much to be a part of the ceremony and to know what happened there.

Her aunt and uncle were quite close to her, and they had told her of her parents' death. They arranged to have the funeral video recorded. After the service, they were able to sit with their niece at the hospital and watch the service together.

Some of the staff at the hospital were concerned that watching a recording of the service would be upsetting to the girl. A few even found it macabre and wondered if showing this to Hana was truly appropriate. These concerns are understandable. Indeed, some children would not have made this request or found watching a recording helpful. For Hana, however, it was just the right thing. She felt included in the ritual of saying goodbye to her parents. She felt respected and affirmed because the family had found a way to respond to her wishes about attending the funeral. She was able to participate in the funeral in the company of her aunt and uncle, who were now to become her guardians. Their shared grief about this tragedy helped them strengthen the important bonds between them.

Wanting to Say Goodbye

The parents of a toddler were concerned when their daughter began slurring her speech and having difficulties walking. The father had ALS (amyotrophic lateral sclerosis, which is commonly known as Lou Gehrig's disease), and the family was already greatly burdened by the demands of the illness. They watched their 2 1/2-year-old stumble at times and even grab her father's cane on occasion to steady herself.

The child's pediatrician referred her to a neurologist and developmental pediatrician for further evaluation. The pediatrician asked several questions. Did the child also walk without difficulty at times? Yes, she did. Did she sometimes speak clearly? Yes, most certainly. Did she ever engage in play in which she mimicked her parents by putting on her mother's scarf or her father's cap, for example, or saying a phrase exactly as one of her parents did? Yes, just like all children, she mimicked and learned from the adults around her.

The child showed no neurological problems on the physical exam. It gradually dawned on the child's parents and her health care providers that the girl had been exhibiting normal behavior by imitating her father. This episode helped her parents understand more about the ways in which she was being affected by her father's illness. They then felt more comfortable being open with her as her father's illness worsened. They made sure her preschool teachers were aware of the situation.

The father died a couple of years later when the girl was starting kindergarten. She had continued to develop a close and strong relationship with him. At his funeral, she wanted to open the casket to see him again. At first, her mother wasn't sure this would be helpful. She had heard stories about young children being traumatized by viewings of deceased loved ones. Then she thought about her own experience. She had wanted to see her husband one last time, and opening the casket just prior to the funeral had been a comfort to her. She realized that because her daughter was asking for this as well, it would most likely be helpful for her. They arranged a private time after the service to have the casket opened, and together they said goodbye to this man they loved.

The next day, the mother told the story to the girl's teacher. The teacher watched for any signs of disturbance or upset but thought that the child was responding appropriately to her father's death. She exhibited sadness at times, talked about her father openly, and interacted regularly with other students.

CONTINUING EFFORTS TO FIND MEANING

Children's adjustment to a major loss is not completed in several months or a year. As children continue in their development and become more capable of understanding what has happened and what it means to them and their family to lose someone whom they love, they will try to find a new and more satisfying meaning for the loss. As time passes, they will face new stressors, learn new skills, and have new opportunities to cope and adjust.

For many children, the second year after a death brings new challenges that may be even more difficult than those of the first year. By this time, there is less support in place. Things have essentially returned to normal for the children's friends, neighbors, teachers, or coaches. People tend to make fewer extra efforts to check in with them. At the same time, the numbing effects of acute grief have usually worn off. In the first year after a death, children and families often experience special occasions in a sort of fog because everything is radically different. The family may not even try to make them festive or important.

For many children, the second year after a death brings new challenges that may be even more difficult than those of the first year.

Yet, when they come upon birthdays, the holidays, or the start of a new school year for the second time without the family member who died, it is clear that these important family events will never be the same. The intensity of these second-year experiences can be quite a blow to children who were expecting to start feeling better.

Sometimes children experience difficulties or raise concerns years after a death. For example, a 2-year-old might adjust reasonably well after the death of her mother, but then have many new questions and concerns at age 7. Now that she understands what a heart attack is, she may worry that she will have similar medical problems or begin to become very concerned about her father's high blood pressure. She may also start to ask questions about the circumstances of her mother's illness or death (e.g., Did she exercise regularly before she died? Had she ever been told that she had heart disease?).

An adolescent might have a challenging first year after the death of a family member and then have a couple of years where things seem back on track. Suddenly, while making the transition to college, a great deal of anxiety and uncertainty emerges.

These are examples of the ways an important loss stays with us throughout a lifetime. A boy who lost a father at a young age will probably ask himself as a preteen and adolescent, "What kind of guidance would my dad be giving me if he were still alive?" As he moves on to a career or college, he might ask, "What sort of work would my father think was good for me?" If he marries and has children, he will wonder, "What advice could my dad have given me about being a father?" When his own children are the age he was at the time of his father's death, he might worry acutely about his own mortality. Sad feelings from that time in his life may resurface. He will continue to miss the modeling his father might have given him about being the parent of an adolescent, the parent of a young adult, and a grandparent.

Educators who understand this ongoing quality of grief in children are better prepared to recognize the presence of grief responses in students who have experienced the death of a family member or friend in the past. Ongoing sensitivity and support for these experiences can be extremely helpful for children. This topic is discussed further in Chapter 8.

CUMULATIVE LOSS

Some communities experience extremely high rates of ongoing violence. In neighborhoods where there is significant gang-related activity, the deaths of teens, young children, and others may be so common that individual children there have experienced many losses. This is described as cumulative loss.

Educators in these communities may have the impression that their students do not want to talk about death or the impact of these losses. "This happens all the time here," one teacher remarked sadly after several students were shot on their way home from school one day. "They're used to it."

Even when death and violence are common, children do not get used to the situation. In fact, generally they become more sensitized to these issues as they continue to have these experiences. Each death may bring up the unresolved feelings of prior losses, which further adds to the sadness, stress, and anxiety. Each death or traumatic experience, therefore, is incrementally more difficult, so much so that children may feel the need to deny their feelings and reactions to avoid feeling overwhelmed. They may then appear to dismiss concerns or show no reaction.

Children want and need to talk about the important things that happen in their lives. This includes violent deaths that touch them in some way. They are looking for guidance about how to express their thoughts and feelings, how to make sense of these terrible things happening around them, and how to cope best under such challenging and frightening circumstances. It is important to give them opportunities to express themselves and to be heard by concerned and caring adults.

Multiple Losses Over a Short Period of Time

We often think of cumulative loss as something that occurs in situations where gang activity or levels of community violence are high. It can also be seen after a disease outbreak or pandemic that results in multiple deaths within the same community or after a large natural disaster. It may materialize in situations where multiple losses occur over a brief time span. Sometimes, students or staff navigate their way through one loss in a fairly straightforward manner but find it difficult to deal with another loss that occurs soon after.

For example, a school that seems to be progressing well after a student has been shot on campus might experience a great crisis when one of the coaches dies of a heart attack just a few weeks later. Both student and staff reactions may bring up responses that are more closely related to the earlier incident.

Who's to Blame for This?

A first grader discovered a loaded gun at home. He picked it up, it discharged, and a second student was struck and killed. The incident was devastating to students and educators at their school. This district had experienced gang-related shootings and deaths, but this accidental death was different. Some educators felt confused by the inadvertent nature of the event. Although they could blame a perpetrator in a gang-related shooting, they could not blame the first grader for this tragedy.

Several weeks later, the school closed for a weekend holiday. Over the break, the ventilation system malfunctioned and the temperature throughout the school building became very high. When students and educators returned, students in classrooms with pets discovered that all of the pets had died.

The staff were very upset—more than would typically be expected for this type of loss. They were enraged about the effect this event was having on their students. A number of individuals were highly vocal about finding out who was to blame for the malfunction.

On the surface, the staff appeared to be overreacting to the loss of the pets. In the context of the earlier death, however, it was clear that the losses had become intermingled. The loss of the pets occurring so close to the loss of a student was overwhelming to many. For staff, the second loss also offered a clear pathway to assign blame that had been absent in the first incident.

A Shooting on a Military Base

An armed gunman fired shots on a military base. The nearby child care program went on immediate lockdown. Phone signals were scrambled during the incident, and parents were unable to reach the program to check on their children.

None of the children were harmed, and no shots were fired at the child care center. However, there were deaths and injuries on the base resulting from this incident. Most of the military personnel on base had experienced combat and seen death. They were able to put these losses into the context of their role as servicemembers—the deaths were painful for the survivors, and they were also a known risk of the job. Military staff know they are putting their lives on the line every day.

However, being unable to check in with the child care program in the midst of a threat was highly distressing for the parents. Their training and experience did not prepare them for this.

A few months later, one of the children in the child care program died of natural causes during naptime. Parents and program staff were overwhelmed by this death. They reached out to the National Center for School Crisis and Bereavement (NCSCB) for assistance. "We need someone to come and help us deal with this," they explained. "We don't know what to do." This community was well-prepared to cope with their emotions after a violent shooting that resulted in multiple deaths. However, the death of a child by natural causes was troubling in a completely different way. It also became mingled with their continuing grief over the losses of their fellow servicemembers.

In situations where students are experiencing multiple losses over a short period of time, offer opportunities to discuss all losses. It is helpful to normalize the experience of comingled grief and to recognize and affirm the effects of cumulative loss.

––––––––

It is helpful to normalize the experience of comingled grief and to recognize and affirm the effects of cumulative loss.

––––––––

DIFFERENT CULTURAL VIEWS OF DEATH

Death is a vital and essential part of every culture. Beliefs, rituals, and practices about death vary from culture to culture, as well as from family to family. When an educator and a student have cultural differences, educators may hesitate to talk about death with the child or the family (Schonfeld et al., 2015). No one wants to say something insensitive when a family is grieving.

It would be virtually impossible for any single person, especially a busy educator with many daily demands, to become completely versed in all of the practices and rituals about death in different cultures. At the NCSCB, we have worked with families from many different cultures and have found two general guidelines to work well in virtually every interaction. First, be competent and comfortable in your own culture, and second, know that every family is unique.

Be Competent and Comfortable in Your Own Culture

The most important guideline to understanding other cultural views on death is to be genuinely competent in your own culture. A sensitive and thoughtful person who can support a child in one culture will usually find it possible to work well across cultures. The same kinds of general questions and concerns come up for children in all cultures. These include concern for self (e.g., "Will I be okay?"), concern for others (e.g., "Will my other family members and/or friends be okay?"), and questions about the meaning of death (e.g., the Four Concepts About Death). For an example of a cross-cultural comparison of young children's understanding of death, see the article by Schonfeld and Smilansky (1989).

When people focus on differences across cultures, it is easy to feel uncertain about offering support to someone from a culture other than one's own. One culture may not speak the name of the dead. Another may name the next-born child after the person who died. One culture may believe each tear shed creates another hardship for the deceased, so families are quiet and restrained at funerals. Yet another culture may believe that the open expression of grief demonstrates the depth of love felt, so families weep with great emotion at the service.

Instead of trying to learn all of these features for every culture in a community, educators can simply remember in a general way that there are different cultural traditions, practices, and beliefs. Families are usually quite grateful when a concerned educator or other helper asks directly for specific information about these matters. At the NCSCB, we have worked with families and professionals from cultures throughout the United States, as well as internationally in cultures as varied as those in Asia, the United Kingdom, Europe, Scandinavia, Latin America, and the Middle East. We often find ourselves saying, "I am not familiar enough with your culture and belief system to know how best to offer my assistance. Can you give me some suggestions about how to be helpful?" We have had great success by simply saying to people, in one way or another, "I'd like to learn about your culture. I'd like to know how to be helpful."

Every Family Is Unique

Another problem with a content-based approach to cultural differences about death is that each family interacts with these cultural elements in different ways. If you think for a moment about your own culture, you'll probably be able to identify approaches to grieving that vary from family to family. Some families adhere very closely to their culture's perspective on death, whereas others follow these precepts more loosely or not at all.

For this reason, it is also important to check in at the family level on attitudes about death. Educators can ask an individual or the entire family for guidance. For example, a teacher can say, "Help me understand how you and your family will go through this and how I can be helpful." Cues are usually immediately offered, such as whether the name of the deceased is used, what the time frame for the family's rituals may be (e.g., burial within 3 days, a memorial service in 2 weeks), and whether strong religious beliefs are a part of the family's understanding. When we make assumptions about how a grieving family relates to their cultural traditions, we may miss important opportunities to offer support.

An Amish Family Remembers

When we were working with an Amish family who had experienced the death of a young child, we were surprised to see a framed photograph of the girl on the wall. Amish people do not allow photographs of themselves, especially if faces are recognizable. For them, photos are considered a sign of vanity and a form of graven image.

The grandmother told a story of seeing her granddaughter out in the yard one day, talking to a tourist with a camera. She went out to see what was happening. The girl turned to her with great excitement and said, "Look, Grandma. He has taken my picture and is going to send us a copy! Please let him send us a copy! I've never seen a photo of myself!" The grandmother, touched by the girl's enthusiasm, decided to allow this. Soon, the family received the photo, and the girl was pleased to see it.

Shortly after this, the girl died suddenly and tragically. The grandmother touched the photo and said, "I am glad now that we have this. It is all we have of her, you see."

This is a good example of an individual family finding its own way on a specific matter of belief, one that had particularly powerful meaning for them at the time a death occurred.

OFFERING CHILDREN SUPPORT THAT HELPS

Educators enter their profession because they care about children. It is difficult to see children struggling to cope with a death. It can also be disconcerting to feel confused by children's reactions to death. Educators may be uncertain about how to communicate with grieving students, an especially frustrating experience for those who are skillful communicators in other subjects, such as administrative review, school budgets, policies, math, or writing.

This is why it is so useful to understand the ways children typically understand death and know about some of the factors likely to affect grieving children. It prepares educators to offer powerful support that can help students cope well, move forward in their lives, and continue to succeed academically. The following chapters further discuss the specific kinds of support that help grieving children.

Key Concepts

- **Children grieve in individual ways, just as adults do.** Every student's situation is unique, and children's reactions will vary. So will the time line for their adjustment.
- **Children may experience a range of emotions after a death.** These often include confusion, guilt, and anger.
- **A number of different factors affect the way children respond to a death.** These include differences in how children are as individuals, their coping skills, and the family situation.

- **It can be difficult to identify distress in grieving children.** Even children who appear to be doing well may be struggling with their feelings and in need of support.

- **In most situations, it is best if children are encouraged to attend funerals or memorials of a family member or close friend.** Children gain many benefits by being part of these events, and educators may be able to guide families in making decisions that support their children.

- **Children who have experienced cumulative loss become more sensitized, not less, to these issues.** Children do not "get used to" death, even if they live in areas where death and violence are common.

- **Although every culture has a different approach to death, educators can best offer support by first becoming genuinely competent in their own culture.** Families are usually grateful when a caring educator is able to ask how to be of help or offer support.

4

Support for Grieving Children: First Steps

Schools and educators can take concrete steps that will help bereaved children. These include understanding how to be present with and express support for grieving children. Communicating clearly and effectively with children and their families is key. It is also essential to remember that grief is a painful process. There is nothing that anyone—family member, educator, therapist, etc.— can say or do that will take away the pain or make the loss less powerful. That is not the goal of bereavement interventions.

GOALS OF INTERVENTION

What are the goals for educators who are taking steps to give grieving children and their families support? They involve helping children in the areas that are most likely to present challenges after the death of a family member or friend. The following are six goals for educators helping grieving children:

1. **Decrease the sense of isolation.** Grieving children may pull back from family members because they do not understand, or are not sure how to respond to, the grief they are experiencing. They may not want their own feelings to create more of a burden. They may feel guilt or shame associated with the loss. If the person who died was a family member, they may wonder what their role is in the new structure of the family.

   Grieving children also often pull back from peers because they may not believe that their peers will understand or be able to help them cope with their strong and confusing feelings. They may not know what to say about the death or their grief. They may feel uncomfortable at the attention people give them, at a time when they are feeling overwhelmed, awkward, or vulnerable, or with friends' attempts to offer support. Or, they may be uncomfortable because their peers seem to be ignoring their loss. They may feel distracted or overwhelmed and less able to keep up

41

with the usual social give-and-take of their friends. They do not want to be singled out or seen as a victim.

At the same time, peers may be reluctant to reach out to their grieving friends because they are unsure of what to say or how to be of support. This can be a lonely and troubling consequence of children's grief. When educators address the topic of death in school, either as planned coursework or in response to teachable moments, they provide all children with knowledge, skills, and increased comfort so that they are more able to share their feelings and receive and offer support.

Although most children want to help their friends, without guidance, they may make insensitive comments, ask repetitive or detailed questions about the death, or even tease a grieving peer. This may reflect their own anxieties and discomfort, but the consequences for grieving children can be painful. In one study of 35 parentally bereaved children ages 6–15 years, 20% had experienced "direct, raw taunting about their loss" (Cain & LaFreniere, 2015, p. 219).

Grieving children often pull back from peers because they may not believe that their peers will understand or be able to help them cope with their strong and confusing feelings.

---

2. **Increase academic function.** Common responses to death include difficulty concentrating, easy distractibility, frustration, anger, difficulty sleeping, anxiety, and feelings of sadness. It is easy for school performance to slide under these circumstances. Support that helps children cope with their feelings also prepares them to move forward academically.

3. **Increase the likelihood children will talk with their family.** Generally, the most important source of support for grieving children is their family. Many families, however, are unsure about how to talk about a death with their children. Children may not realize these conversations are important or may not know how to get started. When children have opportunities to talk with educators and identify their feelings, communicate their concerns, and hear words of support in response, they learn how helpful this can be and appreciate that adults are prepared to provide support. This can encourage them to seek more support from their family as well.

4. **Increase the likelihood of talk and support among peers.** Students who have participated in lessons about death and grief will understand more about the process and may be more comfortable reaching out to a peer who has experienced a loss. Educators can also provide practical advice about what to say to a grieving peer or how to provide support. Students who have previously *given* support to a grieving peer may be more open to receiving similar support themselves if they experience a loss. Students who see an educator talking with a bereaved student, even if they do not know the details of the conversation, have a role model

who shows them that contact is important. When grieving students are more comfortable talking about their experiences, perhaps because they have received support to do so from an educator, they are more likely to reach out to peers as well.

5. **Identify problems in the family.** Often children provide information that brings to light difficulties within the family. Sometimes the most helpful intervention for a child is an appropriate referral for a parent struggling with depression or anxiety.

6. **Connect with students on something of immense importance.** Students respect their teachers and other educators. They emulate them when they believe educators genuinely care about their welfare. There are few gestures that can express caring more effectively than paying attention to a child's needs after the death of a family member or friend.

These goals may sound like a lot to aim for, but they can be achieved in fairly simple ways that do not usually require a great deal of time. The steps described below outline a foundation for making these connections with students. In the remaining chapters, you will find additional suggestions for creating effective lines of communication with students, working with families, supporting students with complicated grief, and providing support over time.

BEING WITH GRIEVING CHILDREN

As a culture, we do not often talk openly about death and the grief process, especially when children are involved. Because of this, it can be difficult to understand something as straightforward as how to *be* with children who are grieving. What does one say? How should one act? What if you have feelings of your own about this loss? What if you *don't* feel strongly about it?

The following are some suggestions for how to act and what to say to grieving children:

- **Be present and authentic.** Children are sensitive to dishonesty, and they can often tell if someone is not being truthful. Being genuine involves finding ways to show concern and emotions that ring true for both educators and grieving children. Most educators have emotional reactions when they hear a student has suffered the loss of a close family member or a friend. An educator who is upset and tries not to show it will not be as effective as one who can speak directly about these feelings. A teacher might say, "I was sorry to hear about your brother's death. I feel very sad that he died. I know you must have some feelings about this, too. Would you like to talk about your brother or tell me what these last few days have been like?"

    Similarly, someone who does not have a strong emotional response should not try to manufacture one. There are effective ways to express caring and concern for children in both circumstances that leave the door open for children to recognize the support. When done properly, children can trust the genuine concern and understand that educators are interested in hearing more from them. For example, if a school counselor did not know the person who died, it would be inappropriate to say, "I will miss her, too." It would make sense to a child, however, if the counselor said, "I didn't know your friend, but I can tell she was someone who was very important to you. I feel sad that you had to experience such a loss."

- **Listen more, talk less.** It is fine to share personal feelings and express caring and concern, but it should be kept brief. Keep the focus on the children who are grieving and give them plenty of space and time to talk.

- **Avoid trying to cheer up students or their families.** Remember, an educator's goal is not to take away the pain of this grief. Powerful and painful feelings will be with the survivors for some time. Comments and efforts meant to cheer people up or find something positive in the situation usually are not helpful.

- **Allow emotional expression.** Young people going through grief are often told to "be strong," "toughen up," or cover up their feelings. A more helpful intervention is to suggest they are probably having many strong feelings and invite them to talk about this. Expressing emotions is an important part of grieving. This may mean watching someone be angry, selfish, or grief-stricken.

Keep the focus on the children who are grieving and give them plenty of space and time to talk.

- **Demonstrate empathy.** Educators can reflect back what they see students express, directly or indirectly. They might describe emotions they see ("It seems like this has been confusing and painful for you") or feel themselves ("I feel sad that you had to lose someone you care so deeply about"). They might restate something a student says ("So your mom has been very sad"). They might, through body language and brief comments, show that they are listening carefully ("I see," while nodding and encouraging the student to continue) and share some of the student's affect (becoming quiet and matching the facial expression and demeanor to the feelings the student is sharing). These reflections should be offered with compassion and without judgment.

- **Stop harmful reactions when safety is a concern.** Some children react to grief with angry outbursts. Expressions such as these are natural and show that children are willing to experience some of the truly deep feelings that accompany profound grief. Allow grieving children to cry, shout, kick the floor, or throw down a book. If such behavior poses a risk to the grieving child or others, however, it should be stopped. Property damage is also not necessary to this process and is not helpful to children.

When children do not have an opportunity to experience and talk about their grief, they often find it difficult to make sense of their experience and move on. Inquiries from teachers or other school staff can be immensely important in these circumstances. The following story offers a compelling example.

Can Someone Just Be Honest?

Seventeen-year-old James worked after school at a local restaurant. One afternoon, he received a call from a relative with the terrible news that his older brother had just died in an auto collision. His parents were on their way to meet with the police. An aunt and uncle would be by to pick up James and take him home where he could be with his younger brothers and sisters.

When the aunt and uncle arrived, they were under the impression that James did not know about his brother's death. They smiled and made small talk and acted as if nothing was out of the ordinary. Back at the family home, they gathered the children around the television to watch a movie. They chose a comedy. James could not figure out what he was supposed to do. Was he supposed to pretend he was happy? Laugh? Act as if he did not know about his brother's death? Should he tell his younger siblings what had happened? "Can someone just be honest?" he kept asking himself.

By the time his parents returned home and told all of the children about the death, a good 4 hours after he had first learned about it, James was completely confused about his feelings and responses. In the weeks and months that followed, he talked little about his brother's death. He rarely showed emotion about it. He kept on with work and school. He focused on graduating from high school and following through on his long-standing plans to join the Navy.

These were difficult times for his parents. His mother struggled with powerful grief, and for several weeks, she was unable to return to work. She found it difficult to do her usual family tasks—shop for food, prepare meals, get the younger children ready for school. James stepped up and took on more of these responsibilities. Everyone was impressed with how well he was coping and the maturity he showed in helping his family.

After a few months, as his mother's acute grief started to improve, James began having more problems with his brother's death. He experienced outbursts of anger or crying. He had troubling dreams. He felt empty at times and hopeless about the future. He missed his brother more deeply, and the feelings seemed to be getting worse rather than better.

After several months, his mother brought James to talk with a bereavement counselor. At first, James could not explain why he was having these increasing problems. As he told his story, however, he realized that he had never really had a chance to experience and express the terrible grief he felt about his brother's death. He had felt a need to keep things together for himself and his family while his mother was struggling so much with her own feelings. There never seemed to be anyone for him to talk to. As she improved, his own feelings and reactions became stronger, to the point where he now felt distracted and disturbed by them.

James needed to have a place to talk about his own story—how he learned about his brother's death, how he felt about it, what this emptiness would mean in his life. His grief, however, once it emerged, was not unusual or complicated. In fact, after just a couple of meetings, he felt more settled, clearer about how he was experiencing this loss, and hopeful again about the future. He did not feel a need for further meetings. This was a simple intervention that a teacher or school counselor could have offered as well. James went on to graduate and pursue his career in the military.

What *Not* to Say

The following are some examples of well-intentioned statements that are generally not helpful to grieving children or their families.

"I know exactly what you are going through."

It is not possible to know what another individual is going through, especially in a matter as profound as the loss of a loved one. Even if you have lost family members, close friends, or a spouse, your own experience is as distinct as those of the children you teach.

What to say instead:

- "I can only imagine how difficult this must be for you."
- "I wonder what this is like for you."

"You must be incredibly angry."

Anger is a natural reaction in the grief process, but it is impossible to know what someone is experiencing at any given time. Telling people what they ought to be feeling is not helpful.

What to say instead:

- "I wonder what kind of feelings you're having about this."
- "Most people have strong feelings when something like this happens in their lives. Has that been true for you?"
- "What have the last few days been like for you?"

"I know this must be difficult, but it's important to remember the good things in life as well."

Watching someone grieve is difficult. The desire to cheer up children or their families is understandable, but it is not helpful. What grieving families need is permission to fully experience and express their immeasurable grief or anger, confusion, relief, or whatever other feelings they are having. Comments that begin with "at least," such as, "At least your mother is no longer in pain"; "At least you still have another brother"; or "At least your friend is in a better place now," should generally be reconsidered. Attempts to cheer up or reassure those who are grieving may quiet their expressions of grief, but they do not lift the powerful feelings or help them process their loss.

"You'll need to be strong now for your family.
It's important to get a grip on your feelings."

The most important opportunity we can offer grieving children and their families is that of expressing their thoughts and feelings fully. Grieving children are often told they should not be expressive—that they need to grow up fast, keep it together for their family, manage their feelings, and not feel sorry for themselves. These messages tend to hold children back from experiencing the deep and powerful feelings they are having, without helping them cope or adjust any more effectively.

————

The most important opportunity we can offer grieving children and their families is that of expressing their thoughts and feelings fully.

————

"Both of my parents died when I was your age."

Avoid statements that compete with children's experiences of loss. Children who had one parent or a sibling die may feel their loss is not as meaningful if the focus is shifted to someone who has suffered even more. Similarly, comments about another student who lost both parents last year may make children feel their situation is not as significant.

"My 15-year-old dog died last week. I feel very sad, too."

It is impossible to compare losses and generally not useful to attempt to do so. As much as possible, keep the focus on the children's experience and need for support.

Does Grief Go Through Stages?

Many people are familiar with models that describe the stages people move through in the grief process. Perhaps the most well-known stages are the Five Stages of Grief developed about 50 years ago by Elisabeth Kübler-Ross (denial, anger, bargaining, depression, and acceptance). Although these models may help us understand something about the range of experiences people have in relationship to grief, they do not by themselves accurately predict the sequence of reactions most people go through most of the time. In fact, people, including most children, experience many of these kinds of feelings at different times throughout grief. Grief is not a simple linear process. Rather than trying to apply children's experiences to any specific model about grief, it is more useful to take steps to understand what an individual child is experiencing at the present time and tailor support to the child's unique needs.

COMMUNICATION: THE HEART OF THE WORK

Communication is the heart and soul of working with bereaved children and their families. When educators help initiate the conversations, they help children gain the skills and confidence to continue them with others.

We encourage educators to address the topic of death and loss proactively. As described in Chapter 2, it is important to discuss death in a general way with all students before any loss is identified because it provides information and anticipatory guidance around the matter of death and grief. It is also essential for educators to actively open communication when they know a specific student is experiencing grief. Educators should not wait for students to approach them. A student may not realize this is an option or feel secure enough in taking the first step.

A vital power differential exists between students and teachers or other school staff. This is often a good thing. It helps educators offer trusted guidance in learning and maintain order when necessary. However, this same difference in power makes it difficult for students to approach an educator with questions about something as troublesome as death. This is not so surprising, really. Even adults are often reluctant to tell others about personal experiences of grief. They may hesitate to tell a boss or supervisor about a death, or they may minimize the challenges and distress presented by their grief. Children who observe this deference or hesitation in a parent or other family member might be even more likely to avoid troubling their teacher or coach.

Similarly, however, an educator's status can open up possibilities with children. Educators' authority communicates experience, wisdom, and an ability to determine what topics are appropriate to discuss. Children are often quite responsive when a teacher, counselor, or other educator suggests they talk about a recent death, and they usually appreciate the opportunity to do so.

Getting Students to Talk

Students may be more likely to discuss a death with an educator if the circumstances make the topic approachable. Educators can help set the tone for a conversation by creating the following context:

- **Students feel they have permission to talk about their loss.** Children realize that the topic of a death is often uncomfortable for people. They are more likely to feel that they have permission to open these conversations if they already know an educator is willing to discuss challenging matters. They may remember a teacher saying, "You can always ask me about anything, even if it seems like something difficult." They may know peers who have felt supported when they talked to school personnel about troublesome topics. An educator can also specifically extend an invitation to an individual child to talk about a recent death.

Students are more likely to feel that they have permission to open these conversations if they already know an educator is willing to discuss challenging matters.

- **Students sense the educator is listening genuinely.** This means the educator is emotionally and intellectually present during the conversation and is responding directly to what the student says. Unhelpful comments should be avoided (see the earlier section "What *Not* to Say").

- **Educators have discussed death, grief, or other difficult topics in the past.** Educators who have already addressed difficult topics with students have demonstrated their ability to listen, teach, and think and learn about them. Students have confidence that the educator can handle the conversation personally and will have something useful to offer.

Steps to Invite the Conversation

This section offers some steps that educators can take to start and sustain communication with grieving students. (More detailed examples of each of these steps are given in Chapter 5.)

- **Express concern.** Let students know directly that you have heard about the death and are thinking about them.
- **Invite the conversation.** Ask a simple, direct question, such as "How are you doing?" This invites students to engage.
- **Listen and observe.** This can take patience. Some students may need time to figure out what they want to say. Some may communicate in nonverbal ways.
- **Offer reassurance.** Feelings of grief may be strong, powerful, surprising, and unfamiliar. It is helpful for students to know that these are typical reactions. It may also be useful for them to understand that the feelings change over time and generally become easier to experience. This can be a bit nuanced—the point of the message is not to dismiss the student's feelings or imply that they will "get over it" after a while. Rather, it is to reassure them that the intensity of acute grief will usually shift over time.
- **Continue to make contact.** Students' thoughts, insights, and feelings change over time. Many will appreciate ongoing opportunities to talk about the ways their experiences are changing.

These types of interventions give children an opportunity to find their own best way through this process. Such conversations help them make meaning of their loss while continuing to move forward in their lives.

Communication Challenges

In the same way that there are factors that increase children's likelihood of talking to educators about grieving and death, there are also reasons why children who are grieving do not readily approach educators about their loss. For example:

Students may feel overwhelmed.

They may not know where to begin. They may feel unable to manage the burden of trying to cope with their own complex feelings while protecting the feelings of others who do not necessarily want to talk about death and grief. They may worry that if they start to express their feelings, they will embarrass themselves by beginning to cry in front of their peers or, worse yet, be unable to stop crying once they have started.

What to do:

- Initiate a conversation.
- Express your concern and interest.
- Start simply with one or two open-ended questions (i.e., questions that cannot be answered with a single word, such as "yes" or "no").
- Offer to speak in private outside of class.
- Ask the student when a good time would be to talk.

――――――

Students may worry that if they start to express their feelings, they will embarrass themselves by beginning to cry in front of their peers.

――――――

Students may lack a clear sense of what support would be helpful.

Students may not fully understand what has happened or the implications that the death has for their life. They may not have personal models for seeking support. They may not realize that talking to someone, such as an educator, would be helpful. In addition, they may not think educators have anything useful to say.

What to do:

- Ask open-ended questions.
- Include some questions that guide students toward useful answers. For example, ask students how they are doing, how their family is doing, what kinds of support they are finding, and so forth.

Students may not want to stand out from their peers.

When everything else in their life feels like it is in turmoil, children may want to feel like they are just regular students, doing regular things. They may be embarrassed by the idea of receiving any sort of special attention.

What to do:

- Offer a private conversation.
- Seek out a one-to-one conversation in a typical setting, such as the playground, a common area, or the classroom during a student–teacher conference that everyone is having about a homework assignment.
- Acknowledge the concern directly. For example, make a statement such as, "I've sometimes talked to students going through a loss who wish everyone would just treat them normally instead of making a big deal about it. I wonder if you're feeling like that."

Students may feel more comfortable turning to peers.

Students may not think of educators as a resource for this kind of support. This is especially true of adolescents.

What to do:

- Acknowledge the importance of receiving support and ask students who they are able to talk to.
- Ask if there is an adult in their lives with whom they can talk about these things.
- Offer to be available if students wish to talk at some future time.

They Acted Like Nothing Had Happened

Teresa was a 16-year-old high school junior when her mother died. She came from a close family and was able to get helpful support from her father, siblings, cousins, aunts, and uncles. She had several good friends who came to see her in the period immediately after the death, and most spent the day of the funeral with her. Everyone talked about the ways they had loved or respected her mother, the ways they missed her, and how they would keep her memory alive in the future.

Teresa returned to school a week after the funeral. She felt ready to bring her attention back to her studies, but she also knew that everything was going to feel different to her now. She wondered what her teachers would say and how she might respond. Would one of the school counselors contact her? Would she cry? If she did, would she feel okay about it?

Her teachers didn't say anything. No counselor contacted her. No coach or club sponsor spoke up. Former teachers did not approach her. "It was so strange," she said later. "The school acted like nothing happened, like nothing was different. But for me, everything was different."

Teresa didn't have a specific idea about what she expected or wanted. "I just knew they should have done something. It wouldn't have even mattered that much to me what it was—just someone acknowledging that I'd gone through this incredible experience that had completely changed my life."

She was lucky to have strong support among her family and friends. However, the transition back to school would have been easier for her if even one or two educators had spoken to Teresa directly about her mother's death.

Talking About Religious and Spiritual Issues

Public school educators and those working in secular private schools are usually wary about any discussions that might touch on religious or spiritual issues. Many wonder whether discussions about death and grief will cross the line and set the educator up for parental complaints or other problems.

It is important to remember that the Four Concepts About Death are a set of facts and principles that do not conflict with religious and cultural beliefs. At the

NCSCB, we have used these concepts extensively in many different religious and cultural settings and have never experienced any meaningful disagreement about them. We know of no religion that has a conflict with these concepts.

We suggest that educators' interventions focus on clarifying the Four Concepts About Death and allowing children opportunities to describe their thoughts, feelings, and other experiences. These conversations are unlikely to create conflicts about religious beliefs with families of any faith or of none.

Religious concepts themselves are usually quite abstract. We agree that outside of parochial schools, educators will not be teaching these abstractions. If students do ask questions specific to religious tenets, educators can acknowledge that different families have different religious beliefs. For example, if a child asks what heaven is like, it is appropriate to acknowledge that different families have different beliefs about heaven. Educators can suggest that they talk to their parents for more help understanding this issue.

In the work of the NCSCB, we have never experienced complaints about religious matters from parents. We think it is prudent, however, for educators to have a set statement that can be used in response to questions about religious beliefs in discussions with any students, including those who are experiencing grief. Educators may choose a response such as, "Your question touches on religious beliefs, and there are many different opinions about this matter. In our school, we respect different religious beliefs, but we do not teach about religion. This is why I am going to ask you to talk to your parents about this. I think they can better help you answer this question."

If a parent does complain about a conversation, the educator can easily repeat back the standard statement and clarify that no inappropriate teaching occurred. In addition, when an educator uses this statement consistently in such instances, other students can affirm that this is the typical protocol. This can help everyone be clear about any conversation that took place and keep their focus on the needs of the grieving student.

It is also useful to recognize that these more abstract questions are often rhetorical in nature for older children. When grieving children say, "Why would God let something like this happen?" they may simply be asking the same question adults ask at times such as these. They are not asking, "What is my religious belief?" Rather, they are saying, "How can I possibly make sense of this complex world?" This topic is discussed further in Chapter 5.

ESTABLISH SENSITIVE, EFFECTIVE POLICIES FOR GRIEVING STUDENTS

One of the ways districts and schools can work proactively to support grieving students is to create and implement informed, appropriate policies about grieving students. This allows schools to address students' experiences in consistent, relevant ways.

We discuss policies for when an entire school is affected by a death in Chapter 9 and policies about memorialization and commemoration in Chapter 13. We mentioned the Grief-Sensitive Schools Initiative in the Introduction, which allows schools to take steps to commit themselves to providing a supportive environment to students who have lost a loved one.

You can also find more discussion, along with policy examples, at the web site for the NCSCB (https://www.schoolcrisiscenter.org/).

There are also policies that affect individual students and their families. These might concern excused time from school for funerals, adaptations for academic work when a student is newly bereaved, family requests for on-campus memorial events, standards for social media monitoring, or commitments for all-staff professional development.

As discussed in Chapter 3, in most cases, it is helpful for children to attend the funeral of a family member. When an immediate family member has died, children may be expected to participate in a range of activities and services, sometimes over a period of time. One educator we spoke with mentioned that students from a local Native American tribe participated in a full week of ceremonies honoring a deceased family member. Families may need to travel to services and events. In these types of circumstances, it is helpful to have policies already in place addressing attendance, excused absences, and accommodation for missed exams or project deadlines that do not penalize grieving students.

Similarly, it is reasonable to expect grieving students to have some academic challenges in the days, weeks, or even longer after a loss. Policies can help guide educators as they work with children and families to make reasonable and supportive accommodations. (We discuss academic accommodations more fully in Chapter 5.) They might also address possible educator or school responses to student experiences of grief triggers (discussed in Chapter 8), including what sort of "safe space" options are allowed.

Some districts inquire about significant losses during enrollment or registration. Grieving students can be connected to sources of support in the school or community. This can help teachers and other staff become more aware of students' potential needs for support.

Most districts and schools now have informal and/or formal procedures in place to monitor social media postings relevant to their students, while still respecting concerns for student and staff privacy. These often focus on important issues such as bullying, cheating, violations of the school's standards of conduct, potential threats, or students at risk for self-harm. However, monitoring may also reveal a student who is feeling challenged by a grief experience or one who is being harassed in some manner after a death. Expanding policies to include such instances would be appropriate.

At the NCSCB, we are strong supporters of professional development for educators focusing on support for grieving children. We are sometimes asked, "Who should attend these trainings?" Our answer is that we believe all staff in the educator community should attend. Although we might expect the greatest portion of this work will rest in the hands of teachers, counselors, and other student support personnel, we cannot emphasize enough the importance of the relationships students have with other adults in a school. Individual students might have a special connection with the librarian, a health educator or parent volunteer, a coach, someone in food services, a custodian, or a school safety officer. This is also valuable knowledge for principals and other administrative staff who are interacting with students, helping to set policies, working to support all school staff, and responding to families.

Training for All of Us

NCSCB assisted in a professional development event for a school that made the decision to include all school staff and volunteers in the process. Everyone took part in this 5-hour training. Participants were active and engaged over the course of the training. They appreciated the sense that these guidelines were being set as a standard for educators throughout the school, whatever their role.

After the training, one of the cafeteria workers came up to the trainer. "Thank you!" she said. "After 15 years in this school, this is the first time I was invited to participate in professional development. This topic was meaningful for me personally and professionally. Thank you for acknowledging that support professionals can provide important support to students."

HOW MUCH TIME DOES THIS TAKE?

One obstacle we find when we talk to educators about matters of death and grieving is their concern about how much time the suggested actions will take. Some wonder if they are adequately prepared to do this kind of work. They worry that they may make things worse for children or their families.

"This is too much work," some educators have told us. "We don't know how to do this kind of complicated intervention. This is social work, not education."

Through the NCSCB, we have worked with thousands of schools around the country and throughout the world. We have consistently found that, most often, these interventions take a relatively short amount of time. With a little training and understanding, as is found in this book, educators can effectively help grieving children. They can use the same skills they are already using to teach and listen to children and to communicate with families. Most educators find it fairly easy to address the necessary matters related to grief and death, particularly when they are supported by their colleagues, schools, and districts. (Chapter 14 discusses how educators can receive support for themselves and their colleagues.) The benefits of educator intervention can be significant. In fact, the positive outcomes ultimately *save* time because they help prevent problems such as acting out, poor academic performance, absenteeism, or other concerns.

There will be times, however, when children's problems will take up time that educators do not feel they have. These are moments when the educator's familiarity with the school and local community can be of great help. Educators can act as conduits to other adults—educators, counselors, pediatricians, or others—to whom students feel connected and who may be able to offer the support needed.

The following are some guidelines that can help minimize this problem:

- **Recognize that most people appreciate when educators show concern.** Grieving students and their families may feel confused or uncertain about what the children need and how schools and families, working together, can help. They appreciate learning that there are steps to help make the grieving process easier for children.

- **Most families will take advantage of help that is offered.** When families feel that they are being listened to and have a sense that genuine needs are being addressed, they tend to become more engaged and more likely to accept assistance and follow recommendations. Sometimes being very specific is helpful. For example, educators can say, "Can we meet tomorrow at 4:00 to talk about some of these issues?"

- **A clear focus on death and grieving can sometimes make interactions with families more efficient.** In one instance, a mother was intent on discussing her son's problems with homework. He was not completing his assignments on time, the quality of his work was poor, and he did not respond well to her reminders to do his work. She asked his teacher for guidance about managing her son's study habits. She contacted the teacher repeatedly and complained that her son was not keeping up. She needed additional suggestions.

  The teacher set up a face-to-face meeting and asked the mother how she felt her son was doing after his father's recent death. In fact, that discussion helped the mother understand that her son's study habits were completely understandable given the circumstances. She recognized that the school was making appropriate accommodations for him and that her most important focus at this time in their lives needed to be on her son's emotions, not his homework. This brief and successful conversation ultimately freed up more of the teacher's time for other work.

- **Look for support from others.** Finding like-minded colleagues who can help educators think through the conversations they might have with grieving students is helpful. School administrators can schedule professional development that helps educators address these issues. Educators can also seek advice from a school counselor or other student support personnel in the school or ask if the school could invite a bereavement specialist who would be available to answer questions. When educators feel supported in these activities, they are more likely to follow through and feel successful.

- **Set limits and get others involved when necessary.** Educators who develop effective communication skills, provide comfort and support to children, and learn to effectively express empathy may find they draw many inquiries from students. Former students may come back to talk to a teacher, coach, principal, or school counselor they loved and trusted.

Most educators want to have this kind of impact and appreciate the rewards of good connections with their students.

There may be times, however, when educators are unable to respond to a student's request for support. There may already be too many demands on their time or too many challenges related to grief in their own life. Educators may have other crises in their life at the moment—relationship difficulties, a sick child, a legal problem. Their personal capacity for compassion may simply be exhausted and need restoring.

If educators feel overwhelmed by requests for this kind of support, it is important for them to remember that they do not need to do all of it themselves. Similar to tutoring, children might choose one educator first, but then seek support from other competent individuals if that educator is not available. Other resources can also be used—a school counselor, school or community mental health services, a colleague, or referral to a local children's bereavement program. Educators can also check with a student's family to see if they are involved in a faith community where they could seek support.

- **Understand that ignoring the problem is not a solution.** It is vital that grieving children are guided to appropriate resources. Even an educator who feels stretched too thin to offer substantive personal support can provide a useful referral. "I am so sorry you have had this death in your family," an educator can say. "Let's figure out who you can talk to."

So, what is the best way to make all of this work when offering support to grieving children? The first step is simply to start the conversation by making contact with a grieving student. Once that first contact is made, straightforward strategies are usually quite successful. More specific guidelines are reviewed in Chapter 5.

Key Concepts

- **There are steps that schools and educators can take that will help grieving children.** These include acknowledging the loss and communicating clearly and effectively with students and their families.

- **Grief is a painful process.** There is nothing anyone can do or say that will take away the pain or make the loss less powerful.

- **There are several goals for intervening with students**. These include decreasing isolation, increasing academic function, and helping children get support from family and friends.

- **It is important to understand how to be with grieving students.** Educators will be more effective when they have a sense of what to say, how to act, and how to manage their own feelings about death and loss.

- **Communication is absolutely key to supporting grieving children and their families.** Educators can use a range of strategies to open communication with students and families.

- **Addressing the Four Concepts About Death does not require discussions of religion.** These facts and principles do not conflict with different religious or cultural beliefs.

- **Schools and districts can work proactively to create policies that help support grieving students and staff.** These allow schools to act fairly and consistently in different situations.

- **These interventions usually take a relatively short amount of time.** Once they understand the principles of these approaches, most educators find it fairly easy to address such matters.

5

Communication: Ways to Make Contact and Keep It Going

Even when educators realize that it is important to make contact with grieving students, it can be difficult to decide how to approach them. Some people seem to have a natural comfort level talking about issues such as death, but many find it challenging. They are not sure how to bring it up. They worry that they will say something awkward that will cause children additional pain or discomfort.

These are natural feelings, but they can keep educators from taking those first steps needed to open a conversation. That is why it is important to understand *how* to make contact. There are a number of ways in which educators can make positive and helpful connections after they learn that a student has experienced a loss. This chapter discusses these techniques, which have been used successfully by educators in a wide range of circumstances. They work in complicated situations and in situations that are more straightforward. They work with isolated students as well as with students who have strong family and social support.

The outcomes of making contact will be different; that is, they will be as unique as every student and family. They will also depend on the educators' relationships with the students. The benefit of reaching out in the first place, however, is almost always positive.

WAYS TO MAKE CONTACT

A number of steps can help set a positive foundation for making contact with grieving children. This section highlights four steps that are helpful for educators.

Make the Commitment

When educators hear that a student has experienced a loss, they should make the commitment to make contact. If educators know the student or family well, they should consider contacting the family at home by telephone after first hearing about the death to offer condolences and support.

It is important to remember that even when educators do not know students well, expressing condolences and acknowledging the loss can be very powerful and helpful. It will also make it much easier for students to return to class when they know that their teachers and other school staff are already aware and ready to provide appropriate support.

Find (or Create) the Opportunity to Talk

Usually, this is a private conversation, so it is best if educators can find a moment when they can interact with the student one-to-one. Perhaps the student could be approached privately before or after class, in common areas of the school, or in some other setting. Educators might also choose a regular school activity that provides one-to-one contact, such as while discussing a report or project. The student could also be privately asked to come in a little early or stay after other students have left for a break.

If educators do not work directly with the student and do not have an opportunity for a one-to-one conversation, they can approach the student more generally and express concern. For example, a teacher might approach a student sitting with a couple of friends and say, "It's good to see you back at school. You and your family have been in my thoughts."

Offer Condolences and Support

A simple expression of concern and caring lets students know that their educators are aware of their situation and thinking of them. The following are some examples of condolences and offers of support that educators have made to students:

- "I'm sorry to hear about your father."
- "I just wanted to let you know you've been in my thoughts. I am sorry about your brother's death."
- "I'm glad to see you back here at school. I was thinking about you while you were at your mom's funeral."
- "How are you doing? I've been wondering how things have been for you since your grandmother's death."

Students' responses to these offers of condolence and support can guide educators. The most important thing educators are offering in this first contact is a compassionate presence—someone who is willing to provide support if students want or need it. It is important to listen, but it is not necessary to force a discussion. Remember, there is nothing anyone can say or do that will take away the pain or the loss. Usually, people who are grieving find it most helpful for someone to listen openly to whatever they have to say.

————

Usually, people who are grieving find it most helpful for someone to listen openly to whatever they have to say.

————

Promote Ongoing Communication

Students who are interested in talking more may ask questions, talk about their experiences, or keep the conversation going in other ways. Educators can continue to be guided by student comments. Answer students' questions in simple, age-appropriate ways. Some questions may need to be answered many times, especially (but not only) with younger children.

Honest answers will be most helpful to students. Often, "I don't know the answer," is the best response. Educators can also be mindful about using euphemisms and remember that it is okay, even preferable, to use the terms *dead* and *death*. Open, nonjudgmental responses help students feel that they can honestly express their thoughts and feelings to their teachers and other school staff. Students may not have similar opportunities at home if they feel they must protect a grieving parent.

Children often do not have a sense of what they want to say or what would be helpful, so educators can ask open-ended questions that give students an opportunity to share more about their experience if they wish. The following are some examples of open-ended questions educators have used that keep communication going:

- "How have you been doing over the past couple of weeks?"
- "How's your mom (sister, brother, family) doing?"
- "What's it like coming back to school?"
- "What has this past week been like for you?"
- "What sorts of things are you thinking about these days?"

As mentioned in Chapter 4, educators may also recognize that some of the questions children ask are essentially rhetorical—they do not need a direct answer. They express a sort of philosophical dilemma about human suffering, rather than a search for concrete answers. Even elementary school–age children might ask questions, such as, "Why do people have to die?" "Why couldn't it have been somebody else's mom?" "Why do we even bother loving people if they're just going to die?"

Questions such as these often benefit from comments that give students opportunities to continue expressing frustration, confusion, and pain. The following are some examples of responses that can keep communication going if students make these kinds of comments:

- "It's really hard to understand why these things happen."
- "So many things about death don't seem to make any sense at all."
- "I can only imagine this loss leaves you with a lot of confusion and questions."
- "You're asking the questions everyone asks when someone they love dies. It's hard to make sense of it."

MAKING CONTACT WHEN GRIEF IS NOT NEW

Many children have experienced the loss of a close family member at some point. With a little adaptation, these same principles for making contact also work well with these students.

For example, educators might respond in a direct and supportive way when topics such as death or grief come up in school. These topics may arise in classroom conversations, playground exchanges, or during interactions between students. Educators who respond are letting students know they are listening, they care, and they are available for further communication if students wish.

Educators can approach students by commenting on what they have seen or heard. Open-ended questions that express interest and curiosity often work best. The following are some examples:

- "Can you tell me more about your drawing?"
- "What were you and Maria playing during recess today?"
- "I wanted to let you know that I was surprised and moved by your essay. I hadn't realized you had a sister who died."

Teasing on the Playground

Six-year-old Justin's father died by suicide. He had cut his wrists. Justin's parents were divorced and had not been in regular contact, so Justin and his mother did not learn about the death for several months. Neither of them had been able to attend the funeral. Justin's mother felt very guilty about her ex-husband's death and barely talked about it with her son.

Justin attended school with his 7-year-old cousin, Evan, who began to tease him about the death. When Evan saw Justin, he sometimes made slashing gestures across his own wrists. He taunted Justin, saying, "Your daddy died, your daddy died," as he repeated the gestures.

When this happened at home, Justin would run to his mother crying. His mother, hearing of the taunts, would burst into tears herself. The two of them sobbed together, filled with anguish and grief. Neither seemed able to take any steps to stop the teasing.

This went on for several months. When the principal finally learned of it, she was concerned by the cruelty of the teasing. She asked for help from a pediatrician who consulted at the school. The physician met with both boys and asked them to tell him what was happening between them. Justin said, "He teases me because my daddy died."

Evan quickly responded, "Well, he teases me because I'm fat."

The physician asked Evan if he had ever experienced a loss. Yes, Evan told him, he had once had a pet die. "How did that feel?" he asked Evan.

"Sad," the boy replied.

"Is that how you want Justin to feel?"

"No!" said Evan, seeming to suddenly realize what he had been doing. "I don't mean for him to feel that bad. I just don't want to be teased for being fat."

Justin, a little surprised, said, "I'm sorry. I didn't mean to hurt your feelings either."

"Is there more?" asked the doctor.

The boys looked at each other. No, there wasn't anything else going on. Yes, they would both agree to stop teasing each other.

The entire intervention took about 15 minutes. After that, there were no further problems between the boys. The mother, who was depressed, was referred for mental health services and was able to improve with appropriate support.

If an educator familiar with children's understanding of death had noticed the teasing early on, it would have been possible to resolve these behaviors sooner. The solution was simply a willingness to talk to both students and an ability to understand what each had to say.

TALKING WITH OTHER STAFF

Another helpful strategy in maintaining productive communication with children is for the school staff to talk among themselves about their interactions with grieving children. What kinds of contacts are others having with children who are grieving? What are their impressions of how they are coping with loss? What about children who experienced a death some time ago?

Staff members often have distinct perspectives on each student. They may have different information about the ways a child is coping. One educator might have opportunities to see more of a student's strengths and supports. Another might see more of the challenges and frustrations. Taken together, these observations can sometimes suggest specific support that is needed and who is best suited to offer it. For example, a coach who finds that he can talk with a grieving student about his interest in baseball might be the perfect person to make authentic contact about how the student is coping with his situation.

PROVIDING SUPPORT FOR SCHOOL EXPECTATIONS

Another way teachers and other school staff can keep communication with grieving students open and productive is to anticipate challenges in schoolwork and classrooms. Some students will do fine socially and academically, even after the loss of someone very close. Most, however, will have at least some of the typical responses to grief, such as difficulty concentrating, easy distractibility, awkwardness with peers, and loss of interest in schoolwork.

It is important for students to understand that these are common reactions. If they have confidence that they will receive support as they move through the process, they will feel less anxiety about their mental state and their academic performance. Educators can take steps that help students gain this understanding. Educators, students, and their families working together can provide support that helps students stay on track while accommodating their needs during this early period of grief.

The following are some actions that schools and educators can take to help students stay on track.

Maintain or Increase Contact With the Student's Family

Phone calls and e-mails are usually helpful. Family meetings can also be very useful if the parent or parents are able to meet in person. These contacts can be use to offer guidance about what grieving students often experience, address concerns of the family, and reassure students that school staff are aware of the challenges they are facing at this time. Students and their families feel more secure when they understand strategies are in place to provide support.

Choose an Adult or a Location as a Safe Space

During the first few months after a loss, children may be affected by sudden reminders of the person who died. These are called *grief triggers* (discussed further in Chapter 8). Children may experience outbursts of sadness, uncontrolled tears, feelings of emptiness or anger, or other distracting reactions. In the middle of a class activity or focused personal work, they may find themselves thinking suddenly of their grief. For a brief period, they may feel overwhelmed or unable to concentrate or apply themselves to the task at hand. They may not wish to remain in the room to listen to a discussion of a book passage that reminds them of their mother who recently died. They may worry that they will start crying in front of their peers.

These kinds of experiences can be disconcerting to children. Talking them over with an adult who knows how to listen can help children understand more about the process of grief in general, as well as their own personal experience. They can learn skills and strategies that will help them cope with greater success over time by understanding what is happening (see the Chapter 2 discussion of the Four Concepts About Death), feeling more in control of their environment and their own responses, and knowing how to get support when they need it.

A "safe space" is a place where grieving children can take time to calm themselves if they feel troubled and to seek guidance to move through these incidents. Some possibilities for safe spaces include the counseling office, nurse's office, assistant principal's office, or even an open study hall or library. In a kindergarten class, a student might be offered a special area as a safe space, such as the corner by the bookshelf. These are places where children can temporarily escape any pressures, demands, or unpleasant interactions. Ideally, they will also be able to talk with a supportive, helpful adult as they work through the incident.

Establish a Procedure That Allows Children to Leave the Classroom if They Are Feeling Overwhelmed by a Grief Trigger

For some period of time after a death, it may be useful for grieving students to have permission to temporarily leave the classroom as needed. When children know they can leave if they feel overwhelmed, they will feel less anxious about returning to school after a death and will actually find it easier to remain in the classroom. Knowing they *can* leave makes them less likely to want to leave. It is similar to knowing that you can turn off a scary movie on a DVD if it becomes too frightening, which makes it more manageable than being in a theater with friends where it would be embarrassing to walk out. Most students will never need to take advantage of this opportunity, but they will appreciate the option. Simple communications, such as hand signals, a brief note, or a key phrase (e.g., "I need to be by myself for a while"), that do not draw attention from peers might serve as appropriate notice to an educator. Obviously, older students can be given more independence in these matters. Younger children will need the safety of an attending adult. As schools arrange these procedures, they should apply the same safety measures they would for other situations in which students might leave a classroom.

Let Children Call a Parent if They Wish

When grieving children experience sudden strong emotions, checking in with a parent or guardian can be very helpful. Children who have recently experienced a loss should have considerable freedom to make these kinds of calls.

Provide Passes or Permission for Children to See the School Counselor, Social Worker, Psychologist, or Nurse

One of the best times to talk with grieving children is when they are *ready* to talk. If children wish to see the school counselor, social worker, psychologist, or nurse, educators can help by facilitating these connections in the easiest, promptest way reasonably possible.

Modify Assignments, Tests, and School Projects

Due dates can be extended, tests postponed, or projects simplified.

Assignments and Tests

Grieving students may be out of school for some period of time—a few days or more, depending on the student and the family's circumstances. When students are in school, it is appropriate to continue giving them assignments; however, it is also proper to modify the assignments as needed. Grieving children may need help finding coursework that feels achievable or appropriate in their current circumstances. For example, if members of a fifth-grade class have been working for 4 weeks on a 10-page paper about some aspect of the state's history, a teacher could talk to a recently bereaved student about writing a more focused paper that is only three pages long. Or, if a high school social studies class has been doing research projects on violence prevention, and a family member of one of the students dies violently, the teacher might check to see if that student would prefer to do research on another area in social studies, such as how citizens can place an initiative on the ballot. Sometimes educators change their plans for an entire class if one or more of the students have recently experienced a death that would be unnecessarily revisited by the planned course of study.

Grieving children may need help finding coursework that feels achievable or appropriate.

Testing is often one of the most difficult tasks for students who are recently bereaved. Therefore, educators might exempt students from tests or give the tests less weight in the final grade for students who have recently experienced a loss. Educators might also allow grieving students to take a test privately in a quiet area or allow more time to complete the work. A one-to-one meeting or a special tutoring session with a grieving student before a test might also provide support that students appreciate and can use.

Changing the Course Curriculum

A serious residential fire resulted in the death of two members of a family—a child and one of the parents. Three other children in the family survived. They attended the public schools, and the oldest daughter was in high school.

These deaths had a profound effect on the community. The family was well known. The daughter was popular and had many friends at school who had known and cared about the family members who had died.

An English teacher, looking over the curriculum for the coming year, recognized that one of the books he loved teaching included a scene in which one of the leading characters died in a fire. Reading and discussing the book had always been the most dynamic lesson in the class. He could not imagine giving it up. Then he tried to imagine teaching the book—to the daughter, to her friends, to all of the students who knew this family, and to all who had simply heard about the fire. "There are hundreds of excellent books to choose from. My class will do fine without this one," he said. He changed the lesson plan.

Provide More Frequent Progress Reports to Students and Their Families

Typical grading periods (e.g., semester, quarter, half-quarter) are really too long a span to monitor progress for children in acute grief. In most cases, children will be trying to get back on track with their studies, their interests, and their social life. They may have trouble figuring out how to do this. They often focus more on areas in which they feel inadequate, and they are less aware of areas in which they are doing well.

Frequent progress reports give educators an opportunity to share observations about students' efforts. For example, teachers can ask students how they are coping, clarify anything in the lessons that is not making sense, and help students schedule additional support for learning. They can also comment positively on any contributions or special efforts students have made. These reports offer important opportunities to provide positive feedback about what students are doing well. At a time when they may wonder if their lives will ever feel "right" again, this can be reassuring.

Offer Private Time With Students

Grieving students can benefit immensely from occasional one-to-one meetings with their teachers or other school staff. These might be offered on an as-needed basis, but it can be very helpful to set up a regular private meeting with bereaved students. Even a period of 10 or 20 minutes a week gives students a chance to ask questions about coursework, express feelings about their grief experience, and benefit from the special concern of a caring educator. Such meetings are an ideal time for educators to ask students some of those open-ended questions about their thoughts, feelings, and experiences as they move through the grief process. It is best not to wait until academic failure becomes obvious before offering extra support. By that point, the child has to deal with grief and academic failure simultaneously, both of which alone can feel overwhelming.

It is best not to wait until academic failure becomes obvious before offering extra support.

A Hoodie Moment

Maribel's father died. She returned to her high school a week after his death but continued to feel overwhelmed any time she thought of him. During these moments, she found it difficult to concentrate and almost impossible to respond to classroom discussions. This was especially troublesome during her social studies class, which was structured almost entirely on discussion.

Maribel's teacher noticed that while she was her usual thoughtful self most of the time, there were instances when Maribel was unable to respond to a comment or question. He suspected this was related to her grief. He asked her to stay after class one day.

Privately, he asked Maribel if she was feeling distracted by her feelings of sadness about her father's death. She acknowledged that yes, she often felt inattentive when she thought of her father. She was frustrated and embarrassed that she wasn't being a better student in the class. Her teacher countered that she was, in fact, a very good student. He mentioned that it was quite normal for someone who was grieving to have moments of distraction, and he thought it would help if she could let him know when she was feeling that way. They talked about how she could send him a message about her state of mind during discussions. She typically wore a hoodie to class. She said, "I could put my hood up if I don't want you to call on me."

This was the perfect solution. The teacher could respect Maribel's needs, and because no one else knew the meaning of the gesture, she didn't feel self-conscious about asking for support. They called these instances "a hoodie moment."

"I trusted Maribel to know what she needed," the teacher told us. "And because we had come up with this plan together, she was comfortable coming to class. Otherwise I think she would have stayed home grieving in isolation and would have missed even more classwork. Being in class, even when she felt distracted, was not the same as grieving on her own."

SETTING LIMITS

Children who are grieving sometimes act in ways that challenge educators. They are experiencing many powerful emotions. They may express anger, act selfishly, or say things that are hurtful to other students. They might break or carelessly lose things. They might speak insolently to school staff. Although a sensitive educator can clearly see that these are expressions related to underlying grief, there may still be a need to set limits on misbehavior. There is, however, a fine line between setting limits and being punitive. Of course, educators must take appropriate steps to keep all students safe and to promote a positive learning environment. If limits must be set with grieving students, this should be handled calmly and in a matter-of-fact way.

Sometimes, a simple, straightforward correction can help grieving children gain control of their impulses and behavior. A compassionate frame gives children a chance to see themselves in a better light, and they may strive to match that image. For example, an educator might say, "Stuart, that was an unkind thing to say. Were you actually trying to hurt Jamal's feelings?" This gives Stuart a chance to explain he did not want to hurt Jamal's feelings and that he does not want to be mean to others.

If misbehavior is more serious, or a child does not seem to respond to this type of redirection, the educator should meet with the student privately. This gives educators an opportunity to make direct observations about the behaviors. For example, an educator might say, "I know that sometimes people feel very angry when someone they love has died. I wonder if you've had any feelings like this since your father died." A more direct observation might be, "I haven't seen you behave in this way before. I wonder if the strong feelings you've been having since your father's death are playing a part in these behaviors." It is important to contact the family to let them know about these concerns. They may be unaware of their child's misbehavior or have other concerns or additional insights. It is also important to convey that the call is due to genuine concern about the child's adjustment, rather than to complain about the child's behavior.

If disruptive behaviors occur repeatedly, a family conference would be appropriate. A referral for supportive counseling could also be helpful. These issues are discussed in more depth in Chapter 7.

HELPING STUDENTS THINK ABOUT SOCIAL MEDIA AND GRIEF

Social media is a simple fact of student life today. The vast majority of teens spend time on social media sites, and many younger students do as well. When a child has experienced the death of a family member or close friend, will social media be a good thing, or is it more likely to cause distress and harm?

We believe the question is not whether grieving students *should* be using social media or whether it is appropriate. Rather, it is how best to adapt to its use in this context and in what ways it can be used optimally. Although some adults may be uncomfortable with the use of social media, especially when dealing with sensitive topics, most children and adolescents find these avenues to be comfortable ways to communicate.

Many schools offer guidance to students about social media use, often with a focus on avoiding bullying, reporting harassment, resisting dares and negative peer pressure, and preventing sexual exploitation. We believe it is appropriate—even necessary—to add discussions of grief and other emotional experiences to these lessons. In the same way educators can help all students think about what to say to a classmate who has experienced a loss, for example (discussed in Chapters 2 and 4), they can help students think about productive ways to respond to these events when they learn about them through social media channels.

Online social platforms offer unique and even powerful ways that children can gain support and check in with peers. In fact, many children dealing with bereavement choose these avenues as their preferred methods of communication.

- **They are familiar.** Young people communicate in these ways about all kinds of life events, including some that are quite serious.
- **They are fast.** Students can get immediate feedback on their questions or the experiences they've shared.
- **They offer control.** Grieving students can decide when to read a text or message. They can monitor their reactions and only need to share what they choose. They can opt to be more open and vulnerable with close friends and a bit more distant with others. They can respond when they feel composed and ready.
- **Others may share more openly.** The sense of privacy users often feel with social media can allow classmates to share personal and sensitive responses they might not share as openly in an in-person setting.

There are, of course, challenges in the social media world as well. The "instant" quality of posts and responses may become overwhelming very quickly. People may say hurtful or inappropriate things—both people a student knows and complete strangers can be surprisingly cruel. Grieving students may come across disturbing news items online about their own loss or other deaths. There is also a good deal of misinformation online. For example, normal grief reactions may be characterized by others as abnormal, whereas complex or troubling reactions that call for expert support might be discounted.

This is one of the reasons it is so important for grieving children to also have face-to-face time with supportive peers and adults. Social media interactions will be most helpful when they are balanced with real-world contacts. Relying only on social media can increase the sense of social isolation grieving children may feel.

Online-Only Friendships: When a Friend Dies

Many young people establish friendships that are online only. These might develop through social media, chatrooms, or texting programs. They might also arise through experiences such as online classrooms or webinars, participating as a virtual attendee at a global youth empowerment conference, or joining a youth advisory board for a national voluntary organization that meets online. These connections can be deeply important to students.

In instances where a close online-only friend dies, students will feel the loss keenly. In addition to typical grief reactions, they may have questions specific to this type of relationship: Is my grief justified? What possibilities have I lost because this friend died before I met my friend in person? Should I have made more of an effort to set up a face-to-face time to be together?

Educators can provide valuable support by accepting these relationships as genuine and meaningful and affirming that the grief students are feeling is real and justified.

Educators Make a Vital Difference

Educators are one of the most important face-to-face contacts for grieving students. It is helpful to keep social media influences in mind when talking with students. Especially with middle and high school students, consider checking in about the kind of support they're getting (or not getting) through social media.

Educators might also suggest that parents of grieving students consider monitoring their children's social media feeds or ask their children about the social media content on the sites they use.

There are additional concerns with social media in instances of suicide or when a death affects an entire school. These are discussed further in Chapters 9 and 10.

KEEP MAKING CONTACT

The death of a family member or friend is a common event in the lives of young people. Although the questions grieving children have are sometimes complex, most often they are straightforward and direct. Sometimes they want to understand facts about death. Sometimes they need help understanding how to explain themselves to friends. Sometimes they simply need to know that a trusted, caring adult believes in them and believes that they will get through this confusing experience. They also need to know that an adult is there to provide support over time as they struggle to adjust to the loss.

We encourage educators to use these "making contact" strategies on a regular basis with students, not just in instances of death, but on other matters that may appear sensitive or difficult. The more that educators can express to students that they are listening, they care, and they are available to talk, the more students will be able to come to them with their questions and concerns, whatever the topic may be.

I Don't Want to Say My Dad Is Dead

Sofia's father died near the end of first grade. Sofia's second-grade teacher was aware of the death and made an effort to notice how her student was coping. Sofia was doing well in school.

Sofia was close with her mother and received strong support from her family. Her first-grade teacher described her as bright and talkative. She said that Sofia was always one of the first children to reach out to meet new people and get to know them. In second grade, however, she seemed more reserved with her new classmates, and she seemed uncomfortable interacting socially with several girls who were new to the school.

The previous year, Sofia had talked openly about her father shortly after he died, but her second-grade teacher never heard her talking about her father. Worried that she might be depressed, the teacher arranged for Sofia to see a counselor. The counselor asked her how she was feeling after her father's death, and Sofia readily acknowledged that she was having a problem.

She explained, "My classmates ask me what my dad does for a living. I don't want to say he's dead—it will make me cry."

Sofia and the counselor explored several different possibilities about what she could say. Perhaps she could say he had gone away? No, that wasn't true, and she didn't want to be dishonest. Could she say she didn't want to talk about it? No, that didn't seem friendly. People would think she was stuck up.

Then the counselor asked, "Could you say, 'My father is no longer alive?'"

Sofia thought about this, and then she tried it out. "My father is no longer alive." When she said this, she didn't feel like crying.

"Yes," she said. "I can say that. This solves my problem!"

Prepared with this phrase that said just what she wanted, she returned to her class, began socializing more freely with her peers, and sometimes talked about her father with her new friends.

Key Concepts

- **Some people have a natural comfort level in talking about difficult issues, but many find it challenging.** Educators who feel unsure about addressing grief with students can learn skills that will help them communicate effectively.

- **Techniques for supporting bereaved students work across a range of circumstances and personality types.** In both complicated situations and those that are more straightforward, educators can take steps that help.

- **It is common for grieving children to experience challenges in their schoolwork.** Many children experience difficulty concentrating, easy distractibility, awkwardness with peers, or loss of interest in schoolwork.

- **It is appropriate for educators to make accommodations in assignments and tests for grieving students.** For example, a student might take on simpler assignments, do a paper instead of a test, or receive an extension on a due date.

- **Educators play an important role in providing anticipatory guidance about social media and grief.** They can ask grieving students about their experiences in social media, affirm positive connections, and offer support for troublesome comments or situations.

6

Working With Families

Working with families is something most educators do regularly. They talk with parents at back-to-school nights, open houses, field trips, school meetings, and parent conferences. They communicate through e-mails, memos, phone calls, report cards, class web sites, and newsletters. These ongoing communications help families take steps to support their children's learning and participation at school. They can also be particularly helpful to provide information and support to grieving families when in-person contact isn't possible, such as during summer vacation. This was also dramatically seen during the lengthy school closures characteristic of the COVID-19 pandemic when it was unsafe to meet in person.

Contact with families is especially important for children who are grieving. As mentioned in previous chapters, challenges with concentration and learning are common for grieving students. Most will have some level of school problems for a period of time after a family member or friend dies. Talking with family members helps educators understand more about what the children and their families are experiencing, lets children know that their families and educators together are concerned, and helps everyone have more realistic expectations and understanding about what will happen in the coming months.

Educators can play a unique and important role for families experiencing bereavement.

EDUCATORS' AND SCHOOLS' SPECIAL ROLE WITH FAMILIES

Chapter 1 reviewed some of the reasons that educators and schools can play a special role in helping all children learn about death and helping grieving children cope. For some of the same reasons, educators can play a unique and important role for families experiencing bereavement. The following are some examples:

- **Schools are familiar; teachers and other educators are trusted.** Schools are part of children's everyday lives. The staff and setting are familiar to families. Teachers are respected for their expertise and knowledge. All of these qualities make information from educators valuable to many families.

- **Families are often looking for guidance.** Grieving families are usually challenged by their situation and often have questions about how to help their children. Many families do not seek advice from health care providers, mental health specialists, or faith-based services, but they will have contact with their children's teachers or other school staff. Some may look for guidance online or through social media channels. Even when they have received advice from other professionals, they often have additional questions about what to do for their children and family. Sometimes families are skeptical of advice provided in a counseling or mental health context. The same information coming from a teacher or school nurse, however, may seem less clinical and more "normal." They may be able to accept this guidance more easily.

- **Educators have special knowledge that other providers do not have.** Educators spend considerably more time with an individual child than most health, mental health, or faith-based providers ever will. They see aspects of children's behavior and performance that may not come up around the doctor, counselor, or even a parent. They have a particular understanding of how grieving children are coping with the process of learning, which is less likely to come up in other settings.

- **Children may behave differently at school.** Children may experience and express frustration or sadness at school, but they may cover up those feelings at home. They may feel a need to protect their parents from seeing their grief. They may be taking steps to avoid "rocking the boat," without even realizing that they are hiding their feelings. School is sometimes the setting where children are able to express powerful feelings that they are not revealing elsewhere.

- **Educators are in an excellent position to make referrals that can help families.** Most families may be unaware of bereavement support services within the community, or they may feel that their grief is something they should be able to handle on their own. However, families may accept referrals from educators that they would not as readily accept from other sources.

They Have No One Else to Talk To

One of the authors of this book, David Schonfeld, served for several years as a consultant to an elementary school in a major city. The school had 800 children in grades prekindergarten to second grade.

One Monday morning, David arrived at the school and was immediately greeted by the principal. "We have had a tragic event in our community," she told him. She reported that several children were visiting an older relative's apartment over the weekend with some other children. At one point, the man excused himself, went into the bathroom, and shot himself in the head. The children were alone when they found his body. The principal asked David if he would meet with the children and begin to help them make sense of this tragedy, as well as guide their families to additional services. It turned out that the children were former students of the school, but the principal asked if David would still be willing to meet with them. Knowing his answer ahead of time, she had already arranged for all of these children to be at the school; they were waiting to meet with him. The principal reassured David that she had spoken with the parents of all of the children over the weekend: "They don't know who else to speak to. They need your help right now. It's not like we can just send them to the other schools before we help them deal with what they heard and saw. Their parents sent them here because they knew we would help them."

Thanks to this principal, who was a tireless and effective advocate for her students, their families, and the community, these children were able to begin talking about the experience. They were connected with ongoing services. Their parents, who had turned first to the principal, received the services that their children and families desperately needed to deal with this tragedy. This was clearly a sign of the enormous impact this principal had within her community and in the lives of her students.

OFFERING GUIDANCE TO FAMILIES

In offering guidance to grieving families, educators can support the use of open, clear communication about death and grief. When children receive support from their parents and other family members, it helps the entire family cope. The family sees that it can stay close even though the feelings of grief might be very strong.

When educators talk with parents, many of the same guidelines for talking to grieving children are helpful. After all, most of the communication strategies described in Chapter 4 work with people of all ages who are coping with a loss. They include such things as being present and authentic, being willing to listen, avoiding trying to cheer people up, and allowing people to express their feelings.

————

It is important to stay open-minded and nonjudgmental about the emotions parents might express.

————

Similar to talking with children, it is important to stay open-minded and nonjudgmental about the emotions parents might express. In periods of acute grief, many of our "filters" are down. People often say things bluntly or reveal things that they might not say in other circumstances. Parents may describe frustration with their children, bitterness about the person who died, old family secrets, or other troubles. Educators who set a stage that welcomes these expressions gain important information about their students' home environments and may be able to make better judgments about what will be most helpful for students and their families.

The following are some of the issues that educators can discuss with parents:

- **A parent's role is essential.** Let parents know that their children are looking to them for help in understanding these confusing and troubling experiences. More than anyone else in their lives, children look to parents for guidance about how to cope.

- **Children are concerned about their parents.** Children wonder how their parents are coping. They worry about their parents' health and survival. If someone close to them has just died, does this mean that others they love and count on could die, too? It is important for parents to find ways to offer honest reassurance to their children.

- **Children are also concerned about themselves.** Particularly after the death of a parent, children may worry that everyone else will die and leave them all alone. Who will take care of them, give them shelter and food, and keep them safe? In these situations, children may benefit from knowing that there will always be someone who knows and cares for them. Sometimes it helps to explain that parents make plans for their children just in case of the highly unlikely possibility that their parent or parents, or another primary guardian, would die while their children are still young.

- **Children need support to understand death.** It is helpful for parents to understand the Four Concepts About Death (discussed in Chapter 2), why they are important for children, and how to explain them to children. Educators can review these concepts with parents of young children and offer suggestions about how to discuss them with their children.

- **Direct, clear language is important.** Many of us have been taught to use euphemisms about death. As explained in Chapter 2, it is important to speak gently but frankly with children and to use direct words, such as *death* and *died*.

- **Honesty is essential.** Children must understand the truth about the death of a loved one. The best possible place for them to hear that truth is from within the family. Some deaths are disturbing, such as homicides, suicides, and random acts of violence. Understandably, parents hesitate to share the details of these kinds of deaths with children, especially if they are young. As difficult as it may be, honesty is essential. If the family does not tell children the truth about what has happened, the children will learn the facts at another time. Usually, this will happen much sooner than a family imagines, and often, the circumstances are not ideal. Children may be taunted by a classmate, come across a news report about the death, or overhear a comment by a neighbor. These experiences can be deeply troubling to children, and they often make it difficult for them to trust their family regarding important issues in the future.

Educators may be able to suggest ways to talk about a troubling death to children. As mentioned in Chapter 2, graphic details are not necessary and should be avoided. These are situations in which a bereavement counselor or mental health professional may also be able to help parents find ways to explain the death and help the children cope.

Educators may also be able to suggest additional resources that can help support families coping with grief. For example, there may be a children's bereavement center or hospice program in the community that offers support groups for children and families. Special programs may also be available for grieving children, such as camp experiences. In addition, there are web sites and written materials that can also be helpful.[1]

It's So Hard to Tell My Son

Nate was 4 years old when his father became ill. His father was diagnosed with depression and hospitalized after a suicide attempt, but his parents chose not to tell the boy about this. Instead, his mother simply told Nate his dad was away on business.

After being released from the hospital, the father was enrolled in treatment and prescribed medications for his depression. His condition worsened, and he was hospitalized a second time after a serious overdose. This time, Nate's mother told him his father had to go to the hospital because he was vomiting, but he would be home again soon.

When Nate's father was discharged from the second hospitalization, he returned home. Moments later, he left to go to his office. Once there, he went to the roof of the building and jumped to his death.

Nate's mother was devastated and felt guilty that she had not supervised her husband more carefully when he returned home. She could not bear the thought of explaining to her young son the truth about how his father had died. Instead, she told Nate, "Daddy fell and bumped his head, and he died."

Nate became increasingly anxious after his father's death. He began to have frightening dreams, often about hitting his head. He insisted on wearing a helmet when he rode his tricycle. He was having problems getting along with peers at preschool. He and his mother were referred for counseling.

---

[1] *After a Loved One Dies—How Children Grieve and How Parents and Other Adults Can Support Them* (Schonfeld & Quackenbush, 2019) is a resource for families that follows the same guidelines as this book. It can be downloaded or ordered in hardcopy for free—even the cost of shipping and handling is free. See the References section for full information. Another excellent resource for parents to help their children and themselves after the death of a family member is *Guiding Your Child Through Grief* (Emswiler & Emswiler, 2000).

Nate's mother arrived at her first counseling visit exhausted. Nate had been up much of the night after having another nightmare about hitting his head and dying. She told the counselor about her reluctance to tell Nate about his father's suicide. "I just don't think he is ready to know. I will tell him when he's older—just not yet."

The counselor looked at her. "The explanation you've given him doesn't seem to have been very satisfying for Nate," he observed.

She agreed that it didn't seem to be working. The counselor spoke to her gently. "You may want to reconsider this," he told her. "From my experience, I've seen that children do best when they have an honest, appropriate explanation of what happened."

He went on to point out that it was only a matter of time before someone else told Nate the truth about his father's death. "It is very difficult information to share, I know. But it will be best if it can come from you."

The mother reluctantly agreed, and she and the counselor spent the rest of the session working out how she could tell her son the truth of his father's death. She was able to follow through on this plan. Although Nate continued to miss his father very much, his nightmares stopped, and his behavior in preschool became more appropriate.

Information About Their Children

Educators can describe some of the reactions children generally have to a death. As discussed in Chapter 3, children may become upset by discussions about the death, feel reluctant to talk about it, or feel guilty or ashamed about it. Letting parents know that these responses are common can help reassure parents about the reactions their children are having.

Educators' specific observations can also be helpful for parents. For example, they can talk about how they see the student coping. This might include areas of difficulty, such as a child who has withdrawn somewhat from peers or is having difficulty concentrating in class. When possible, it is also helpful to comment on areas of strength. The child might be reaching out to friends for support or doing good work in some areas of study. The educators can affirm that it is clear the child's attachment to the family is strong and important.

Educators can also review what the class is studying and discuss the type of work that is forthcoming. They can describe how the student is doing academically and talk with the parents about any accommodations in lessons or tests that might be appropriate. Again, it is important to normalize these periods of academic challenge for grieving children. The goal is to reassure parents that their children are getting appropriate support, not simply to suggest that there is a problem parents must address.

Guidance About Funerals

It is important for children to be offered the opportunity to participate in funeral and memorial services. In most cases, it is better for children when they do attend these services. The subject of funerals is discussed in detail in Chapter 3.

Parents may ask educators for guidance about whether their children should attend funerals. Educators may be the only professionals who interact with the parents or have the opportunity to provide such advice before the funeral occurs. Educators can play a valuable role in helping parents understand why this can be so important to children's grieving and ongoing recovery after a death.

CHECKING IN WITH PARENTS

Bereaved children are coping with many challenges as they make the effort to understand what has happened in their lives. When family members are also struggling, this can create challenges for children. The death of a family member can result in depression in a parent, increases in fighting or domestic violence, financial stresses, and other problems.

Educator–parent conversations offer an opportunity to see how well the parents and the family are doing as a whole. When the person who died was also important to the parent or parents—and this is typically the case when children lose a family member—they will likely also be struggling with grief.

Sometimes an educator's window into a family reveals valuable information that has been missed by others. Educators may learn that a parent is not coping well (Krell and Rabkin [1979] present a model of how parental guilt after a death can significantly alter family dynamics and how parents interact with surviving siblings), the house is in chaos, the family does not have money for food, or the family has relocated to the overly crowded home of an extended family member. They may see ways that the family's response to the death is creating problems for the children. Although educators cannot personally solve such problems, they can help arrange referrals and support for a troubled family. This can be a great help to students.

An Open Invitation

Grief is not a quick process. Children who have lost a family member or friend will feel the effects strongly for some time. The trajectory of grief is different for every child, and how this influences school and family life will also be different.

Some children go through an acute period of grief and gradually feel better over time. Others do well for a period of time and face challenges later. Some have a difficult period, do better for a period, and then have difficulties again. When children are struggling, issues may come up at school or at home. The signs might be falling academic performance, difficult social relationships, or increasing conflicts with parents and family.

When educators talk with parents about grieving children, it is important to leave the door open for additional talks in the future. Both educators and parents have important information about how children are coping. Their willingness to share these observations can help children over time in all the domains of their lives.

Ongoing Contact With Families

Chapter 5 describes ways educators can make initial contact with families after a death, often by telephone. The goal of this first call is simply to express your condolences, let the family know that they are in your thoughts, and answer any immediate questions they may have, such as about funeral attendance. This is usually the most a parent is ready for immediately following a death.

At a later point, often after students have returned to school, educators can make contact again. In this instance, the goal is to talk with parents about how their child is doing in school. The following are some suggestions about what to say and do when meeting parents:

- **Make it personal.** Ideally, educators and parents can meet face-to-face. When this is not possible, telephone contact can be made. Although some people are quite comfortable with e-mail and instant messaging, we do not recommend this, at least for an initial meeting. There is a great deal of nuance in discussions about grief, and it is easy to miss something essential or miscommunicate with these formats.

- **Normalize the contact.** Educators should explain that it is a good idea for educators and parents to meet any time a child experiences the death of a family member or friend. This allows educators and parents to work together to offer the best possible support for children during this difficult period.

- **Focus on academic and social issues.** Educators should let the parents know that their interest is in both the child's academic performance and their social and emotional health.

- **Let parents know that they are helping the educator.** During this conversation, educators will be able to draw information from parents that helps educators make the best plan for the child. Parents have something valuable to offer.

Let the parents know that your interest is in both the child's academic performance and their social and emotional health.

The timing of these meetings will vary from one family to another. Most families will be grateful to hear from their children's teacher or other school staff. Many will feel relieved that the educator is expressing concern and interest. Some parents will be eager to come in and talk about these matters right away. Others may feel too overwhelmed and need more time before they can manage such a meeting. Even when everything is done well, some parents may still prefer to keep their family's loss private and not accept an educator's assistance.

It is important to respect parents' wishes if they are unable to meet; however, it is also helpful and appropriate to continue to make contact with grieving families over time and to make additional efforts to set up a meeting. If a parent declines the offer to meet, the educator should leave the door open for further contact if possible. The educator might say, "I'd just like to check back in a week or so and see if it might work better at that point. I do really want to be sure I'm giving your daughter as much help as I can."

DIFFERENT OUTCOMES

Because every family is different, it is impossible to predict with any certainty what will happen when educators and families talk. At the NCSCB, we have generally seen positive outcomes from these meetings, and we highly recommend them. However, there can be challenges.

When It Does Not "Work"

It is no surprise to educators that some of their students live in difficult circumstances and that some of the parenting they receive is less than ideal. These problems can feel especially acute in the context of grief and loss. A struggling family struggles even more. A child who has already been dealing with hardship is dealing with even more.

Sometimes parents do not acknowledge or address their children's needs around bereavement. They may insist that their children are doing fine and do not need any special attention. They may be unable to acknowledge their children's needs because they are too distracted by their own grief. Some parents have personality or mental health issues, or they are dealing with alcohol or other substance abuse problems that make it difficult for them to ever consider their children's needs in depth.

Sometimes parents simply do not know *how* to address children's needs about grief. They may come from cultures where death is not discussed openly. They may have lived a protected or untroubled life, and therefore, they may be facing complex challenges for the first time. Their spouse may have been the one to handle the "emotional" things, and if that is the person who died, they may feel at a complete loss.

Parents may also have a different belief about what is the right thing to do. They may believe their children can cope with the challenges of grief entirely through prayer and religious observances. They may believe that indulging children's emotions at times such as these makes them weak. They may believe, despite evidence to the contrary, that children do not feel these matters deeply and do not need any special consideration.

We have also seen instances where parents make decisions about what to tell their children that are not helpful. They may denigrate the dead, criticizing a parent who suffered a drug overdose or died in a car crash while speeding.

They may obscure the truth, refusing to describe how a family member died. We have known parents who felt unable to tell their children that a sister or brother had died, and they instead carried on a pretense that the child was in the hospital and would come home again.

These are challenging situations. The best course an educator can take is to continue to strive to make an alliance with such families. If educators suggest that these parents do not have their children's best interest at heart, a positive alliance will not be possible. In most cases, such parents *are* greatly concerned about their children but do not know how to meet each child's needs or feel unable to do so. Educators who can create an alliance with a family may be able to provide gentle guidance to parents in some of these situations. They can emphasize, with the authority of their expertise as well as their compassion for the family's situation, the importance of telling children the truth.

There may also be instances in which families are simply unwilling to participate in educator–parent conferences. After making several offers to meet, teachers may have to let go of their intentions to set up a conference.

The best guidelines in these situations are familiar to educators: Keep trying to do what you know works best for students and be willing to step back when you hit the limits of what you can do. After some time has passed and the parents have started to adjust to the loss or come to realize the distress their children are experiencing, they may be ready to accept the educator's offer to meet. Educators can seek the advice and assistance of the school counselor, nurse, psychologist, or social worker who may be able to reach out to the family as well.

Of course, any time an educator has reasonable suspicion or evidence that neglect or abuse is occurring, a report to the proper authorities is necessary. This is true even for a family struggling with recent grief.

When It Does "Work"

Educator–parent conferences that "work" are not necessarily easy encounters either. Grieving parents may express deep feelings of loss, be very emotional, or have some trouble following the conversation. Just like their children and all people who are in acute grief, they are likely to have trouble with concentration and feel overwhelmed.

Parents who become engaged in these conversations may also pose some difficult questions. However, this can actually be a sign of success—parents are interested, involved, and concerned. They are looking for guidance and willing to hear suggestions. For example, families often describe some dilemma or question about their child and then look to the educator for an answer—"What would you do if it was your child?"

In general matters, such as whether to tell the truth about a death or let a child attend a funeral, educators can safely offer appropriate guidance. "I think you can trust that your child is able to hear the truth about this death, and that will be the healthiest thing." In more complex situations, however, it becomes necessary to reflect the question back to the parents. For example, a grieving mother says her 10-year-old son, whose father died 2 weeks ago, has decided he wants to spend his entire summer with his grandparents. In a situation such as this, the best course is to help the mother continue to assess the situation so that she can make a good decision. A helpful response might be, "I don't really know all of the concerns in your family and with your child, so I can't make the best judgment. But let's talk about what you feel you should do." This might also be a point to involve a school-based mental health provider, if one is not already working with the family, to offer more specific guidance.

Giving parents an opportunity to engage in these types of discussions can be helpful to them, to their family, and to grieving students. Educators can model how to engage in gentle, frank conversations about death. They can show respect for the range of feelings and responses parents are having, and they can show compassion for the concerns parents experience for their children. They can reassure parents that a wide range of responses to death are common, and they can offer resources for additional support.

All of these steps reinforce the importance of parents in their children's lives and the power of their relationships. There is probably no other time in the lives of children when it is more important for parents to understand how vital they are to their children's success and well-being.

Key Concepts

- **Educators and schools play a special role with families.** They are a familiar and trusted resource, and grieving families often look to their children's teacher or other school staff for support.

- **Educators' observations and suggestions can be helpful for parents.** They can reinforce the importance of parents' roles, describe common reactions children have to a death, and share specific observations about how their children are doing with peers or in schoolwork.

- **Specific guidance is often important for families.** For example, parents may appreciate learning about the Four Concepts About Death, the importance of being honest with children, or how to support their children in building an appropriate and useful understanding of death.

7

Special Concerns for Bereaved Children

Mourning a death is a challenge for any child. Some children, however, have additional circumstances that make this process even more complicated. Circumstances of the death or characteristics of the family may complicate matters. Bereavement after deaths that are sudden and violent, stigmatized, or highly publicized can be more complicated. Line-of-duty deaths of individuals in military or police services also raise a number of unique issues. Some children have difficulties understanding or otherwise making sense of the events leading up to a death. This can make it even harder for them to move forward through the grieving process.

When educators recognize students who are bereaved, acknowledge their loss, and make themselves available for ongoing conversations or contact, they offer immensely valuable support. For students with additional challenges, educators and student support personnel may need to guide families to other resources, such as a bereavement counselor or mental health provider, to make sure those children have the support they need.

In this chapter, we review some of the circumstances where the need for referrals or additional support may be more likely. These include complicated mourning, major secondary losses, students in transition, students with disabilities, and students who have lost a loved one to a line-of-duty death. Educators who are aware of the additional demands that can arise in these situations will be better prepared to offer realistic, necessary support.

COMPLICATED MOURNING

Although mourning is often a complex and difficult process, there is usually a sense of transition over time. In the first days after a death, surviving family members and friends often ride a roller coaster of emotions. They might sob uncontrollably at one point, feel empty and without emotion 20 minutes later, share fond memories and laughter an hour after that, and then begin sobbing deeply again.

A week or two after the death, they might be having similar responses, but there is a sense of change and movement. The deep sobbing might still occur, but less often. Although the exact features of grief are not the same from person to person, the sense of gradual shifts and change is common. Usually, some months after the death, the feelings of grief have less intensity, although they often continue to be strong.

In some situations, however, people seem to "get stuck" at one particular, difficult point of the mourning process. Instead of gradual improvement, the situation may become increasingly difficult. That is, the feeling of positive movement—of change or progress—is still absent months after the death. Individuals may also demonstrate unusual or particularly severe reactions, such as intense guilt. They may be unable to draw on inner resources or external support. They cannot adjust to the new reality of life without their loved one. Mental health providers call this *complicated mourning*. (See Rando [1993] for an excellent textbook for clinicians on the topic of complicated mourning.)

> **In some situations, people seem to "get stuck" at one particular, difficult point of the mourning process.**

What Complicated Mourning Looks Like

At first, complicated mourning may look like any other mourning process. The degree or nature of reactions, the extent to which they persist, and the fact that they sometimes get worse instead of better are striking. People suffering from complicated grief might experience any of the following:

- **They may not move forward in their grief process.** The loss of a close family member or friend often brings ongoing feelings of sadness or despair. At first, it may be difficult for grieving people to imagine ever enjoying life again. Over time, they find some things that bring moments of pleasure—a beautiful sunset, a funny movie, a dinner with family and friends. As time moves forward and the death is increasingly distant, they find the moments of despair happen less frequently and the moments of enjoyment occur more often.

  In complicated mourning, this shift in the pattern of sadness and enjoyment may not occur. Each day may feel as difficult as the first day of grief, and this continues over a period of months or even years.

- **They may have difficulty managing the ongoing responsibilities of their lives.** Over time, most grieving people are gradually able to resume the responsibilities in their lives. For children, this would include school and perhaps other activities, such as working at an after-school job (for older students); helping out with household chores; or participating in clubs, sports, or other extracurricular activities. For adults, this usually includes work or caring for children or other family members.

They keep gas in the car and food in the kitchen (most of the time). The house gets cleaned (perhaps not as thoroughly as before), and the lawn gets mowed (at least occasionally).

In complicated mourning, these responsibilities may continue to feel overwhelming. Children continue to have difficulty concentrating in school. They may not be interested in other activities, or they may find they simply cannot do what they once did easily—pass a football, play a song on their guitar, or sit through a club meeting or religious service.

- **They have problems with social connections.** In acute grief, some people push away friends or family for a period of time. They may feel like no one can understand what they are going through. They may question the meaning or purpose of their relationships and the social activities they used to enjoy. Children may be confused about the ways their own feelings have changed and feel unsure about how to act around family or friends. This is one of the reasons grief can be isolating. Over time, however, grieving children and adults who have experienced this kind of isolation find their way back to social connections that have meaning for them. Some of their relationships may change, but they find they can feel close to people again.

  In complicated mourning, people may isolate themselves from many or all of their friends and family in an ongoing way. The relationships do not improve after a few weeks or months. They resist the attempts people make to spend time with them. They may become engaged in social media or online sites where others focus on hopelessness and despair, and negative coping strategies are promoted.

- **They cannot stop thinking about the deceased.** When we first lose people we love, they are in our thoughts constantly. "She would have loved this movie." "He will never get to ride his bicycle along this beautiful road again." "This party would be great if only she were here." Sometimes, it may feel as if we cannot get away from such thoughts. They intrude on everything we do.

  Over time, these thoughts usually continue, but they are less frequent and less intrusive. We know how much she would have enjoyed a book or movie or television show, and we can go ahead and enjoy it as well. We think of him when we walk along his favorite country road, and we are able to truly enjoy the beauty for ourselves. We miss our loved one, but still can have a pretty good time at the party.

  In complicated mourning, it may be difficult or impossible to enjoy life. Thoughts of the deceased are constantly present, and the person's grief is relentless. Disturbing images of the loved one at the moment of death may intrude repeatedly. Longing for the deceased is powerful, and survivors may have difficulty accepting the fact of the death. There is no hope, no bright moment, no satisfaction or happiness. The absence of the loved one taints everything.

- **They may abuse alcohol or other drugs.** Sometimes, people who are grieving find themselves turning to alcohol or other drugs more than they did before the death. They may be trying to calm their nerves, get some sleep, or numb their pain. Eventually, most will realize that substance use is not helping them cope with their grief, and their use will drop back to previous levels.

  In complicated mourning, people may continue to use substances more frequently. They may abuse prescription medicines. Problems with use may worsen over time, and they may show signs of a substance use disorder. Although younger children do not often abuse substances, adolescents experiencing complicated mourning may.

- **They may have persistent thoughts of suicide.** Many people who lose a loved one have moments when they wonder whether life is still worth living. They cannot picture themselves ever feeling happiness again. They may imagine or believe that their own death will allow them to see their loved one again. If these thoughts occur, they are usually transient—they come and go. As with most symptoms of grief, they tend to be more common early in the process and become less common over time. There are likely to be "thinking about it" moments, rather than persistent and troubling thoughts of suicide. Educators who become aware of thoughts of suicide by students or their family members, even if seen soon after the death, should involve a school mental health provider to ensure the person's safety.

  In complicated mourning, when thoughts of suicide occur, they are more likely to be persistent and have great force. This might include making specific plans, such as how and when the suicide will take place. People experiencing this kind of grief may actually begin to follow through on their planning, perhaps taking steps to put their affairs in order or think about when and how they will do it. This level of planning and preparation, or even significant thoughts of suicide in the absence of such planning and preparation, is an unusual response to grief and represents a psychiatric emergency. Care is required immediately, even if the person is reluctant to seek help or resists doing so.

- **Emotional, mental health, or learning problems present before the death worsen significantly.** People coping with the stress of grief often experience difficulties with preexisting conditions. These additional challenges can range from mild to severe. For example, people who had mild and occasional anxiety or blue moods before the death might find they have anxiety or depression serious enough to warrant treatment. People who have had moderate depression for some time that was treated successfully with therapy or antidepressants may find themselves dealing with more complicated symptoms that no longer respond well to their existing treatment. They may need to try new medications or receive therapy more frequently for a period of time.

Children may develop, or experience, a worsening of many different conditions. These include such things as anxiety, depression, school refusal, oppositional disorders, attention problems (e.g., attention-deficit/hyperactivity disorder), or obsessive-compulsive disorder. They may need special attention and additional support to cope with these challenges for some period after the death.

In complicated mourning, the worsening of problems may be dramatic in some way. The symptoms become much more severe, or children may not respond to usual supports and assistance.

Often, children who are experiencing complicated mourning show typical symptoms of depression. These might include such symptoms as irritability or anger, feelings of hopelessness or worthlessness, or withdrawal from family and friends. Children may show either an increase or decrease in appetite and begin sleeping much more, or much less, than usual. Difficulty concentrating and physical complaints, such as stomachaches, may also occur. Feelings of guilt are common.

Children who have a parent experiencing complicated mourning are facing tremendous burdens. They may fear for their parent's welfare. Their home life may become disorganized because essential household tasks are not getting done. At a time when they most need emotional support and reassurance, they have a parent who is unable to give it to them. It can be devastating for a child to realize that all he or she has to offer is not enough to make a parent let go of the grief and "come back" to the world.

Professional intervention is recommended for children and adults who suffer from complicated mourning. In many cases, a combination of therapy and medication helps people work through their difficulties and begin to move forward in the process of grieving. It is quite important that parents experiencing complicated mourning get treatment or intervention so they are better able to care for their children.

Even when children suffering from complicated mourning are referred for mental health services, the role of educators in offering support is important. Educators play a unique role in children's lives. Mental health providers cannot duplicate this—they offer a different type of support. The comfort children receive from a caring, concerned educator continues to be meaningful and valuable to children, even in these most difficult circumstances.

Children who have a parent experiencing complicated mourning are facing tremendous burdens.

When Complicated Mourning Is More Likely

Anyone might experience complicated mourning. This can occur for children and adults who have excellent social support, strong coping skills, and no previous history of emotional difficulty. However, there are factors that make complicated mourning more likely for children. (Several of these factors were highlighted by the Institute of Medicine in their summary of factors associ- ated, in the literature, with an increased risk of psychological morbidity for children following the death of a parent or sibling. See Osterweis et al., 1984; see also Schonfeld & Demaria 2016.) As with many other elements of grieving, these include circumstances of the death and circumstances in the lives of the students and their families.

Circumstances of the Death

No death is easy, but some deaths are more difficult to understand or imagine— why it happened, how it happened, why it happened to this person. The fol- lowing are seven examples of deaths that may lead to complicated mourning:

- **Deaths caused by traumatic circumstances.** Deaths due to traumatic circumstances usually occur suddenly. They often involve significant elements of "bad luck" or fate. For example, if the person had not been standing on that particular corner, if the driver of the car had left home 60 seconds later, or if someone else had been working on patrol rather than their mother that night, the death would not have occurred. These are often deaths that are also painful to imagine. The deceased might have suffered. There may have been disfigurement or mutilation of the body. The person may have been alone at the moment of death.

- **Deaths by violence.** Violent deaths are a particularly difficult form of traumatic loss. Similar to other deaths by trauma, it is painful to imagine the moment of death and the effects on the body.

Living With Grief and Fear

Kendra, a 9-year-old girl, lived in a large city with her mother, Laurette. Laurette worked as a bartender and occasionally dated men she met at the bar. She didn't always show the best judgment about the men she invited into her life. One of her former partners was a man with a history of violence, and Kendra watched in horror one day when he threatened to kill her mother. He turned to Kendra and said, "And I'll kill you, too."

One evening about a year later, Laurette came home after work to an impa- tient daughter complaining that they were out of cat food and that her mother needed to go buy some now. Laurette sighed, picked up her purse, and headed out to the local convenience store. She didn't return to the apartment, and after several anxious hours, Kendra called an aunt who lived in another state.

The aunt called the authorities in Laurette's town and learned that her sister had been shot and killed in the parking lot of the convenience store. The aunt called Kendra's grandfather, who lived near Laurette's apartment. He came over immediately, had Kendra pack a bag, and drove off with her to her aunt and uncle's home. There, she was informed of the tragic circumstances of her mother's death. She never returned to the apartment she'd shared with her mother.

Kendra's aunt and uncle took custody of her. This was a difficult transition for her. Her relatives lived a quiet life with structure and rules that were unfamiliar to her. She missed her old independence.

She was not allowed to attend her mother's funeral. She had not taken any mementos from the apartment and had nothing of her mother's to remember her by. The entire family was vague about the details of the death. They seemed embarrassed about how Laurette lived her life and the fact that she was murdered. They believed it was better to focus on the future rather than dwell on the past.

Kendra was furious about the way she was being treated, and she acted in ways that showed this. She was disrespectful to her aunt and uncle. She refused to follow their rules. She didn't want the new clothes they bought her. Sometimes she cursed at them. "In this house," they told her, "we insist on respect."

"No one is respecting me!" she shouted back. "No one will tell me anything! You're treating me like a little kid."

She began acting out at her new school, creating disturbances in the classroom and conflicts with her classmates. She didn't want to make new friends. She didn't want to learn new things. She refused to talk about her past life. Her teacher reported that she often seemed anxious and distracted.

It was clear that something needed to be done for Kendra, so she was referred for counseling. The counselor asked her if she would talk about some of the things on her mind. Kendra told him she worried that she would be murdered just as her mother was. At first, this seemed to be an understandable reaction to the circumstances of her mother's death, but as Kendra continued to talk, the counselor realized that there was more to the story. Kendra believed her mother had been murdered by the man who had threatened them both. She was living in terrible fear that he would track her down. Sometimes, she believed she saw him in crowds searching for her.

The counselor spoke with the family about Kendra's concerns. They were surprised to hear this story. Kendra was able to give identifying information about the man who had made the threats, and the police were able to locate him. He had been arrested before Laurette's murder and had been in custody since that time. He was not a suspect in her mother's murder.

Kendra's family began to talk to her more about her mother and what the police were doing to find the murderer. She was reassured that this was someone who did not know her and could never find her. As they continued these conversations, they were able to talk with her about other thoughts and feelings she was having about her mother.

The counselor met with Kendra again, and they talked more about her mother. Kendra complained that she had not been able to take any of her mother's possessions. She didn't have any of their family photographs. If she'd had the chance, she would have taken along some of her mother's shirts, one of her bottles of perfume, and a stuffed animal her mom kept on the bed.

Laurette's apartment had not been emptied yet, so other family members were able to gather some mementos for Kendra. She received a package with some of her mother's possessions, as well as the family photos. These remembrances meant a great deal to Kendra.

Her aunt and uncle took Kendra to visit her mother's gravesite. Although she was still upset that she had missed the funeral, this at least gave her an opportunity to say goodbye to her mother. She made her aunt and uncle promise they would bring her back again in the future. They readily agreed once they realized how important this was to Kendra.

After this, Kendra didn't feel she needed to talk further with the counselor. By now, the family was being more open with Kendra, and she responded well to their greater honesty. She began to follow the family rules more successfully, and sometimes responded to their efforts to show affection. She calmed down in school and began to apply herself to her classes.

One day, her uncle invited her to the school's father–daughter dance. Kendra snorted. "You can't be serious," she said. "What a stupid idea." After a while, though, she changed her mind and told her uncle that she would like to go. They both enjoyed the event, and it was the beginning of a time of increasing closeness for all of them. Once Kendra was reassured about her own safety and could trust her aunt and uncle to be honest with her, she moved on in her grieving and was able to adjust successfully to her new life.

- **Deaths that are not socially sanctioned or the impact of which is not appreciated.** Some deaths are more troublesome socially, and people may find it more difficult to talk about them. They may not know what to say to survivors. Gossip or rumors may surround such deaths. Bereaved family members may experience a sense of shame. As a result, survivors may not ask for or receive the same level of support they might for other types of deaths.

  These might include deaths from suicide, certain diseases (e.g., HIV), or drug- or alcohol-related causes. The grief of survivors when someone dies while *committing* an act of violence is another area that may not be acknowledged. Children are sensitive to the stigma surrounding such deaths and may be more hesitant than usual to acknowledge their feelings or seek support.

  People may underestimate the impact of a death on someone when they do not understand the personal connection of the survivor to the deceased. Deaths of an estranged former spouse or miscarriages early in pregnancy often result in far more impact than friends or colleagues realize. Survivors may grieve with limited social support. Deaths of stepchildren or half-siblings who spent most of their time with another family may not be recognized in the same way as the death of someone who always lived with the family.

- **Sudden deaths.** When deaths are sudden and unexpected, the pain of loss is not necessarily greater; however, the shock of it can be traumatic and can interfere with the usual processes of coping with grief.

- **Deaths after a long illness.** Long illnesses place immense difficulties on families. The person who is ill may deteriorate slowly over a period of years while the family struggles to provide care. Financial circumstances often become challenging. The person who is ill may be irritable and difficult, and the physical and mental processes of decline can be agonizing to witness.

  Even in the most loving families, people going through these experiences find themselves wishing, at times, that death would be hastened. They do not wish to see a loved one suffer, and although people talk about this less often, people sometimes wish to be relieved from their own suffering related to the demands of the illness. Confusing feelings of guilt, relief, regret, and sadness are not at all unusual in such circumstances, and, when strong, these may contribute to episodes of complicated mourning.

- **Deaths seen as preventable.** Sometimes a death seems preventable. If someone had continued talking with a loved one for 30 seconds longer, the person would not have been hit by the truck. If a family member had decided to take the person to the emergency room a few hours earlier, doctors might have saved his life. Sometimes, these impressions have some basis in fact—if the seatbelt had been fastened, if the medication had been given properly, or if the mother had never gotten involved with the violent boyfriend, then death might have been averted. Powerful feelings of guilt contribute to the risk for complicated mourning.

- **Public deaths.** When deaths receive public attention for any reason, children and families may face special challenges in coping. Sometimes the recognition is positive—a family member may have died a hero for saving someone or died while in military service. Other times, the attention may be about more troubling matters—a family member died during a crime or in macabre circumstances.

  The additional attention these deaths receive places burdens on children. Other people have their own ideas and attitudes about what occurred, and children are likely to hear comments from peers and adults. Disturbing posts or images may appear in social media or online.

  There is less of a sense of privacy about these deaths and the process of grieving. Survivors may find themselves in the public eye much of the time. They may feel embarrassed about how they are reacting to the death and worry that they are not living up to what society and peers expect of them. They may be ashamed if they cry in public or worried that if they do not cry, people will question how much they cared about the deceased.

  There may be public demands on the family, such as appearances at communitywide memorial services. Children may not see the events the same way that those from the community do. They may not feel grateful that their father was a hero, for example, but instead angry that he put himself at risk and abandoned the family by dying.

Circumstances of the Student or Family

A number of family or individual circumstances can increase the risk for complicated mourning. The following are several examples of these situations:

- **Emotional problems.** Children with current emotional problems or those with a previous history of problems are more likely to have complicated grief reactions. Typical problems include such things as anxiety disorders or depression. In addition, some children have family members with emotional or mental health problems. This can also increase the risk for complicated grief reactions among children or their family.

Children with current emotional problems or those with a previous history of problems are more likely to have complicated grief reactions.

- **Ambivalent relationship with the deceased.** Some children are ambivalent about family members who die. They may have lost a mother who abandoned the family when they were very young. The person who died may have abused them in some way. They may have felt jealous of the person. They may have resented a parent's limits or restrictions. They may gain benefits as a result of the death, such as greater status within the family or more freedom or respect.

  These ambivalent feelings are difficult. Children may feel relieved or indifferent about the death. They may have true and deep feelings of loss as well as confusing feelings of satisfaction. When such dissonant feelings occur, complicated mourning is more likely.

- **Struggles for autonomy and independence.** High school students have begun to break away from their parents in anticipation of leaving the family home for college or work. At some level, most long for freedom. Often, teens resent adult supervision and the restrictions in their lives. Many families go through periods of turmoil related to adolescent rebellion or the struggle for autonomy. However, as adolescents move through these times of transition, they typically also have periods where they want and need to approach their parents for advice and support. Those who have left the family home still look forward to return visits. Although they may seem "ready" and even eager to leave their parents, a parent's death in late adolescence can be a particularly stressful loss.

- **Intense or dependent relationship with the deceased.** Some children may have had an unusually close or intense relationship with the person who died. This might have been an especially dependent relationship. It might have been a relationship that offered important support that was not available from others, such as a deaf child who lost the only person in the family who understood and used sign language. For some children, the person who died may have been the safe relationship in a family storm—a grandmother who provided a haven from physical or sexual abuse by the mother's boyfriend, or an aunt who always helped get the schizophrenic father to the hospital when he decompensated. Losing someone so essential to everyday survival can contribute to the risk for complicated mourning.

- **History of other losses or stressors.** Children who experience loss, even when it involves the death of a close family member, are usually fairly resilient. When they can turn to others for support and guidance, they usually learn to cope and move forward. However, when children go through multiple losses over time or experience other serious stressors, the response to new stressors, including grief, can be more difficult.

  This encompasses a wide range of possible circumstances. A child who has already lost one parent, for example, will have a much more difficult time losing a second parent. Children who have been emotionally, physically, or sexually abused have lost much of their innate resilience. Children who have already been witness to death and loss (e.g., coming from a war-torn country, growing up in an area where they have lost classmates and family members to violence) have already spent many of the natural resources they were given. Cumulative loss of any type can increase the risk of complicated mourning.

- **Lack of social support.** Grief is both an intensely personal and a social process. It is important for people who are grieving to receive support from others. Grieving children need touch, reassurance, a listening ear, patience, and acceptance. These are not things they can get on their own—they must be delivered by another human being.

  Some children do not receive this kind of support. Their families may be incapable of offering it, and they may not have strong relationships with peers. They may be the quiet kids at school who do not cause problems, do not stand out, and do not receive much attention. They may not give any indication that they need or want such support—indeed, they may not be aware themselves that they need it. Children who have little or no social support are more likely to experience complicated mourning.

DEATH AND SECONDARY LOSS

Another factor that can make it harder to adjust to the death of a loved one is secondary loss. When children lose someone close to them, they experience the immediate and direct effects of that death. In most instances, especially if the deceased is a parent or primary caregiver, they also experience additional losses in their lives. Examples of secondary loss include the following:

- **Changed relationships.** When people die, they leave behind a circle of work associates, friends, and family members. Children have their own place in this circle and often enjoy the relationships within it. However, if the deceased was the center of that circle, when the center is gone, the circle itself may dissolve.

Even when children receive support about the loss of a family member or friend, they may not receive support about the loss of these relationships. They no longer get the special attention from the secretary at their mother's office. Their aunt and uncle do not come by much any longer now that their father has died. Their brother's friend who used to come over and play guitar, teaching them a few chords along the way, no longer drops by.

Sometimes, relationships that seem fairly incidental to adults have tremendous importance to children. This is especially true for children who have limited support in other ways or who are dealing with family problems.

Sometimes, relationships that seem fairly incidental to adults have tremendous importance to children.

- **Moving.** When a parent or other family member dies, the family may have to move. A move to a new neighborhood, city, or state can create a stressful transition for children who are already grieving. After the death of a family member, it often seems as if everything about the world has changed. When children must also relocate, this becomes literally true. In addition to this death, they also lose familiar places, their school, and their friends.

- **Lifestyle.** When a parent or other source of financial support for a family dies, the family's financial circumstances often change. Families can lose their homes, their sense of financial security, their ability to fund their children's college education, and their ability to comfortably purchase other things they want or need. Surviving parents may need to work more hours or at a more demanding job and, therefore, be less available at a time when children especially need their presence and support.

  Some families must move into smaller, less-expensive living spaces. They may move from a single-family home to an apartment, or from a three-bedroom apartment to a one-room place, which may mean less privacy, more crowding, and, usually, more family tension.

  In some instances, children may also experience a distinct shift in class or social status after the death of a parent. They may not be able to participate in special school programs that involve extra costs. They may need to purchase secondhand clothing for the first time in their lives. They might suddenly become eligible for subsidized school lunch programs. All of these changes can add additional layers of emotion, such as shame, anger, or sadness, to the grief they are already experiencing.

- **Peer group status.** Children may also experience shifts in peer group status related to some of these changes. If they move to another area, they must reestablish themselves in a new peer group. If a popular friend died, it may disrupt their connections to others in their circle of friends. If a family loses financial resources, children may no longer be accepted or feel comfortable in their former peer group. If their family member or friend died with some taint of scandal, children may withdraw from their friends or be avoided by them.

Although, as adults, we would like to think that issues of status are not important at such times, children and teens can be quite sensitive to these matters. For some children, the shift in status will be substantial.

- **Shared memories.** Families share important memories—"The day you were born," "The mischief you used to get into when you were a toddler," "Your first day of school." Children love to hear these stories told and retold as they grow up. The stories make them feel special, and they help affirm their sense of place in the family. They provide a sense of continuity as new memories and stories are woven in over time. Sometimes, new bits of information come out—"One time, you were going to get punished by Grandma because of your mischief, but she just couldn't stop laughing."

  It is an extraordinarily powerful experience to have someone hold this special set of memories about you—the unique, singular person you are. Therefore, when children lose someone who has these kinds of memories about them, they lose a thread to their own sense of self. No one else knows them in quite that way, and no one else will ever know them in quite that way again.

- **Shared visions and plans for the future.** Although most children are strongly oriented to the present, they also have plans for the future. Their family members are part of those plans. When a family member dies, these visions change. Will graduating from eighth grade mean as much if the parent or grandparent is not there to see it? Will the swim meet next month matter? How will a student choose a college or complete applications without this person's support? What about the planned drive down the coast or the imagined trip to Hawaii? Children have many things in the forefront or background of their minds that can be affected by a death.

- **A sense of security and safety.** In our daily lives, all people tend to make certain assumptions. We probably assume, for example, that we will walk out of our door in the morning as we always do and go to work or school, see our colleagues, have lunch, and perhaps take a little walk in the afternoon. We assume that we will come back to our home after work and find it intact. We expect to see our family members for dinner and have conversations in the evening as we always do.

  This is called the *assumptive world* (for further discussion of the assumptive world and its impact on bereavement, see Rando, 1993). These assumptions are the things we automatically count on; they are part of the background in our lives. Generally, it is good to be able to make these assumptions. This frees up our attention so we can focus on the things that are changing every day in our lives—a new project at work, a bill that needs to be paid, a special visit with an old friend. It allows us to go through our day without becoming overwhelmed with all of the tragedies that *could* occur.

When children or adults experience a death, they experience the loss of this assumptive world. They assumed, before this event, that they would see their family member or friend again. They then realize that much of what they had taken for granted was really an assumption. Now, because this person has died, they lose their ability to trust any of the assumptions they make.

Children sometimes feel this loss more acutely than adults who have already had experiences with death. How can they trust that they will see any of the people they love again? How do they know that they will not die as their family member or friend did? How can they be sure that anything will ever feel normal again? This loss of an everyday presumption of safety and security can lead to feelings of vulnerability and anxiety. People grieve not only the death but also the loss of their ability to trust that things—almost anything—will be okay.

––––––––

When children or adults experience a death, they experience the loss of this assumptive world. They assumed, before this event, that they would see their family member or friend again.

––––––––

Making Grief More Challenging

These experiences of secondary loss reinforce the primary grief experience. A young girl who has lost her father is struggling to regain some sense of normalcy in her life, but every day, she is reminded of his absence by the crowded conditions of the new, small apartment where her family had to move. A young man who has been planning to go to college cannot stop thinking about his mother's death because he cannot imagine how to make his decisions, or finance his education, without her. An 8-year-old boy whose favorite aunt has died wonders who will tell him at his next birthday about all of the things they did together when he visited her farm, the way she had done as far back as he can remember. When secondary loss experiences are powerful and lasting, mourning may become complicated.

Way Too Many Changes

Eight-year-old Dylan's mother died after a long struggle with cancer. One way his father coped with all of the painful memories of his life during her illness was to change things. He bought a new car. He switched jobs. He moved the family to a new home. Then he met and began dating a new woman. Within a year of his first wife's death, he had remarried.

Dylan found all of the changes unsettling. He had to adjust to a new school and new friends, and now there was a new woman living in his home. He had trouble accepting his father's new wife as a part of the family so quickly, even though he liked her. He told his counselor, "He treats her like she's a queen. I mean, she shouldn't just be a maid, but she shouldn't be a queen, either. She should be somewhere in between."

Dylan had a number of reasonable and appropriate issues related to grief about his mother's death, but all of these were worsened by the extraordinary number of secondary losses he experienced.

GRIEF AND STUDENTS IN TRANSITION

Students go through many transitions in their lives. They may begin with pre-school and then move to elementary school. They graduate to middle school. They move on to high school, and then perhaps college, trade school, or the military.

Young people often experience other transitions as well. A divorce can change the configuration of their family. A job transfer may mean the family moves to a new state. An aging grandparent may move into the house, or an older sibling may move out.

Children are more vulnerable during times of transition. They are more likely to start new, risky behaviors, such as smoking, drinking, or drug use. Experiencing a death around the time of a transition can make grieving more difficult. In addition, transitions are also times when grief issues from an earlier loss may reemerge. For example, a child who lost a parent while in third grade and then had some school difficulties may have received support, gotten back on track, and returned to satisfactory schoolwork. However, when he moves to a new school in seventh grade, he has to shift classrooms several times a day and is no longer in the company of familiar classmates and teachers. He then begins to have school problems again.

Students may also feel heightened effects of bereavement during their high school years when academic performance becomes especially important. College-bound students in particular feel pressure about grade point averages (GPAs), advanced placement classes, and SAT scores. They want to develop effective interview skills. Some are making extraordinary efforts to build résumés for college applications by participating in school clubs, doing volunteer work, or taking part in other extracurricular activities.

These endeavors are stressful for any student. For bereaved students, they may be especially challenging. They may be unable to perform at their best if they have experienced a recent loss. The heightened pressures of this time can also bring up difficulties related to earlier losses.

Students are also sensitive to the statements made by family members after a loss. Older students often take on additional responsibilities in the family if a parent has died. They may help younger children with homework, do grocery shopping, drive siblings to their baseball games, and keep the lawn mowed.

They may also be providing emotional support to surviving parents—talking to them late at night, encouraging them to return to social activities, offering a shoulder to cry on. If the surviving parent becomes dependent on this support, it is more difficult for the student to make a transition to college, especially if this means leaving the area. A parent who says, "Your help has been wonderful, and I am so grateful for all you have done," is expressing important appreciation. However, if that parent adds, "I could never do this without you," it makes leaving for college even more difficult.

Some of these students will change their plans and choose to attend nearby colleges that allow them to stay geographically close to their families. Some will go away to college and find that they are unable to tolerate the distance from their families. These students may drop out so they can return to their family home.

Sometimes, postponing independence from the family is what works best for the student and the family. This may be a time when it feels right for everyone to be close together. It is important, however, to support young people in making their own choices about these matters. If they stay close to their family because they feel enmeshed and unable to free themselves from the weight of their family's grief, it will not be a helpful course of action for anyone in the family. Such students may develop feelings of resentment, frustration, guilt, or shame, or they may experience symptoms of complicated mourning or other emotional problems. (Additional issues regarding transitions are discussed in Chapter 8.)

STUDENTS WITH DISABILITIES

Students with disabilities are as unique as students who are typically developing, and there are no hard-and-fast rules that apply to all of them. As we discussed in Chapter 2, when students with learning differences and/or developmental disabilities experience the death of a family member or friend, it is likely that they will need more reassurance, patience, and understanding than other children.

Death challenges most people's understanding. Adults as well as children may not initially understand what has happened, or they may need to hear information more than once. Younger children are especially likely to need repeated explanations about such things as the Four Concepts About Death, what happened to the deceased, how their own lives might change, what kind of support they can ask for, and where they can receive support.

These issues are often simply a matter of degree with students with intellectual and neurodevelopmental disabilities. They may ask the same questions many times. They may want to listen to an explanation many times. Students may hear an explanation, accept it, and then decide later that they still are not quite sure what it means. Concrete examples are usually helpful, and conversations about the meaning of death and their relationship with the deceased may be revisited often.

School communications with family members are especially important with these students. Educators will want to offer support in helping students understand what has happened. To do this, they will want to gain a sense of what has been explained already and how the death is being discussed in the family. They may be able to offer guidance to parents and other family members. Again, these are basically the same steps recommended for all students, but the extent of discussion may simply be more—just as it is with other topics in their education and their lives.

Parents of children with disabilities may also find it particularly upsetting to have discussions about the death. Having to explain in simple and direct terms what the death means and what impact it has on the family, especially repeatedly, is difficult for the parent who is also grieving. If a parent has died, surviving parents may be so worried about what will happen to their child who has a disability if they also die that they may be unable even to begin the conversation.

Special education teachers, or general education teachers who know students well, are often the strongest resource when their students with intellectual or neurodevelopmental disabilities have faced the death of a family member or friend. Educators are often among the most skilled and trusted communicators in their lives. They are familiar with the concepts that students are likely to grasp easily, as well as those that will be a challenge. They know how the students respond when they are frustrated, frightened, or confused. They have already addressed challenging topics with them, such as difficulties with peers, classroom behavior, emotions, and other sensitive issues.

UNIQUE CHALLENGES IN LINE-OF-DUTY DEATHS

In the same way that virtually all educators will work with grieving children, most will work with children who have the potential to be affected by a line-of-duty death. There are almost two million children of active service members in the United States. Most live in civilian communities, and more than 80% attend public schools.

Most schools also serve family members of police personnel. Each year, more than a hundred law enforcement officers in the United States are killed in the line of duty. Each of these deaths touches the families of other law enforcement officers. Educators can expect to find children affected by line-of-duty deaths in schools throughout the nation.

There are three essential points to remember about students affected by line-of-duty deaths.

1. **Most grief experiences are similar.** In most ways, children and family survivors of line-of-duty deaths experience grief and coping with loss much as others do. They have similar thoughts, feelings, concerns, and needs.

2. **Some grief experiences are distinct in important ways.** Survivors of line-of-duty deaths are coping with unique issues within a unique

culture. Most people outside the military or law enforcement world are unfamiliar with these issues.

3. **Educators can make a difference.** When educators are aware of the distinct issues facing these families, they can plan and provide more effective support.

Parents, spouses, and children of law enforcement officers and military service members understand their family member is at risk for injury or death. Living with this knowledge on a day-to-day basis requires some effort. Many practice a type of healthy denial that helps them cope. "Nothing will happen to my mom because she isn't working in combat situations." "My dad is smarter than the bad guys, so I know he'll be okay."

When educators are aware of the distinct issues facing these families, they can plan and provide more effective support.

When a line-of-duty death occurs, these presumptions can be profoundly challenged. There are a range of responses that children and families might have. For example:

- **The world becomes more dangerous.** Because the possibility of death is a fear the family has been coping with all along, the ability to go forward and continue to use healthy denial or make presumptions about a stable world may be disrupted. Many things about the world that once felt safe and secure are now likely to feel dangerous or threatening.

- **Children regret not being "better."** Children may regret not staying more connected with their parent or loved one. They often feel they should have been "a better kid," more attentive, or more available. They may think, "I should have known this would happen. I should have spent more time with my dad and not gotten into trouble so much."

- **Families may feel relieved.** In addition to shock and grief, some family members may actually feel a sense of relief when the constant worry about their loved one ends, just as people sometimes do when someone dies after a long illness. This can bring up feelings of guilt and shame.

- **Children may feel resentful.** Children understand that their loved one made a commitment to serve and protect their community or country. They may be resentful that, because of that choice, the person is now dead. They may feel guilty about wishing he or she had not chosen to serve.

- **Questions of honor can be confusing.** There are many causes of line-of-duty deaths, including deaths from accidents or natural causes. These may not seem particularly "heroic." In cases where an officer or service member dies by suicide, children are likely to sense the confusion and perhaps shame of adults around them. They may be told this death was not heroic or that their loved one has done something wrong.

In addition, these deaths tend to be sudden and intentional ("Someone *wanted* to kill my family member"), and information about them is public. Although children may hear accolades about the heroism of their loved one, they are also likely to see social media posts that denigrate the deceased because of their role as a police officer or servicemember. Funeral services are often highly public and follow military or service traditions that may leave little opportunity to focus activities on what would best meet the needs of the children. The children may also feel self-conscious about the attention or angry that their family isn't allowed to grieve privately.

Further information about support for student survivors of line-of-duty deaths can be found at the web site for the Coalition to Support Grieving Students (https://www.schoolcrisiscenter.org/) in the Resources section.

WHEN MORE IS NEEDED: REFERRING FOR OUTSIDE SERVICES

Many children will benefit from additional services to help them cope with their grief. Children who are experiencing complicated mourning or who have particular challenges related to the loss (such as those outlined in this chapter) that place them at higher risk of complicated mourning, *even if their mourning does not yet appear to be unusual*, are especially likely to need this extra support. The extra support can guide them through the grief process in a manner that helps them continue participating in school and learning. It can also support them as they sustain and build on the existing relationships in their lives.

Signs that children need additional support might include any of the following, particularly when the behaviors are new or become markedly worse than they were before the death:

- **School problems or failure.** Some difficulties with school are common immediately after a death. If they persist, students need further support.
- **Aggressive or delinquent behaviors.** Students may develop new problem behaviors, or earlier problem behaviors may worsen.
- **Guilt.** Feelings of guilt are extremely common after a death; however, when they are persistent, marked, or related to a rational sense of responsibility (e.g., when a child drowns while under the supervision of an older sibling), counseling is recommended.
- **Apathy.** Students who were once connected to peers, classroom activities, or school programs may stop feeling that sense of connection and thus become apathetic.
- **Self-destructive behaviors.** Among adolescents, self-destructive behaviors might include new or increased use of alcohol or other drugs, reckless driving, or risky sexual behavior. Younger children might take physical risks, such as jumping off walls or riding their bicycles dangerously.
- **Social withdrawal or isolation.** Formerly sociable students who no longer seek out interactions with peers may be withdrawing because of a complicated grief reaction.

- **Talk of suicide.** This is always a concern, no matter what the circumstances. Children who talk of suicide should be seen by a mental health professional right away.

Educators sometimes state that they are not appropriately trained to make assessments about students' mental health. However, educators are familiar with the personality and performance of specific students, as well as with the behaviors typical of all students. This leaves them in an excellent position to observe students' behaviors and notice when something has changed or is out of the ordinary.

When questions arise about whether a student needs additional support, our general advice is to go ahead and make a referral. Almost all grieving students will benefit from extra attention at this time. If students *are* suffering from complicated mourning, a referral could make a significant difference in their present and future success in school and in their relationships with family and friends.

Professional Resources

Resources for support include:

- School counseling services

- A pediatrician or other health care provider

- Bereavement support groups for families and children

- Community-based mental health services

In these more complicated situations, children usually need to be seen by professionals. However, an educator's or school's awareness and sensitivity to the issues can make an immense difference in a child's ability to get that extra help in a timely and appropriate fashion.

Key Concepts

- **For some people, the process of grief is more complicated than usual.** This is sometimes called *complicated mourning*.

- **The degree of reactions and persistence of grief are key features of complicated mourning.** Whereas most people begin to feel a sense of positive movement after a few weeks or months, those with complicated grief may find their ability to cope becomes worse instead of better.

- **Children may experience complicated mourning themselves, or they may have a parent who is experiencing complicated mourning.** Both circumstances present immense challenges to children.

- **There are some situations in which complicated mourning is more likely.** This includes times when there is something especially troubling about the death or when there are challenges in the student's family situation.
- **Children often experience secondary loss after the death of a family member.** This might include changes in living circumstances, finances, or social situations.
- **Children are more vulnerable to emotional and behavioral problems related to grief at times of transition.** This might include changing schools, moving, or experiencing a change in family constellation.
- **Students who require supports around learning and understanding may have additional challenges coping with the death of a family member or close friend.** These students may need more attention and help understanding and coming to terms with the loss.
- **Students who lose a family member through a line-of-duty death will experience grief and loss much as others do but will also face unique circumstances and challenges.** Educators who are familiar with these unique circumstances can offer more effective support.
- **Children experiencing complicated mourning usually benefit from assistance from other professionals.** Educators play an important role in helping students gain access to this kind of help.

8

Providing Support Over Time

Grief changes over time, but for most of us, the death of someone we care about stays with us in some way throughout our lives. This is especially true for children. As they continue to develop and grow, they are able to bring more complex understanding to their experiences. As they revisit the death over time, it will have new meaning to them.

The following are three things to remember about the way grief proceeds for children and adults:

1. **Grief proceeds on its own terms.** Chapter 7 describes the quality of grief *changing* over time; however, there is no set time line for grief. It should not be expected for the bereaved to be "over it" after 6 months or a year or any other particular period.

2. **Grief affects many different domains in life.** It influences feelings; thoughts; behaviors; and relationships at home, work, school, and various social settings. The ways children might show the effects in school, perhaps by being distractible and finding it difficult to concentrate, are discussed in Chapters 4 and 5. They are likely to have similar thoughts and experiences in other pursuits as well, such as sports, clubs, community service work, or activities related to their faith community.

3. **The expression of grief is personal and subjective.** No two people react in the same way to the death of a family member or friend.

PROVIDING STUDENTS WITH SUPPORT OVER TIME

Feelings of loss are reexperienced in many ways as children grow, mature, and gain new insights. Children commonly have these experiences during the following:

- **Holidays.** Family holidays are not the same after a family member dies. Children miss the familiarity of their loved one's presence.

- **Transitions to a new grade or school.** The absence of a classmate or family member can be powerful at these times.

- **Special events, awards, and graduations.** Celebratory events, especially when they involve families coming together, can heighten awareness of the absence of a family member or friend.

- **Rites of passage.** As children and teens grow toward adulthood, they take a number of important steps toward maturity—first bicycle, first out-of-town trip on their own, first date, first job, first prom, first car, high school graduation. These rites are different from one family or peer group to another, but the inability to turn to a specific family member or friend for support, to experience the person's sense of pride, or to share the excitement or satisfaction often brings up feelings of grief.

Experiences involving revisiting grief may be fairly straightforward for children—something they recognize and cope with well. These experiences might also be difficult, however, because they may be overwhelming and unexpected. They are also frustrating because it makes children feel out of control, and they can be distressing because the feelings are unpleasant and uncomfortable. Children may have feelings of shame or anxiety when these signs of grief arise.

It is helpful for bereaved children to understand the effects of grief over time and to determine how they can receive support for these feelings as they arise. Educators can offer guidance that helps children expect a range of feelings at different times.

Feelings of loss are reexperienced in many ways as children grow, mature, and gain new insights.

Responding to Grief Triggers

Triggers of grief are common in bereavement. Grief might be triggered by anniversaries or other important events. The family holidays, the deceased's birthday, the start of a new school year, or a father–daughter dance, for example, might bring up sudden and powerful feelings of sadness. Everyday occurrences can also act as triggers—walking by a familiar corner or seeing a television show the deceased person used to enjoy.

A wide range of events can act as grief triggers in school settings. A student might come across a photo of a place the family visited on vacation a year ago. In music class, students might sing one of the deceased's favorite songs. A health class might discuss a new medicine that helps people survive the very disease that caused the death of a friend. A student might make a cruel or thoughtless joke about death. A new set of math problems might remind a student of how much she misses the help her father used to give her with her math homework.

In addition, grief triggers often catch people off guard. They can be troubling to children who are trying to keep their school day on track while trying not to think about the person who died. The emotional responses can be mild and brief. A student might have a resurgence of sadness and a few moments of distraction, and then be able to focus again. Such emotions can also be powerful and deep, bringing on sudden tears or sobs and evoking overwhelming feelings of emptiness.

Educators who observe emotional responses to grief triggers can help students find a safe place to experience their feelings and regain their composure. This might be the office of the school counselor or school nurse, if they are available. There might be a safe place for students to step out of the classroom for a brief time—a hallway, the library, or the main office.

Common Grief Triggers

The following are common triggers for grief that children may experience:

- Listening to a song

- Hearing a piece of information on the news

- Certain smells and sounds

- Special occasions (e.g., birthdays, holidays, Mother's and Father's Day, graduations)

- Lost opportunities (e.g., recitals, sporting activities, father–daughter dance, prom)

Helpful Responses When a Child Experiences a Grief Trigger

The following are some options for offering support if a child experiences grief triggers:

- Choose an adult or location as a safe space the child can go to if strong feelings of grief arise.

- Establish procedures to allow the child to leave the classroom with prior permission if he or she is feeling overwhelmed, so the student doesn't attract the attention of peers when about to cry. This can make it more likely that the child will seek needed support.

- Let the child call a parent or family member if needed.

- Provide permission and encouragement to see the school counselor, nurse, psychologist, or social worker to talk.

- Offer private time with a teacher or other educator to discuss feelings, concerns, or other matters.

It is important that the student have a chance to talk with someone about this experience. Teachers can invite students to talk with them for a few moments after class, and they should be sure to do so if a counselor, nurse, or other support person is not available. Occasionally, a student may want to call a parent. Students should understand that these responses are natural and may continue to occur. For most people, they occur less frequently over time, although they may continue to be powerful. See Chapter 5 for further discussion about responding to grief triggers.

Students and families continue to be affected by grief, and they will appreciate the sensitivity of an educator who offers ongoing support about their loss.

Ongoing Support for Students and Families

Educators can take a number of steps to offer support to grieving students and their families over time. Although these are not likely to be as intensive as the kind of assistance teachers offer immediately after a death, they can play an important role in guiding students along in the process. Students and families continue to be affected by grief, and they will appreciate the sensitivity of an educator who offers ongoing support about their loss.

The following are some suggestions that students and families have found helpful:

- **Help preserve memories.** Children sometimes worry that they will forget the person who died, especially if they were quite young at the time of the death. Stories, pictures, and continued mention of the person who died can help children sustain their memory of the deceased. This reinforces their sense of having known and been known by this person.

  Educators who know students who have coped with a death at some point in the past can invite them to write, talk, or draw pictures about the person. This lets students know that the educator is supportive and concerned, as well as available to talk about these matters if they wish.

  Students may want to share some of their stories with the educator or their class. It is important that this be a matter of choice. Some will want to share information about their family member or friend who died, and others will not.

- **Affirm the importance of strong feelings.** This is something educators can do directly with bereaved students or in a general way with all students. Children and adolescents can benefit from opportunities to learn how to identify, describe, and cope with emotions. They can learn that strong feelings are something everyone experiences. Students might identify people who can give them support when they have strong emotions. They could develop lists of ways to cope with feelings, such as taking deep breaths, talking to a friend, talking to an adult, playing with a pet, and so forth.

It is helpful for bereaved children to understand that their feelings are a sign of how important the person was to them. When this understanding is paired with skills for coping with strong feelings, children are less likely to be distressed by powerful emotions that arise as part of ongoing grief.

- **Maintain or increase contact with the family.** As mentioned previously, it is important for schools and educators to contact families after a death occurs (see Chapter 6). Families and educators together can assess how children are coping and plan accommodations in schoolwork if necessary, as well as other means of support. These sorts of contacts continue to be helpful over time. If there are concerns about a student's behavior, early attention can prevent problems from starting or make it possible to resolve them more quickly if they do develop.

  Some time after a death has occurred, if educators notice grief reactions that seem especially strong, it is a good idea to check with the family. Difficulties may also be showing up in other areas.

- **Support contact between the family and the child's health care provider.** As mentioned, after a death has occurred, children often worry about their own health and that of others in their family. They are also experiencing greater stress than usual, which can cause a range of physical symptoms, including headaches and stomachaches.

  Educators may have opportunities to encourage families to contact their children's pediatrician or other health care provider. These providers can help identify complaints that stem from physical illness, emotional distress, or a combination of the two. Health care providers can also direct families to community resources that support families experiencing grief, such as bereavement support groups, community mental health programs, or camps for children who have experienced the death of a family member. Health care providers may offer to talk with children to see what they understand about the death and how the children and their family are coping. Sometimes they can help children express concerns that they are not discussing with the family.

- **Remember and recognize 1-year marks and other important dates.** Families remember the date of a loved one's death, and the school community remembers the date of the death of a student or staff member. Children will be aware of these days as well. Typically, they will find themselves thinking of their family member or friend more often, and more intensely, around this time.

  It's generally best to avoid using the term *anniversary* directly with grieving individuals at these times, especially after a school crisis such as an on-campus shooting, because the term is otherwise often associated with celebrations. A more neutral term or phrase, such as "the 1-year mark" or "the passage of 1 year since the death/crisis," may be preferable.

Moving through these moments can be a confusing and lonely experience. Even when students had strong support from friends and community at the time of the death of a family member, people outside the family are less likely to remember calendar markers of the death. A year later, friends have often moved on to other concerns. Schools may be reluctant to acknowledge the 1-year mark of the death of a member of the school community. This can prompt children and staff to think that they are alone in experiencing distress at this time. In addition, special support, such as counseling or bereavement groups, may have already ended. At this time, when their sense of support has diminished, students may find their feelings of sadness increasing. At each subsequent yearly marker, children are likely to experience these same feelings of remembrance and sadness.

When their sense of support has diminished, students may find their feelings of sadness increasing.

Educators can reach out to students around the date marking the death. For example, if a student lost a parent in sixth grade, it would mean a great deal to receive a card from their sixth-grade teacher the following year. The card can acknowledge that the teacher is thinking of the student during what is probably a difficult time.

Similarly, a seventh-grade teacher might mention privately to the student that he or she had heard from last year's teacher about the death and knew that the 1-year mark was coming up. An expression of caring and condolence is very powerful and important.

Schools can provide opportunities to acknowledge the calendar markers of deaths of students and school staff. Chapter 13 addresses the important topic of memorialization and commemoration in schools. Sometimes people worry that an acknowledgement of the anniversary will serve as a painful reminder to children. Children are usually already thinking about the anniversary of a major loss. A genuine gesture of support will be appreciated.

APPROACH TOPICS WITH SENSITIVITY IN THE CLASSROOM AND AT SCHOOL

Because we have such extensive knowledge of world events, we hear constantly about tragedies and deaths around the world. These topics make their way into classrooms regularly through literature, history, health, current events, and other subjects. Knowing that many students have lost a family member or friend, it is important to approach such subjects with sensitivity. It is understandable that some students will find these topics distressing.

Often, educators will not know the specific students who have experienced losses. It would be difficult, though, to anticipate what content or activities might be upsetting to individual students because educators cannot know the full history of every student.

What Educators Can Do

Educators can take some simple steps when they introduce classroom activities or subjects that might be difficult for children who have experienced the death of a family member or friend. Being proactive in this way offers reassurance to all students, while also providing support and understanding to those who have experienced losses. It also models for children how to be empathic and supportive of the needs of others.

The following sections offer some suggestions for maintaining sensitivity in the classroom for children who have experienced the death of a loved one.

Educators can take some simple steps when they introduce classroom activities or subjects that might be difficult for children who have experienced the death of a family member or friend.

Providing Activities That Focus on a Loved One

In elementary school, students often prepare cards, letters, gifts, or drawings for family members. They might make cards for Mother's Day, Father's Day, Valentine's Day, or other holidays. In any given class, there is a reasonable chance that one or more students has lost a parent. In addition, there may be students who have parents who are otherwise absent or who have parents of the same gender. Others may live with grandparents or other relatives.

Educators can approach these activities by asking students to think about an adult who has helped raise them or has supported them in an important way. This discussion can lead naturally into a conversation about the ways we recognize and appreciate people who have helped us grow up and stay healthy and safe. Mother's Day and Father's Day are ways to acknowledge these people.

Students can then be invited to make a Mother's Day card for their mother or a card for another woman who has been an important support in their lives. An educator might acknowledge that students have many different kinds of families, and some of them live with their mothers, whereas others do not.

A Mother's Day Card

Jack's mother died in March. In early May, his third-grade teacher handed students pieces of colorful paper and asked them to make their mothers cards for Mother's Day. Jack froze in his seat, staring straight ahead. The bright paper sat untouched on his desk. He had no idea what to do. Other students in the class knew Jack's mother had died. As they bent to their tasks, they stole glances at him, wondering what he was thinking and how he could possibly do this assignment.

His teacher walked around the classroom, checking on the students' work. When she got to Jack's desk, she saw the blank piece of paper. She said, "Jack, you can just make a card for your aunt or something." She walked on. Every student in the class watched as he slowly picked up a single crayon and began to mark listlessly on the paper in front of him.

When educators know students who have lost a parent, they can approach them privately before these activities. Students and educators can work out an approach to the activity that is positive for the student. For example, in the Mother's Day card activity, a teacher might say something like this:

> Later this week we're going to do an activity that talks about Mother's Day, and I'm going to ask the class to make cards. Your situation is different from classmates because your mother died earlier this year. I wanted to talk to you beforehand so we could figure out if you'd like to do this activity or if you'd rather do something else.
>
> The point of this activity is for all of the students in the class to think about someone who has been important to them—maybe their mothers, maybe someone else—and express appreciation to that person. You can make a card or drawing about your mother if you wish, or you can make a card for someone else who cares for you. You don't need to share your work—I won't call on you—but if you want to share, you can volunteer. Also, if you'd rather, we can come up with a different activity for you to do that doesn't focus on Mother's Day.

Educators can't be expected to know the personal experiences of all of their students, so even if they don't know about any students who have experienced the death of a parent, it would still be helpful to introduce the activity to the entire class by adding:

> Tomorrow, we're going to do an activity that talks about Mother's Day, and I'm going to ask the class to make cards. You can choose to prepare a card in memory of your mother or choose a different woman who has been important in your life. That way, everyone can participate. Please let me know if you would like to discuss this with me.

These simple words let students know that the teacher is aware of the situation, sensitive to feelings that might come up during the activity, and willing to be quite flexible about what sort of activity would be most useful.

Discussing Topics Involving Death

Characters die in novels. Current events often involve upheaval, tragedy, and death. History and social studies classes discuss wars and violence. What effects do topics such as these have on bereaved students?

Topics involving death can be difficult for students who have lost a family member or friend. This is even more likely when there is some similarity between the discussion topic and the actual death. For example, a lesson about the Vietnam War might be difficult for a student who lost a family member in the war in Afghanistan. A lesson about the immune system may remind students of the deaths of family members during the COVID-19 pandemic. A novel that includes characters who are killed in a car crash would probably be challenging for a student whose friends died this way.

One of the best ways to offer support for bereaved students—both those who might be known to an educator and those who are not identified—is to prepare all students ahead of time for the material. Before beginning the study of a novel where a death occurs, an educator might say, "Without giving away the plot, I do want to let you know that one of the important characters in this book dies in a car crash. Some of you have probably known people who have died, perhaps in a similar way. When we read about events like this, it sometimes brings up strong emotions. If any of you have thoughts or feelings about the book that you'd like to discuss privately, please let me know. I'll arrange a time when we can talk."

Similarly, educators can acknowledge that students might have a range of emotional responses as they address current events or discuss history. For example, a teacher might say, "We're going to see some film and photographs tomorrow about the liberation of the concentration camps at the end of World War II. I want you to know that the images are disturbing. I've seen them several times and still find them upsetting. Please talk with me or your family if you think you don't want to watch the film or are unsure. If you do decide to watch the film tomorrow and find yourself having strong emotional reactions, you can let me know so I can excuse you from watching the rest of the film. I want you to remember several things. First, it's common to have such responses. Second, it's important to talk to someone you trust about your responses. And, third, if you want to talk privately about any of your thoughts or feelings after seeing these things, let me know. I'd be happy to set up a time to talk with you."

It would also be a good idea for educators to make a general statement at the beginning of a course that covers such events. Again, educators can acknowledge that students might have a range of reactions to the material throughout the course.

An educator could say, "Many of these subjects can be disturbing. Sometimes they are especially troubling for people who have had similar experiences in their own lives. For example, if your family had to leave an area where there was war or violence, it may be hard to hear about similar situations in other parts of the world. If someone you care about was wounded or killed in combat, it may be difficult to learn about wars. If you do have any strong reactions about the things we're learning in this class or worry that you might, please let me know. I'm happy to talk with you privately, or as a class, at any time about these things."

Teaching About Important National Events

In recent decades, the United States has experienced a number of major events of national importance—events that have transformed us as a nation. These include terrorist attacks, such as September 11th; wars and armed conflict; the terrible consequences of large-scale natural disasters such as hurricanes, floods, wildfires, and earthquakes; and health care crises such as the COVID-19 pandemic. Other events in the future will play an important role in our identity and history, and many of these will involve tragedy and death.

It is important for students to learn about these events to understand more about themselves, their communities, and their country. At some point, the position of these events shifts in our consciousness. They are no longer what is currently happening or recently occurred, and they become a part of our history. When do teachers stop teaching about September 11th as a current, critical matter and begin to address it as a matter of recent American history, for example?

Recent history feels more real to everyone, including students. This means it can be more troubling. Because we live in a country where people are mobile and move often, any classroom might include students who have been personally touched by such events.

Educators do not need to avoid teaching about these events, but it is important to be sensitive about them. They continue to touch real people across the nation, and this may well include students in their classroom. Using the principles described in the previous section, educators can give students advance notice that potentially difficult topics will be covered. They can mention these more current events specifically. They might survey students in a general sense about their experiences (without asking for public disclosures of personal losses) before delving deeply into content. For example, a teacher could ask, "How many of you have heard about Hurricane Michael? Did any of you know people who were affected by the storm?" It is always important to acknowledge that students may have emotional responses to some of this material and that they can talk to the teacher and family members about their thoughts or feelings at any time.

A Special Exhibit

A museum in one U.S. city focused on important social events in the nation's history. It had an excellent exhibit on the history of civil rights, for example. The museum had a lively educational component and was a popular destination for school field trips. Students of all ages found the exhibits interesting and informative.

A few years after the attacks of September 11th, the museum planned a special temporary exhibit about the event to open on the anniversary of the attack. It included photos of the plane crashing into the second tower, the devastation on the ground, and survivors running away from the buildings. There were photographs of surviving New York firefighters and police officers next to their comments about their comrades who had died in the rescue efforts. Images showed the damage to the Pentagon and the crash site of Flight 93 in Pennsylvania. It featured letters and pictures sent by children from across the country to first responders in New York City.

The temporary exhibit was located immediately beyond the main entrance. All of the students on field trips who were planning to learn about the material covered in the museum's permanent exhibits would have to first walk into this room full of powerful, potentially upsetting, and recent images. There was no advance warning before walking into the exhibit. The students would have no preparation beforehand. Educators would not be expecting the exhibit and would not know to prepare students or their families.

Coming upon these images might have been painful for any American. They could be disturbing to children just by the nature of the event and the power of the images, but it would be especially difficult for children who had been close to the event in some way. Some of the children may have had parents who worked in or near the Twin Towers or the Pentagon, some may have lost family members, some may have had friends whose parents were close to the event, and others may have simply seen a great deal of media coverage in the days and weeks after the attacks.

A museum member raised concerns about these issues, and the museum staff responded immediately. They asked the NCSCB for advice, and, working together, a plan for the exhibit was quickly developed. The museum sent out information to educators who were planning field trips to the museum. They developed teaching materials about the exhibit for students of all ages and made these available to educators. They removed a few images that were particularly graphic from the exhibit. When classes of students arrived at the entrance, they were greeted by docents who talked about the exhibits they would see in the museum, including the special exhibit on the September 11th attacks. Museum staff and docents were also given guidelines for talking to children and adults about the exhibit. The museum made sure that the exhibit was well staffed, especially during field trip hours.

Normalizing the Experience of Grief

Schools can also take steps to normalize the experience of grief. They can include information and lessons about death and grieving in regular course-work. They can respond to deaths that have an impact on individual students and the school community as they occur. They might also offer grief support groups in the school setting. Such groups could take a variety of different forms. For example, a children's bereavement center might facilitate a grief group that meets weekly for 8 weeks and is open to any student who has experienced the death of a family member or friend. A school's mental health specialist might host a monthly "Remembrance" group in which students can drop in and talk about friends or family members who have died. The school's counseling services might do specific outreach to students they know who have experienced a loss of a family member or friend, as well as set up a support group for them.

SUPPORTING STUDENTS IN LIFE TRANSITIONS

Life transitions can be challenging times for bereaved students. The loss of a parent can be particularly difficult for children as they move forward in their lives and miss the special guidance and support a parent can give. Even if a death occurred many years earlier, transitions can be difficult. The following sections describe some of these challenging times, and Chapter 7 further describes some of the challenges.

Puberty

Puberty can be a very challenging time for students who have lost a parent. The loss of a same-gender parent can be particularly troublesome at this time. Puberty can be more difficult for girls without a mother or boys without a father.

Girls who have lost their mothers may not have a comfortable source to turn to for information about how to manage menstrual periods and the physical and emotional issues that often accompany them. Tampons or pads? What do I do about cramps? Why do I feel so sad all of a sudden? What do I say to my teacher if I have to leave class because my period just started? What if my friends tease me about having my period?

Boys who have lost their fathers may be confused or frightened by wet dreams; have no clue about how to cope with unwanted erections at school; and struggle with how to respond to teasing, dares, or derogatory comments by peers. What do I do about this changing body? Why do I have these new feelings and urges? What does it mean to be a man?

In classes that discuss puberty and growing up, children are often given assignments that require talking to a parent. In classes about sexuality, students are often told, "If you have more questions about this, you can ask your parents." In a health class that is learning about friends and dating, students might be asked to talk to a parent about things they did with friends when they were young. Although every student should have a parent or guardian, these topics may be difficult to discuss with an opposite gender parent or a guardian the child does not know as well.

Educators can be sensitive to the fact that some students do not have parents who can help them with these assignments. Sometimes a parent has died. Some students may have a living parent who is unavailable for any number of reasons—deployed in the military, in prison, mentally ill, divorced, or living out of state.

This is why it is always a good idea to offer students the option of talking to their parent or another adult they know and trust, such as another family member, a coach, or a counselor. Educators can offer to talk to students and help them identify such a support if students are having difficulty identifying someone for this role.

Dating and Relationships

As children and adolescents mature, they are likely to have crushes and become involved in romantic relationships. Many preteens and teens turn to parents or an older sibling for direct advice at these times. They are also looking at their parents' relationship indirectly—it serves as a model for the ways a couple communicates, negotiates differences, demonstrates caring and love, offers support to one another, and builds increasing intimacy.

If a surviving parent is not in a new relationship, is dating casually, or has had a series of partners, adolescents may miss the modeling of a steady relationship. If the surviving parent has established a new and ongoing relationship, the imperfections of the new partner may seem quite stark to a child who has naturally idealized a deceased parent. This can leave some adolescents feeling frustrated, isolated, and confused. They may engage in riskier types of relationships (see Adams & Deveau, 1987) or simply feel adrift as they try to make their way through these new kinds of relationships.

Many children are raised in single-parent households and may miss a divorced parent in similar ways. For a child whose parent has died, however, the feelings are linked to the deeper experiences of bereavement and the recognition that this person who was so important will never be able to offer support and guidance in these matters.

Transition to College

Educators of older students who have lost a parent may be able to offer support as they near the end of high school. Students must decide whether their next steps will occur close to their family or farther away. As mentioned in Chapter 7, the best answer will be different for different students. It would be helpful for bereaved students to be offered support from a trusted educator. An educator might say, "I know this can be a difficult time for anyone. This is the age where you need to decide whether to stay nearby or go somewhere else after high school. Sometimes, though, this decision is especially hard for students who have lost a parent or sibling, even if the death happened some time ago. If you ever want to talk about this, I'd be happy to listen."

Schools can also take steps to create a "warm handoff" between a high school and a college counseling program when a student has experienced a significant loss. This needs to be done with the student's permission. Explain to students that this process can help them be aware of resources at the college in the event they wish to take advantage of them. In other words, it is not because the school feels the student is not coping well. Often, such students have described their experience of loss in their college entrance essays. Students may not realize that college admission offices rarely share those essays with future instructors or counseling staff.

If the student agrees, a school counselor or administrator can contact the college's counseling office and share background on the student's experience and current status. Ideally, the student can be given the name of a specific individual to contact in the college counseling services.

In instances where an entire school has been affected by a critical incident, schools may make a more general gesture. One high school experienced a mass shooting that received substantial national news coverage. Its counselors contacted all colleges being attended by graduating seniors. They explained that they were touching base to alert the schools about their students' experience. They suggested the colleges reach out to these incoming students as they made this potentially challenging life transition.

Bereavement and Transitions

The following are examples of issues that may come up for bereaved students, especially those who have lost a parent or family member, during school or other life transitions:

- Feeling less secure in the face of an exciting but also frightening change

- Less confidence due to loss of a parent who promoted more independence

- Loss of advice about coursework, college decisions, or future plans

- Worries about increased personal independence and separation from family when a surviving parent or younger sibling is still struggling to cope

- Concerns about choices that will place more financial burdens on the family (e.g., extracurricular activities, college preparatory courses, private or out-of-state colleges)

- Sense of abandoning younger siblings through increased independence or a transition to career or college

- Passing on the role as acting head of household to a younger sibling who is unprepared or struggling with bereavement issues

- Missing support in career decisions (e.g., an adolescent may have wanted to pursue the same career as the family member who died but no longer has the person's guidance and mentorship)

- Loss of a trusted resource for support in making important life decisions

BEREAVEMENT CAN LAST A LIFETIME

At each new stage in their lives, children develop new skills for thinking and relating to others. Bereaved children will use these skills to reach a deeper and more satisfying explanation of a death. In many ways, the work of making meaning from a death never really ends; however, over time, this work becomes less difficult and takes less energy. It may start as a full-time job. Later, it becomes more of a part-time effort that allows other meaningful work and experiences to occur.

Educators who remain sensitive to the needs and experiences of bereaved children over time can offer ongoing support that helps students make sense of these experiences and maintain a positive, productive course in their lives. One of the most important principles we promote at NCSCB is the recognition that grieving can last a lifetime, but it should not consume a life.

———

Grieving can last a lifetime, but it should not consume a life.

———

Key Concepts

- **Grief changes over time.** Although there is no set time line, over time, most bereaved children and adults will experience reductions in the intensity and intrusiveness of their grief.

- **Grief affects many different domains in life.** Feelings, thoughts, and relationships at school or at home may be affected.

- **Anniversaries, transitions, special events, and rites of passage may all lead individuals to reexperience their grief.** At notable times such as these, children and adults often feel their loss more deeply.

- **Any number of experiences or memories can act as triggers for grief.** These may catch people off guard and can be troubling to children.

- **Educators can take steps to prepare students when they introduce activities or subjects that might be difficult for children who have experienced the death of someone close.** Being proactive in this way helps reassure all students while supporting those remembering a death.

- **Bereavement can last a lifetime.** Children who have lost a parent or sibling are especially likely to continue to be affected by the death and experience their grief in some way at each new stage in their lives.

9

When an Entire School Is Affected

The death of a member of the school community—a student, teacher, or other staff member—can have a profound impact on the entire school. Educators will need to provide students with information and support and monitor their reactions and adjustment. Often, virtually everyone will experience some sort of emotional response to the death. This can sometimes involve strong feelings of grief among many or all students and staff.

This chapter discusses some of the strategies that schools can use to notify and provide support for students after a schoolwide loss. Every school should have a crisis response team that has planned for such events and policies in place that provide best for the needs of students, families, and staff. It is also helpful for all educators to know more about what may happen and how they can support students.

GOALS OF SUPPORT

It is important for schools to set up a system for offering students and staff support. This involves including school staff who have experience and skills in providing support after a school crisis and who are available to talk with staff and students in both group and individual settings, as well as consultants and collaborators from other agencies and organizations that can provide additional advice and support.

The goals of support for students include the following:

- **Normalize common experiences of grief.** Advice and guidance help students understand what to expect. They can hear about the range of feelings that are common in these circumstances, the ways people might express their feelings, and the ways people's feelings may change in the short and long term (i.e., the coming days, weeks, and months).

- **Help students express and cope with feelings.** Following a death, talking with students directly helps them to understand what happened and to identify their feelings. They need a safe, nonjudgmental environment in which to express their reactions. In groups, they can learn coping strategies and share their own ideas. These interventions keep more students present in school at these difficult times and decrease the negative effects on learning that often accompany grief.

Proactive interventions keep more students present in school at these difficult times and decrease the negative effects on learning that often accompany grief.

- **Help students find resources and strategies for coping with difficult feelings.** Many students will experience straightforward reactions to the death that are clearly expressed and match the situation well. Some, however, will have more complicated reactions. They may struggle with feelings of regret or remorse, especially if they believe they mistreated the individual at some point in the past. Others may have a sense of survivor's guilt: "Why should he have been the one to drown when we've all gone swimming out at the quarry?" They may feel anxious, fearful, or angry. As previously mentioned, depressed students may experience a worsening of symptoms. Students may also feel despair or have thoughts of suicide, especially when the crisis is due to a death by suicide.

  Talking with a mental health professional with expertise in bereavement and crisis can help students with troublesome feelings find productive ways to express and cope with them. They can also find resources for ongoing support if the difficult feelings seem dangerous in any way (e.g., thoughts of suicide) or do not resolve within a reasonable period of time.

- **Clarify concepts for younger students.** Younger students may have more difficulty understanding death. They are more likely to misinterpret explanations about death.

The goals for staff support are similar. School mental health professionals and qualified consultants may be helpful in providing information and support to staff. They can facilitate discussions about how educators feel being the bearers of this information, ask about their interactions with students, and offer guidance for any situations with students or parents that they are finding difficult or confusing. Educators must also take steps to care for themselves personally at these times, which are discussed in depth in Chapter 14.

MAJOR CRISES AND COMPLEX SITUATIONS

Some types of deaths that may touch a school community are especially complicated. They might involve major crises, such as a natural disaster, an industrial accident, a violent incident in the school (see Schonfeld & Demaria, 2020a, 2020b) or community, or an act of aggression or terrorism that directly affects the local community. Providing support to students after such events involves many of the same principles that are described throughout this book, as well as other important steps (Schonfeld & Demaria, 2018).

Planning for and responding to such major events is not the focus of this chapter or the book, but it is vitally important for schools. For those interested in learning more about how to develop school crisis preparedness and response plans, as well as how to train school crisis teams, we recommend the handbook developed by members of the NCSCB. (See Schonfeld et al. [2002] and Schonfeld [2007]. For an earlier article that summarizes the school crisis preparedness and response model, see Schonfeld et al. [1994]. A brief overview of the School Crisis Response Initiative [Schonfeld & Newgass, 2003] can be freely downloaded at https://ovc.ojp.gov/sites/g/files/xyckuh226/files/publications/bulletins/schoolcrisis/ncj197832.pdf)

School Crisis Plans: Responding to a Death

Schools should have a school crisis team in place that has developed a response plan in the event of a death in the school community. The plan should cover how notification of a death is handled, and it should address such matters as who is notified, how people are reached, and what is said. Typically, this includes the following steps:

- **Notify and activate the school crisis team.**
- **Verify the information.** Check with the family, local authorities (e.g., the police or coroner), or other authoritative sources.
- **Determine what information is to be disclosed.** The family may express wishes on this matter. Find out what information has been publicly released through the press or local authorities.
- **Notify teachers and other staff.** An emergency meeting is often scheduled before classes begin. Teachers are informed of the death and given guidelines for notifying students and offering support.
- **Notify students.** Face-to-face notification by familiar staff in small, naturally occurring group settings is recommended. Homeroom or another class (depending on when the school learns of the death) is often a good option. It is best to avoid delivering such information in large assemblies or over the public address system. Students should all hear the same information (e.g., from a prepared, written statement). They should also be given information about support resources and offered opportunities to talk about their responses to the news. This might occur within a class discussion or by referral to a support room where mental health professionals are available. Options should be made available as soon as students hear the announcement.

Face-to-face notification by familiar staff in small, naturally occurring group settings is recommended. Students should all hear the same information.

- **Notify parents.** Often, this is done by a letter that is sent home with students, sent by e-mail, or posted on the school's web site. This letter should describe the types of support being offered to students and families.

- **Notify other schools as appropriate.** This might include feeder schools, where the deceased was known by teachers or younger students, or schools attended by siblings of the deceased. In smaller communities, it may be appropriate to notify all schools.

Following these steps gives schools a better opportunity to ensure that students learn of the death in an appropriate setting—that is, with a familiar teacher or other educator who has been prepared and is ready to make the announcement. Students can then be connected to support services more easily and effectively.

A Pity About Mr. Sutton

Maddy was walking down the hallway at her high school early one Monday morning before many students had arrived. Her band teacher, Mr. Thompson, walked by reading a memo. She greeted him.

"Hello, Maddy!" he said brightly. "How was your weekend?" Then he pointed to his memo. "Wow. What a pity about Mr. Sutton."

Mr. Sutton was the school's French teacher. He was a prickly, troublesome character as far as many of the teachers were concerned and not well known except by students taking French. Many of those students found him difficult—a teacher with high standards and an unforgiving attitude about late assignments or poor test scores. However, he had a small and devoted following of advanced students who performed well in his classes, enjoyed his unique brand of irony, and blossomed under his focused and carefully planned lessons. Maddy was one of those students.

"What happened?" she asked, thinking he must have broken a leg, had his car stolen, or lost his dog.

"He died of a heart attack Saturday night. And he was only 38. What a shock."

"He . . . what?" said Maddy, confused. She reached out and took the memo from Mr. Thompson's hand. She squinted at the words and tried to make sense of them. "There must be a mistake," she said, growing ashen. "Is this a joke? This can't be real. He . . . he was fine on Friday. He has two kids. What did you say happened?"

Mr. Thompson look startled. "I'm sorry. I didn't realize you knew him," he said, looking and feeling awkward. "Well, I've got to get on to my class," he said rather abruptly, taking back the memo and walking away. "How was I to know?" he thought to himself. "She never said she was taking French."

Maddy stood alone in the hallway, tears brimming in her eyes. She had never known anyone who had died before. She turned around slowly, making a full circle. She saw no one she knew.

When schools have well-designed, up-to-date crisis plans in place, educators will be better prepared to speak with students about a death of a member of the school community. They will know what resources for support are available. They will understand that students may have powerful emotional responses, and they will direct them when appropriate to school mental health staff who can listen to their reactions and guide them through the process. See Chapter 11 for suggestions about how these steps might be different in virtual or online school settings.

After a death that touches the school community, it is common for students, educators, or parents to come up with plans for memorialization and commemoration. These actions can be helpful in the process of bereavement, especially when careful consideration is given to key principles, which are discussed in Chapter 13. Otherwise, the process can generate conflict and controversy.

Making Sure All Students Are Informed

Another important consideration is making sure that all students have been informed about the death. On any given day, some students will not be at school. They may be out sick, on a field trip for the day, or away for an overnight class trip or a band festival. How will students in each of these situations hear the information?

It is difficult for students to come back to a school community that has experienced something this profound when they do not feel included. This can lead to anxiety, misunderstandings, and a sense of isolation.

Although each situation is different, the following are some possible solutions:

- **Schools might call, text, or send e-mails to the parents of students** who are not in school that day to provide the necessary information as well as suggestions about talking with their children.

- **A school administrator might plan to meet a class returning from a field trip to share the news with them.** A call to the teacher's cellphone before the class returns will allow educators to make sure students stay together on their return so they can hear the announcement and receive support. Older students are likely to hear the news almost instantly through texts from peers or social media posts, so it may be necessary for educators to explain what has happened before the group returns to campus.

- **Educators away with students on overnight trips should be contacted by the school.** Copies of the announcement about the death, as well as supportive material for student discussions, could be e-mailed or faxed to educators in most settings. It is usually best to share this news with students promptly. Many are likely to be checking in with families and friends and will hear some of the information from them. Again, students who learn of the news at school will often communicate quickly by text or social media. This can leave students in the difficult position of informing others who have not yet heard the news (e.g., friends, classmates, teachers). This is an unfair burden for students.

- **During summer vacation or over a holiday period, news of a death may appear in local papers or other news outlets.** The school might choose to contact students' families by e-mail or telephone trees to relay the information. Many schools relied on similar mechanisms to notify and support students after deaths during the lengthy school closures in response to the COVID-19 pandemic. In some situations, especially if the death is likely to have a significant impact on many students, the school may decide to open for a day or an evening. Students and families could be invited to come in to talk with counselors if they wish.

- **After a summer or holiday period, announcements may be made in all classes** so that students who might have missed the information during the break are appropriately informed. This also serves as a good opportunity to remind students of supportive services available through the school.

Shared Experiences of Grief

What happens in a school when so many people are sharing an experience of grief? The following are some common occurrences among students:

- **Everything is multiplied.** When one grieving student looks around, he or she sees other grieving students. One person crying might start several other people crying. One anxious student might heighten anxiety in three other students. One act of compassion inspires others. Both positive and negative coping behaviors are likely to be repeated and multiplied many times.

- **Anxiety can grow.** It was previously mentioned that death challenges our assumptions about the things that will stay in place in our world (see Chapter 7). Students may no longer feel assured that their peers or staff they feel close with will be at school the next day; they may also worry about family members. When many students in a school are experiencing this effect, anxiety may become higher for all students.

- **Students come with a range of experience and understanding.** Although bereavement is a common experience among children, many students may have never experienced the death of someone they personally know well. They will be having these experiences of grief, anxiety, and confusion for the first time. Other students are likely to have already experienced a death. They will have some basic understanding about grief—they know it is intense, it is confusing, and that it may persist for a while, but it does not throw you off track forever.

- **Information spreads quickly.** News of death is compelling and raises anxiety for almost everyone. People naturally want to know about these events. Staff and students will talk among themselves about what happened. This creates a ripe environment for passing along information as well as for spreading rumors. This is one reason it is so important to inform the entire school of a death at the same time—it gives all students the same accurate information. Otherwise, some students will hear an accurate statement provided by their teachers, and other students will pick up rumors or bits of overheard conversation. When information is inaccurate or incomplete, anxiety and complicated reactions are more likely.

- **Students are confused about what is expected.** Children and teens who have not experienced grief at a group level, or who have never gone through something this serious, may feel uncertain about what to do and how to behave. Particularly among adolescents, who sometimes have an "imaginary audience" in their minds, there may be some rumination about what is expected. "Did I cry enough? Or was that too much?" "Am I supposed to look really serious and sad even if I don't feel that way?" "Am I supposed to act like I'm actually reading this assignment in class today, when I can't concentrate on anything?"

- **Some students will naturally be more empathetic.** Some students seem to know what to say or do to help themselves, peers, and even educators feel better. These students can provide positive role modeling and emotional support for their classmates. This is one of the benefits of having students share experiences and ideas about how to deal with grief. They can reach out to one another, offer support, and learn from each other. However, it is important to recognize that a student who appears to be handling the situation well may also benefit from support. These students should not be expected to carry extra burdens as the school community copes with the loss.

- **Educators can have a range of powerful reactions.** All of these experiences can be compounded by the fact that teachers and other staff are also having powerful reactions. Educators may have many of the same responses students do—difficulty concentrating, uncertainty about how to act and what to say, confusion, anxiety, and a sense of being overwhelmed by the concentration of grief in the school community.

Often, a few educators have had a special connection with a student who has died. They may have offered tutoring and mentorship to the student, encouraged extra plans or projects, sponsored the student in competitions, or had other opportunities to build a stronger-than-usual relationship. Some educators step into roles almost as surrogate parents. They may be personally devastated by the death of a student they admired and cared about.

When an announcement about a death is made schoolwide, educators may also find themselves experiencing something quite different from their students. If a sixth-grade student dies, for example, the second-grade students may not have known the student, but their teacher who makes the announcement to the class may have taught this student. Similarly, if a teacher or school administrator dies, students may not have known the person well and may have a mild response to news of the death. Their teacher, however, may be feeling grief related to the loss of a colleague or friend, along with a sense of personal vulnerability (i.e., "Could such a death happen to me?").

GIVING SUPPORT TO STUDENTS

As discussed previously, educators can make a meaningful difference in times of grief by establishing an authentic and supportive connection with students. The following are some steps that will be especially useful when a school is reacting to a death in their community. Most of these will sound familiar because they are similar to the steps recommended for individual students experiencing grief.

- **Know the guidelines of the school for these situations.** Schools should make guidelines available to educators through an intranet site or written documents or in other ways. Every educator should have access to copies of crisis plans at any time. Familiarity with the plan should be developed through ongoing training and exercises. If the school does not have crisis plans in place, educators should advocate for their development.

- **Remember that any student may be deeply affected.** It is impossible to know the experiences of every student. Any student may be deeply affected by a death, so it is important that educators speak sensitively about the incident to all students.

- **Be approachable.** Educators who can talk about complex and difficult topics, including death and grief, are more likely to be approached by students looking for support. Educators should take opportunities to discuss these matters in an open, authentic manner; for example, by talking with a class about common grief reactions or by discussing how receiving support for troublesome feelings can be helpful.

- **Listen.** When students want to share, it can be especially powerful for them simply to have an attentive listener. The focus should be on them.

- **Protect students.** The death of a peer or school staff member will be troubling to students. However, educators should take steps to protect students from added distress. For example, emotionally expressive students might be teased by others for crying. Reporters might want to talk to students about the death. A television in a common area might be tuned to a news station repeating details about the death.

- **Make connections.** The strategies described in Chapter 5 can be used to make authentic and positive connections with students. Educators should invite them to talk about their thoughts and experiences.
- **Teach about grief and normalize receiving support.** Educators can help students understand common reactions to grief, including having strong feelings, being confused, feeling out of control, and so forth. They can emphasize the importance of reaching out for support and the power of giving support to others. Educators can also include suggestions about when seeking help is especially important (e.g., when troublesome feelings persist or get worse) and provide resources (e.g., the support room set up by the school after a crisis).

Educators can emphasize the importance of reaching out for support and the power of giving support to others.

- **Be a positive role model.** It is okay for students to see educators' emotions, as well as some of the ways they are coping with their feelings. This helps students understand how to express their own feelings and come up with strategies for coping. For example, a teacher might say to her class, "I was shocked when I heard the news, and I just felt like crying." Or, "When I heard about the car crash, I felt frightened. I was even nervous when I got in the car this morning." Then the teacher could offer an example of coping. "After I cried, I talked to my husband (or sister, friend, partner), and it helped me feel better. Who is someone you could talk to if you were feeling sad?" Or, "I took a couple of deep breaths, made sure my seatbelt was fastened, and made sure I was attentive the whole time I drove here."
- **Watch for signs of distress now and over time.** Educators can use the guidelines reviewed in Chapter 7 to identify students showing signs of distress. They should then provide referrals when appropriate. Although a school crisis plan, including drop-in counseling support, may be in place for a week or so, powerful feelings might come up for some students for weeks, months, or even a year or more after the incident.
- **Seek personal support.** These experiences are deeply emotional for educators. Crisis response plans should provide support for them as well. Educators should consider visiting the staff support room or talking with one of the staff made available to them, such as through an employee assistance program. This is useful even when educators do not feel a strong need to do so but feel it may be helpful. This provides good role modeling for students and colleagues. We also find this type of support helpful for people who are coping well with a loss, and we recommend it to educators who have worked in a school setting that has experienced a crisis or death.

REACHING OUT TO STUDENTS AT HIGHER RISK

As mentioned in Chapter 7, some students have a higher risk for emotional distress after a school death. A well-planned crisis response plan takes the special circumstances of these students into account. For example, a member of the crisis response team might spend the day following the schedule of a deceased high school student to be available to talk to classmates in any of the student's classes. A mental health specialist might make individual contact with the student's best friends. One of the counselors might speak with the student's teammates on the basketball team or members of clubs the student had joined.

All students should have an opportunity to meet privately with a mental health professional if they wish. This meeting could include a check-in about the student's feelings, as well as some advice and guidance about other feelings that may arise in coming days, weeks, or months. It is also important for students to know where they can go if they wish to talk with someone about their feelings or to address questions in the future.

All students should have an opportunity to meet privately with a mental health professional if they wish.

Students who have a greater risk for more complex reactions include:

- **Students who were close friends of the deceased.** Students who were close to the deceased or who felt a special connection in some way are likely to have strong grief reactions.

- **Students who shared a class with the deceased.** Classmates of the deceased are more likely to have had close personal connections and respond more strongly to the death.

- **Students who shared extracurricular activities with the deceased.** This would include clubs, sports teams, community-based groups, faith groups, and groups in other nonschool settings.

- **Students who had a complicated or difficult relationship with the deceased.** When relationships are troubled, there is a greater likelihood of more complex reactions after the death. A student who had ended a romantic relationship with the student who died might feel guilty. Someone who just had a bitter argument with the deceased that ended with threats of violence by the student who died might feel a sense of relief and then a sense of guilt. A student who had a secret crush on the person might feel unable to express grief openly, even if it is quite strong.

- **Students who shared some meaningful characteristic with the deceased.** This might be some feature that heightened the surviving student's sense of identification with the deceased (e.g., "We both drew manga comics"). It might be some characteristic related to the cause of death. For example, if a student dies of a chronic disease, other students with the same disease have a greater risk of distress. If a student who has been bullied dies by suicide, other students who are being bullied may be at risk for suicidal behaviors. Students who are using or experimenting with drugs may be particularly affected when a peer dies of a drug overdose.

- **Students with a history of prior losses or emotional difficulties.** The death of a friend or classmate will often act as a trigger for grief about earlier losses or bring up feelings about past or current difficulties, such as parental separation or divorce.

- **Students who have already known someone who died from similar causes.** Having previously known someone who died of similar causes is also likely to act as a trigger for earlier grief experiences.

- **Students who may worry about similar losses.** A student whose mother is ill with cancer may become very upset when a teacher dies of cancer.

- **Students with preexisting conditions.** Students with mental health issues, such as depression or anxiety disorders, may have a more difficult time coping with their feelings after a classmate's death. Anyone who has expressed suicidal thoughts or participated in self-harming behaviors may be at particularly high risk.

UNIQUE CASES: SUICIDE AND HOMICIDE

Suicide and homicide raise unique concerns for schools and students. When there has been a homicide, particularly when it is gang related, friends of the deceased may feel a need to avenge the death. This can lead to escalating cycles of violence, as well as further injury and death. Other students may find that fear for their own safety is their primary concern initially, which interferes with their ability to grieve the death of a friend or peer.

When a student dies by suicide, other students who are feeling hopeless, helpless, and isolated may find thoughts of suicide emerging. This may be especially likely if the death results in attention that feels positive to an isolated or depressed student. For example, other students at the school might say, "I feel terrible about this. I'll never forget him. I'll always regret not being a better friend." A student who feels left out and overlooked might yearn for that kind of attention as well.

It is important to talk about these deaths carefully and without glamorizing the victims in any way, but still acknowledging the grief of survivors who lost a friend and a classmate.

Teachers can be proactive and set the tone for students. This would include educating students about warning signs of suicide and emphasizing that thoughts of suicide are not a normal response to grief. Schools can distribute information about hotlines and support services. The act of seeking support can be destigmatized. Students should also be encouraged to speak to an appropriate adult if they are worried that a friend or peer is thinking about suicide.

See Chapter 10 for more information about responding to a suicide within the school.

Was It Really an Accident?

A school was notified that a 13-year-old boy at the school was accidentally stran-gled when the cord of his hooded jacket caught on a tree branch in his back yard. He was alone at the time this happened, and his body was discovered later.

The school crisis team informed teachers of the incident and provided a writ-ten announcement that they could read to their classes. The statement indicated that the cause of death was believed to be accidental strangulation. Teachers were told that the medical examiner was continuing to investigate the death. Teachers were also given guidelines for discussion with their students, including information about common reactions to news of a death, resources for support, and opportunities for students to make comments or ask questions.

The crisis team also let teachers know that there might be questions about the cause of death. They understood that students might find it difficult to believe that a 13-year-old died accidentally this way. Students might reasonably wonder if this was a suicide or perhaps an instance of someone playing a fainting or choking game.[1] Teachers were offered suggestions for how to answer these questions.

If someone asked, for example, "Wasn't it the choking game?" they could respond by saying, "We don't know if it was, but it sounds like you may have heard something about this issue. Let's talk about that. What do you know about the choking game?"

If a student said, "A friend of mine said that guy killed himself," the teacher could reply by saying, "We don't really know if that's the reason for John's death, but suicide is an important issue, even if it wasn't what happened here. Let's take a few minutes to address some questions or concerns you may have about suicide." The teacher could then guide the discussion to general issues about suicide. Who would students go to if they were feeling sad? What are some warning signs that mean it is important for someone to get help? Who could they talk to if they had concerns about a friend's mood or behaviors?

Teachers were also given some guidelines to help them talk about the prob-lems with rumors and speculation and to encourage students to stick to what was known in the discussion. This approach allowed teachers to focus on the concerns and anxieties of the students, even in the face of incomplete information about the student who died. The materials from the school crisis team prepared teachers realistically for the experiences they would have with students. It also allowed the school, despite some challenging circumstances, to provide appropri-ate intervention and support for the students after this disturbing event.

---

[1]Fainting or choking games are used by children as a means to create a partial or complete loss of consciousness by hyperventilating (sometimes followed by then applying pressure to the chest) or using ligatures around the neck or other means of strangulation, which often involves the assistance of other children. This can lead to a short period of lightheadedness or feeling "high." Severe injuries, brain damage, and death are possible.

DEATH OF A PROMINENT PERSON

Sometimes someone prominent in the nation or the community dies. It might be a politician, an actor, an athlete, or a popular musician. It might be a basketball player who dies suddenly on the court during the game, witnessed by hundreds or (if televised) millions of fans. Or it may be a popular athlete, such as the death of basketball star Kobe Bryant in a helicopter crash in 2020. Death might result from a highly public event, such as the 1986 space shuttle Challenger disaster, which was witnessed by students of all ages everywhere in the country. Similarly, the Sandy Hook Elementary School shooting in Connecticut in 2012 and the school shooting at Marjory Stoneman Douglas High School in Florida in 2018 had deep impacts on students and educators across the nation because of the prominence of the tragedies.

These incidents can be expected to create many of the same kinds of reactions as a death in the school community. Students may have heightened anxiety about their own safety and that of family members and friends. They may worry about their future. Children dealing with challenges or deaths in their own families may experience greater distractibility, anxiety, and emotionalism.

For the most part, educators will find the same skills they have used in other situations concerning death and grief useful at these times. They should help students recognize their emotional responses and make sense of the event. What emotions are they having? What kinds of things can they do to feel better? How can they ask others for support? How can they support each other?

It is also important to protect children from unnecessary trauma about the incident. Turn off television stations that are showing the incident repeatedly or endlessly analyzing reactions. Keep the focus on positive coping. Remind students that emotional responses to such events are expected.

Students may have heightened anxiety about their own safety and that of family members and friends.

Putting Guidelines in Place That Support Effective Practice

The NCSCB has developed practical guidelines on how schools can respond to the death of a student or staff member. These can be freely downloaded from the web site of the NCSCB at https://www.schoolcrisiscenter.org/resources/guide-responding-death/ (for death from any cause) and https://www.school crisiscenter.org/resources/guide-responding-suicide/ (for death due to suicide). Sample notification letters, which can be downloaded as template Word documents, can also be found as part of these guidelines.

BEING GRIEF SENSITIVE AFTER A
LARGE-SCALE CRISIS: ONE PRINCIPAL'S STORY

A large high school (more than 2,000 students) experienced an on-campus shooting. The shooter was an enrolled student. Two of his victims died; other students were injured. The shooter took his own life at the end of the incident. Three months after the event, we spoke with the principal to learn more about how the school addressed student bereavement within their crisis response and to hear how students were coping.

How Did Your School Respond in the Immediate Aftermath of the Incident?

Decisions about how to move forward were definitely a collective effort. We had a number of stakeholders involved in our recovery plan—our superintendent, assistant superintendents, director of student services, and director of mental health services put as much time into the planning as I did. I can't imagine trying to navigate this process without their active involvement. We also involved a variety of parent groups on campus. Many times, these groups are the eyes and ears for parents, and we knew involving them early would provide comfort to the larger parent community.

As a site principal, I was also dealing with literally endless e-mails and other communications. Staying organized would have been impossible without the help of someone who could help me vet and prioritize these communications. This was critical. My wife is a counselor in the district, and she was able to step in for this task at the outset. As she returned to her own school, my office manager assumed this role. And our site admin team—our assistant principals—did the bulk of the work putting everything into place.

I believe that when you have a group of good people, you get good ideas. Our experience bore that out.

For 2 weeks following the shooting, we did not officially have school, but we did have an open campus where students and parents could engage in a variety of activities. These included one-to-one therapy, group therapy, and a variety of activities such as yoga, art therapy, sound baths, blanket making, pet therapy, and coloring. We also had an open gymnasium for basketball and volleyball.

I believe these activities helped the parents as much as the students. It provided reassurance that things were going to be okay. In my opinion, the parents who participated in these activities were better prepared to help their children. Perhaps the best coping strategy students received during this time was developing the confidence to be on school grounds.

My staff is pretty amazing. The day after the shooting, the teachers met and got into a conversation about upcoming lesson plans and how to adapt these. They did not want to use materials that might retraumatize students. So, for example, one class was set to work with the book *Of Mice and Men*, which depicts a shooting between friends. That teacher chose another book. A history class was about to begin work on World War I, which usually included historical videos of actual combat. The graphic videos were set aside. Teachers talked about ways to check in with students about what material they were ready to work on. I know a few students asked for an alternative assignment in a class that was studying *Night*, a memoir about the holocaust. I think this will be the norm here for a couple more years.

Students returned to regular classes 2 weeks after the incident. Staff continued to be thoughtful about how to help students cope. For example, we immediately froze student grades to the day before the incident. Students could only raise their grades from that point to the end of the semester. Over the next 4 weeks, teachers implemented light academics. Most teachers dedicated the bulk of class time to small-group activities or activities that allowed students to engage with one another.

For many students, being in class was still too stressful. We allowed these students to visit our Wellness Center, where they could meet with mental health professionals. We modified the school day for other students who were having a difficult time resuming classes. We wanted them to experience the success of being at school, even if for a short period of time.

We were working with Dr. Schonfeld during this period of time. He provided staff with a script to help teachers engage in dialogue with students about grief and trauma. This was a beneficial tool. If I were to highlight the most effective tool we implemented following the students' return to school, it would be the staff's intentional focus on student behavior and mood.

How Did Students Express Grief in This Period?

Not surprisingly, we saw a range of emotional expression with students. Especially early on, we saw some very physical reactions—deep crying, sobbing. Some students didn't want to be in class while they were having these responses. Some wanted to withdraw and be by themselves. Of course, we did not want them to become isolated. We established a Wellness Center during the first 2 weeks following the shooting. It was staffed with a number of counselors. We could refer students there, and they could obtain one-to-one counseling or other support.

We also found that much of the grief students expressed was really more about unrelated experiences in their past—traumas and losses that were revisited by this incident.

Students had different responses to the return to academics. Some wanted to discuss the incident, but only briefly. Others wanted to discuss it in an ongoing way and did not want to move on to coursework. It was difficult to find a balance that worked for everyone. We continued to offer services at the Wellness Center for students who wanted to carry on with these discussions or for other students who needed additional support.

We also saw anger and confusion about what had happened, especially among the shooter's peer group. Even now, they continue to be conflicted about what happened. They're trying to understand why he did this. These friends feel that he was a victim, too, and should be recognized in memorial activities. While I understand that something was troubling him, and I wish we had known and been able to give him support, I do not believe including him in memorial events would work for the family and friends of his victims.

We've set up a weekly group for his friends, where they can meet with a counselor to express and affirm their feelings. I want them to know that they have our support, too.

Quite a few students voiced concerns over campus safety and asked what we would be doing to improve this. Most of their suggestions revolved around metal detectors or additional police support on campus. For the first month back, we had parent volunteers on campus to help with supervision. We did this to provide students with a sense of safety.

I feel like everyone in the school community—staff, students, parents— has worked hard to strengthen our coping skills and keep us moving forward. Sometimes though, when it seems like we're doing well, we get a reminder that everyone is still fragile. A couple of weeks ago, one of our campus security golf carts ran over some trash and made a popping noise. As a result, about 1,000 students ran off campus. Clearly, our students are not feeling 100% safe or secure yet.

Several students were injured during the shooting. They are now all back at school, and they are absolutely leading by example. Every day they show up and walk by the same place where they were shot. They are all positive, upbeat, and outgoing. I know these attitudes help them get through their own days, but they are important to the rest of us as well. They demonstrate so much strength to others—including me. If they can go forward and keep their outlook positive after everything that has happened, then so can I.

What's Next?

We're just about 3 months out from the incident now. In many ways, the students are coping better than the staff. They appreciate that we have returned to regular academics. As a staff, we refer to this as "a return to rigor but with more flexibility." I am constantly asking students how their classes are going, and they all appreciate the great flexibility teachers are providing. This might include re-takes on exams, less homework, chunking their learning into smaller segments—because we're still seeing a lot of students with decreased ability to concentrate. They are working more in small groups. In fact, I think teachers who have switched from lecture-driven classes to more small-group activities are having more success getting their students to stay focused.

As we get back to the business of learning, I am also interacting constantly with staff to know what they need to help students. Of course, if I ask 100 staff,

I'll get 100 answers! But we work to find steps that will be meaningful to a majority of them.

As a principal, I want to continue my practice of meeting with different groups of students each week to get a sense of the pulse of the school. This is one of the best ways for us to give students an active voice in the choices we are making and what our recovery will look like. We will only succeed if we have students contributing to our plans.

I also know that we are preparing for the long haul. It can be a matter of years before a school gets back to its baseline in terms of safety, security, academic performance, and staff satisfaction. This is exhausting work, and we need to stay motivated to keep it moving forward.

As I reflect on these things, I think about heroism. People talk a lot about the heroic efforts of the day when the violence happened. We are grateful to our first responders. But my staff is also heroic. Our students are heroic. Their families are heroic. This is heroism. You step forward. You give it your best. You make a difference. As difficult as this can be, I feel fortunate that I get to do this work surrounded by such an outstanding group of heroes.

Key Concepts

- **The death of a student or school staff member can have a profound impact on the entire school.** Often, virtually everyone will have some sort of emotional response to the death.

- **It is important for schools to set up a system that offers students and staff support at such times.** This includes the services of school staff and consultants who have experience and skills in providing support during such crises.

- **Particular issues should be considered in school settings in which many people are sharing a grief experience at the same time.** For example, responses may be more intense, people may feel anxious, and rumors may spread quickly.

- **Steps similar to those that support individual students experiencing grief will be helpful when a group experiences a death.** Educators can make a meaningful difference by establishing an authentic, supportive connection with students.

- **It is important for schools and educators to reach out to students at higher risk for emotional distress after a school death.** This includes close friends of the deceased, classmates, and others who had some special connection to the person.

- **Deaths by suicide or homicide raise unique concerns.** These include taking steps to prevent other students from harming themselves or others.

10

Responding to a Death by Suicide

When a member of a school community dies by suicide, the impact is felt deeply by virtually everyone in the community. These deaths are even more likely than others to bring up feelings of confusion, doubt, blame, guilt, and anger. They typically touch a large circle in profound ways. Even when the deceased is someone a student barely knew, the death can have great emotional impact.

Because this book focuses on the grief that emerges after a death, we do not address suicide prevention in depth here. It is a complex topic that goes beyond the scope of this text. However, we encourage educators to bring attention to the issue of suicide prevention and seek resources to make such efforts part of their school or district's program.

Schools and districts need to have a range of plans, practices, and policies in place for responding to a death by suicide—a process called *suicide postvention*. Educators should have a general familiarity with these plans. Although a comprehensive review of postvention policies and practices is beyond the scope of this book, we have included some general guidelines about how to support grieving students after a death by suicide. As mentioned in Chapter 9, the NCSCB has developed practical guidelines on how schools can respond to a death by suicide that can be freely downloaded from their web site (https://www.schoolcrisiscenter.org/resources/guide-responding-suicide/).

It is important for students and staff to have opportunities to discuss their reactions to and feelings about these complicated incidents. Clear, consistent information about the death is vital. Rumors are especially likely after a death by suicide. These can be harmful to students and painful for the family of the deceased. Students and staff also need guidance on steps to take if they find themselves or people they know struggling with thoughts about suicide.

Misunderstanding and myths about suicide are common. These can heighten anxiety in students and educators alike and may be reinforced in comments made about the deceased in face-to-face or social media interactions. It is necessary to counter the myths and provide constructive guidance for coping with a death by suicide.

Schools and educators need to be prepared to offer additional outreach to vulnerable students whose own risk of suicidal thoughts and self-harm may be increased by a death by suicide.

Suicide Affects Children and Youth

Suicide is the second leading cause of death for children and youth ages 10 to 24. For every young person who dies by suicide, several hundred others have made attempts. Each year, approximately 3% of high school students make a serious attempt that requires medical treatment. More than one of every six high school students has seriously considered suicide. Approximately one in seven has made a plan. Suicide is believed to be widely underreported—many of these deaths are classified as unintentional or accidental.

FIRST RESPONSE: THE SCHOOL CRISIS TEAM

As with other types of death or other crisis events, the school crisis team should be activated when a school learns of the suicide of a student or staff member. It is this team's responsibility to gather accurate information about what has occurred by checking with family members and local authorities. The team should determine what the family would like shared within the school community as well as anything that has already been reported in the media or by local authorities.

Once the death has been verified and accurate information gathered, the team can develop a plan to notify school staff, students, and parents. They should mobilize appropriate support systems for students and staff, such as having mental health professionals available on campus for students, staff, and parents.

Language Is Important

When talking to students, it is important to use the phrase "died by suicide." These words underscore that educators are willing to discuss this difficult topic. Avoid saying "committed suicide," which may imply blame or criminal behavior. Always include a message about the importance of students talking with a trusted adult about any concerns they have for themselves or others. If students hear someone describing suicidal thoughts or intentions, they must speak up and reach out to a trusted adult for assistance. Students need not, and should not, protect the privacy of that conversation.

Letting Staff, Students, and Parents Know What Happened

It is ideal for staff to meet before school when possible so a unified plan can be established. All staff can be briefed on what has happened and how to interact with students. A death by suicide must be acknowledged but not sensationalized. Facts can be shared (e.g., name of the deceased, that this was a death by suicide, when it happened), but graphic details are not necessary. For example, the school might share that this was a death by self-inflicted gunshot (if this information is public knowledge, already known by many students, and/or shared by the parents to be communicated with peers) but will not need to address the location of the wound, where the body was discovered, how long it had been there, or what resuscitation efforts were made.

When educators are all able to hear the same information about what has happened, misinformation and rumors are less likely to take hold across the school. When staff have an opportunity to openly discuss this death with one another, it reinforces that it is okay to discuss the topic sensitively and frankly with students as well.

Ideally, students will learn of the death from a familiar educator who shares a prepared statement in person. As with any death affecting the school community, this is best done in small, naturally occurring groups such as homeroom or a first-period class. The news should not be delivered in a large assembly or over a public address system. School staff should keep in mind that students or staff may already have heard about the death through social media, although their information may be inaccurate or incomplete.

_____

When staff have an opportunity to openly discuss this death with one another, it reinforces that it is okay to discuss the topic sensitively and frankly with students as well.

_____

A letter for parents notifying them about the death can be sent by e-mail or posted on the school web site. It should acknowledge this was a death by suicide, offer suggestions on how to support their child, describe support services being offered to students both within and outside the school, and offer parents a chance to talk with or meet with school personnel for further guidance.

Parents often experience great anxiety for their own children after a death by suicide in the school. It is important that parents stay engaged with their children and be available to talk or answer questions. However, we have seen situations where parents become so anxious they have considered asking their children about current suicidal ideation almost daily. Parent meetings at the school can help families find a constructive balance that includes checking in with their children, being available to talk about what has happened, and allowing their children to process this experience and move forward on their own time line.

Help Students Understand the Mental Health Connection

In the aftermath of a suicide, it is essential to explain to students the connection between mental health problems and suicidal actions. Students need to understand that there is a difference between the mental illness called depression and the feelings of sadness all humans experience.

Here's an example that might be used with younger students.

Everyone feels sad sometimes. However, some people have a mental illness called depression. They stop feeling happy about anything at all. It is hard for them to make good choices or decisions.

Most people with depression get better, although sometimes they need the help of a doctor or therapist. Sometimes, a person with depression feels the only way to stop feeling so sad is to die. They may not even realize that they could ask for help or that a doctor or therapist might have some ways to help them with their sadness.

When someone we care about dies by suicide, we have many different feelings, including feeling very sad. Feeling sad after the death of someone you know and care about is normal. It does not mean you have depression. It is important to talk to your parents and other adults about your feelings so you can have some help to feel better. They can answer questions or discuss worries you have about what happened.

In the aftermath of a suicide, it is essential to explain to students the connection between mental health problems and suicidal actions.

With older children and adolescents, it is important to also address the connection between depression, substance abuse, and other mental health problems. Emphasize how critical it is that people dealing with these issues talk to a doctor or mental health provider who can help them see a greater range of alternatives. Remind them that most people with depression respond well to treatments, such as medication or counseling. Tell students that it is always important to talk with a trusted adult about suicidal thoughts or concerns, whether these are their own or those of a friend or acquaintance.

Students need to understand that there is a difference between the mental illness called depression and the feelings of sadness all humans experience.

Why Talking About Suicide Is Difficult

There are a number of reasons it's difficult to talk about suicide. One of the most common is an old myth—the belief that talking about suicide might give students the idea to harm themselves. Instead, these conversations open up possibilities for greater understanding. They allow students to express their thoughts and feelings and learn coping strategies. They may help students better monitor their own impulsivity or feelings of hopelessness (which can be factors in suicidal thoughts or behaviors). They also provide opportunities to connect students with support services if necessary.

There is considerable stigma placed on suicide. Families may feel ashamed, confused, responsible, or otherwise conflicted by the suicide death of a family member. People who had thoughts of suicide in their past, or perhaps made a suicide attempt, often express feelings of shame about those experiences. It is not unusual to hear blame placed on parents or friends of someone who has died by suicide—"A better mother would have known her son was depressed!" "Good friends would have stopped this from happening." Some people avoid mentioning suicide as a way of avoiding the discomfort they feel or criticism they fear.

Another challenge is the complexity of suicidal thoughts and behaviors. After a suicide, it can be difficult to make sense of what happened. Some people find it hard to empathize with someone who has attempted or died by suicide— "What was going on? Why didn't they reach out for help?"

On the other hand, some students might express identification with the deceased—"We are all so stressed out. I can understand how this might happen." (This offers an excellent opportunity to emphasize that stress is a universal human experience and that stress alone is not the reason someone thinks about suicide or acts on impulses.)

Students may also describe their own troublesome feelings or those of friends. These might include guilt about not preventing the death or thoughts about self-harm or suicide. The emphasis here can be on normalizing the human state of having emotions—everyone feels sad, stressed, or troubled at times—and the importance of seeking guidance when troublesome emotions persist or get worse. Schools should provide opportunities for students to talk with a trained mental health specialist, and educators can encourage students to participate in these services.

In these conversations, educators should take steps to avoid romanticizing or glamorizing the individual who died. Although it is appropriate to acknowledge the person who died, it is also important to avoid gestures that might make these acts seem appealing to depressed or isolated students such as by holding formal commemorative events to honor the memory of the person who died. We don't want students to reach conclusions such as, "No one even noticed him in this school until after he killed himself."

Discussion should focus on the grief of students and staff after having lost someone important in their lives or sadness for a life that ended too early, rather than focus on the means of death or suggesting that the deceased was a "hero" or more worthwhile or noteworthy as a result of suicide. An important goal of suicide postvention is to encourage others who may be considering suicide to seek and obtain needed help, without normalizing the act of suicide. Comments such as, "He did what anyone would do in that situation," should be avoided; instead, it should be explained that suicide is not a logical act. Rather, suicide is usually associated with mental illness (e.g., depression) or substance use. People who die by suicide often are not thinking clearly and make poor decisions as a result. Weave into these conversations the important message that students should never honor a peer's request to keep a plan for suicide secret. In most situations, individuals who mention thoughts or plans of suicide are ambivalent about ending their life and will later appreciate a friend's intervention that prevented their death. Even if this does not occur, it is better to have a friend who is upset with you than a friend who died.

Social Media: Harm and Help

Many students will find information about what happened online or through social media. They may read sensationalized accounts with unnecessary detail about the death. They may see comments that are critical or dismissive of the deceased—jokes, blaming, charges of being "cowardly," or even suggestions that the world is better off without this person. There may also be posts critical of the deceased's peer group—"Why didn't his friends do more to help him?" "What's wrong with that school?"

These are uncomfortable issues for anyone to address. However, they offer educators an excellent opportunity to talk about the power of positive messaging on social media. When educators talk about these resources with students, it is important to recognize the value these platforms have for many young people. Unfortunately, we live in a time where people can post long statements or troubled manifestos before they die by suicide. People have left voicemails as they take action to end their lives. There are individuals who have livestreamed their suicide.

In conversations, educators must be ready to hear about these troubling instances and engage students in discussions about how to experience and express grief in a constructive fashion. This includes such things as recognizing and speaking about personal anger—whether online or in person—in a way that does not discount others' perspectives or make them uncomfortable.

It also means helping students think actively about the resources and information they pursue on social media and online. Where are they most likely to see or hear positive, constructive messages? What are positive things they can post or share? What messages will express compassion and hope to their peers? What messages would they like to read themselves as they go through this difficult process?

A quick online search will provide you with a number of organizations that offer sound information about suicide prevention and grief after a suicide. Encourage students to seek out these kinds of resources and support.

Was It Suicide? How to Have These Discussions When Cause Is Uncertain

Suicide carries a stigma. It is not uncommon for family members to ask a school not to disclose suicide as a likely cause of death. This is especially true when the cause of death has not been confirmed by the medical examiner—a process that may take several weeks.

As we discussed in Chapter 9, it is generally best to respect the family's wishes while still addressing the topic of suicide forthrightly when students ask about it. Here's an example of what an educator might say to students:

> We are all saddened by John's death. It is still under investigation, and the family does not agree with media reports that this was a death by suicide. They believe it was an accident. However, many of you have asked questions about the news reports. Let's talk about suicide in general because I want you all to understand this important topic.

In this way, the family's wishes can be respected at the same time the students' needs are being met.

What Students Need to Know: Points to Always Include

After sharing the basic facts about a death by suicide and answering students' questions, be sure these points are covered.

- **Talk to a trusted adult if you are concerned about yourself or others.** Suicidal thoughts and intentions should never be kept secret. Don't worry that a friend will be angry if you talk to an adult to get needed help. Most friends will ultimately be thankful for the assistance; reassure children that they did the right thing, even if their friend is upset.

- **Know about resources for help.** Offer suggestions for information web sites and suicide prevention hotlines. Emphasize that students can touch base with these resources at any time, whether there is a crisis at hand. They can ask for information or talk about a friend or family member. There may be local resources that are a good match for your school. You can also tell students about the National Suicide Prevention Lifeline web site (suicidepreventionlifeline.org) and 24/7 hotline (1-800-273-8255). Post these numbers in classrooms, counseling offices, libraries, health clinics, school web sites, and other appropriate locations.

- **Remember, no one is to blame for someone else's death by suicide.** It is common for people to experience conflicting feelings about a death by suicide, including a sense of guilt for not taking steps to prevent the death. The point of these discussions is not to blame anyone, but to encourage everyone to reach out for support if they or someone they know is troubled by thoughts of suicide.

   There have been instances in which one person, or a group of people, have harassed or bullied another person on social media, face to face, or through messaging apps, or even encouraged someone to follow through on suicidal intentions, possibly contributing to a death by suicide. The issue of blame is more complicated in such situations. Professional guidance with a mental health specialist would be recommended for a student in this situation—or whenever there is significant or persistent guilt feelings, even when the guilt seems unwarranted to others.

PROVIDING SUPPORT SERVICES AT SCHOOL

It is important for schools to offer crisis, grief, and related support services after a death by suicide, geared toward both students and staff. About half of U.S. adults know someone who has died by suicide. A good number have struggled themselves with depression and suicidal ideation. Quite likely, any school staff community includes such individuals. Educators may also have their own doubts about what has happened and be struggling with feelings of guilt or blame.

Facilitating discussions with students about suicide after the death of a member of the school community in the context of these personal experiences can be particularly difficult for educators. It can also be challenging for administrators to make the necessary leadership decisions after a suicide if they have reactions to a personal or family history triggered by the death.

Educators should follow the guidelines and suggestions in Chapter 4 as they engage in discussions with students. This includes keeping the focus on students and listening more than talking. Self-disclosure about past experiences with suicidal ideation or behaviors is generally not appropriate. Employee assistance programs or other providers can help staff examine their own feelings and experiences and cope more effectively with the loss.

Having mental health staff who can offer support to students gives educators an opportunity to refer students to knowledgeable adults who are a step removed from the immediate loss. These providers can help students express their grief and focus on coping behaviors that allow them to continue to attend to their studies. They can facilitate referrals to other resources for students who might need additional mental health services.

I Wish I Had Spoken Up

A teacher was speaking with a crisis counselor after the suicide of one of his students. He was struggling with powerful feelings of guilt about the incident. "I feel like I am responsible for this death, at least in part. I believe my student killed himself because he was gay and he felt hopeless about his future. This is not an easy community for gay people.

"I'm gay too, but I've never discussed this with my students. I can't help but feel that if I had been courageous enough to be out and to be a positive role model for this young man—maybe to reach out to him and talk to him about these things—this might never have happened."

The counselor affirmed the teacher's experience and gently reminded him that these types of feelings are common after a death by suicide. She asked him to speak for a bit about some of the ways he had been a support for his student. It was clear that the teacher had a genuine and rewarding connection with the student. She reassured him that he was not to blame for his student's death and affirmed that there were understandable reasons the teacher had chosen not to be out in his teaching role in this community. She encouraged him to monitor the intensity of these feelings over the coming weeks. If their power did not diminish, she suggested he reach out again for support.

Time to Send the Letter

A high school student made a serious suicide attempt and ended up on life support. The superintendent and school counselor drafted a letter to explain the situation to students and their parents, but 2 weeks later, the letter still had not been sent. A meeting was called with school administrators and district staff.

The school counselor asked why the letter had still not been sent. The principal responded, "Our legal office said sending this letter will create a liability exposure. Since the student didn't die, they feel we don't have an obligation to follow our protocol on student suicide."

The counselor disagreed. "But this is still having an impact on students and staff. He's on life support! Students know this. They have questions."

The team couldn't reach an agreement.

Finally, the principal spoke up. "One of my parents died by suicide. I just haven't been able to talk about this incident with our students. I've been avoiding dealing with it because it's been so painful for me. But I realize at this point I can't do that. If another student attempts suicide, I'll feel responsible."

Despite his personal experiences, the principal saw that the choice not to talk about the suicide attempt was far worse for him and his school. The letter was sent, and students and families were notified and counseled. Afterward, this principal became a highly effective advocate for informed school policies and practices about suicide and suicide attempts. He has helped other administrators who find themselves in similar situations.

Students at Higher Risk

In Chapter 9, we described students who are likely to benefit from additional emotional support after the death of a peer. These include close friends, those who shared classes or extracurricular activities, individuals who identified with the deceased, those who had a difficult or complicated relationship with the deceased, and those with a history of similar losses. Similar outreach needs to be pursued after a death by suicide.

In addition, school mental health professionals should reach out to students with mental health conditions, particularly depression. They should follow up with students who demonstrate concerning behaviors after the death, such as increased impulsive or disruptive behavior, withdrawal from friends or family, abandoning extracurricular activities, increased alcohol or substance abuse, or a significant change in academic work.

Continue to monitor those impacted by the death over time. Certain dates or events may trigger intense emotions (e.g., homecoming, parent day, graduation, 1-year marker of the death, birthday of the deceased). Offer supportive services at these times when needed.

Should Educators Review Risk Factors for Suicide With Students?

Students may benefit from understanding more about the kinds of comments or behaviors that suggest someone may be at risk for self-harm and should be told how important it is to talk to a trusted adult if they ever have concerns about themselves or someone else. We call these "warning signs" of suicidal thinking or actions. These can include, but are not limited to, such behaviors as increased impulsive or disruptive behavior; withdrawing from friends or activities; using more drugs or alcohol; or comments reflecting hopelessness, lack of a reason to go on living, a sense of being a burden to others or not belonging, or an interest in suicide (e.g., "The world would be better without me," "I'm not going to stay around for this," "I think I'm going to kill myself."). Whenever students make statements or engage in behaviors that raise concerns about self-harm, educators should refer students to, or seek advice from, a school mental health professional who is qualified to do an assessment for suicide risk.

More general lists of "risk factors" can be less helpful because they are often quite broad. When students are told that suicide risks are greater when people are younger than 24 years old, are stressed, get inadequate sleep, have experienced trauma, and feel isolated, many students in the class will fall into these categories. This invites students to self-identify as someone at risk. This can lead to overidentification with those at risk for suicide, which may contribute to, rather than help prevent, self-destructive or suicidal behaviors.

About Suicide Clusters

One of the reasons it is essential for schools to take active, informed steps after a death by suicide is because this can help prevent additional self-harm or suicide among students. A number of schools and districts across the nation have experienced suicide clusters, where, after an initial death, one or more other students attempt or die by suicide. Sometimes these occur in the same location as the initial death or in the same manner.

These are extraordinarily complicated situations that require outside consultation and assistance. This is a time to examine the school climate, explore protocols for supporting distressed students, and create a plan for building a different environment in the school. This is a process not just of recovery, but of prevention. It requires the engagement of schools, parents, students, the community, and outside experts.

We strongly recommend that any school experiencing more than one suicide over a brief period of time immediately contact the NCSCB (https://www.schoolcrisiscenter.org/) or other organizations trained to deal with these events.

Memorializing Someone Who Dies by Suicide

The ways we commemorate and memorialize members of the school community have a significant impact on the ongoing emotional health of students and staff. It is always important to avoid glamorizing the means of death, no matter the cause, but this is especially vital in cases of suicide. We do not want to suggest to vulnerable students that they might gain positive attention through self-harm. Chapter 13 addresses commemoration and memorialization in detail.

Our challenge in deaths by suicide is how to help people grieve someone in ways that help the grievers without increasing distress or risk in them or others. The goal is not to commemorate what the deceased did that ended their life but rather to remember who they were when they were alive. We want to recognize that people care about them. This can be a delicate line to walk, but it is a necessary one.

We discourage dedicating a yearbook to a student who died by suicide or creating a testimonial page to honor that student (or, really, after the death of a student from any cause, in order not to create inequities). However, neither is it appropriate to delete all pictures of the student. Removing any record of the student's life as part of the school community might suggest that the student was indeed "invisible." This may cause marginalized students to feel even more devalued. It also makes it very difficult for students who are friends or relatives to grieve their loss.

Putting Familiar Principles to Work

Suicide is a special case. However, the steps educators can take to best support students who are grieving the loss are similar to those that have been emphasized throughout this book. Be present and authentic. Listen attentively (and listen more than talk). Provide opportunities for children to experience and express their feelings. Normalize common experiences of grief, and link students with support when grief becomes more challenging. Help decrease children's sense of isolation. Support conversations with family and friends.

The more effectively we can do these things, the greater is our likelihood of success in helping students cope successfully with a death from suicide and the better we can support suicide prevention.

Key Concepts

- **Suicide is a leading cause of death for children and adolescents.** All schools need to have plans, policies, and practices in place in the event of a death by suicide.

- **Students and staff need opportunities to discuss their reactions to and feelings about a death from suicide.** Deaths by suicide touch many people and raise complicated and confusing emotions.

- **Students and staff need guidance on steps to take if they find themselves or others struggling with thoughts about suicide.** It is not unusual for a suicide death to bring up thoughts of suicide for others, even individuals who were not especially close to the deceased. Preventing further suicides is one of the primary goals of a school's response to a suicide.

- **Talking about suicide is difficult.** Frank, sensitive discussions that use the words "died by suicide" help students understand that educators are ready to discuss these challenging issues.

- **Schools need to have plans in place to reach out to students known to be at higher risk for suicidal thoughts or behaviors,** as well as students who demonstrate behaviors suggesting they may be at risk. This may involve ongoing work over a period of time.

- **Schools experiencing suicide clusters should call in experienced consultants.** These are extraordinarily complicated situations that require outside consultation and assistance.

11

Applications Beyond K–12

In recent years, we have seen greater attention given to the issue of grieving students in the K–12 setting. The growth of the Coalition to Support Grieving Students (https://grievingstudents.org/) and the establishment of the Grief-Sensitive Schools Initiative (https://grievingstudents.org/gssi/) have helped share important knowledge and broaden the reach of these efforts.

OTHER LEARNING ENVIRONMENTS

Of course, children, adolescents, and young adults are also found in settings beyond K–12. The principles outlined in this book can be adapted for use in a variety of settings such as prekindergarten (pre-K); college and trade schools; after-school programs; summer camps; home schools; online schools; private, parochial, charter, and other nonpublic schools; and boarding schools. They will also be useful among community-based organizations serving children and youth.

In this chapter, we review some particular points to keep in mind in these settings—issues that may be different from a public school, K–12 environment. Remember that it is also helpful to offer planned coursework on the topic of loss and use teachable moments to discuss death and grief even if a death has not occurred. These steps give children, adolescents, and even young adults opportunities to understand more about death and grief generally. This provides a foundation of understanding that may be useful in the future should they experience the death of a peer or family member.

Pre-K

As we mentioned in Chapter 2, even very young children grieve the loss of a loved one. In that chapter's vignette, "All Gone," we described 21-month-old Eva and the way she demonstrated her understanding of the irreversibility of her grandmother's death. Educators working with pre-K children who have experienced a death can use similar language, ideas, and stories to help them understand the Four Concepts About Death.

Family involvement is usually greater in preschool settings. Parents are often involved as regular volunteers. This means that when a parent dies, the impact on all students may be greater than it would be in a K–12 setting. Students and parents alike will be affected by such a loss.

In these circumstances, the school can arrange to talk with all students about what has happened. In some schools, this will work best if parents are invited to participate with their children in the conversation. Schools may also wish to offer a special parent session to help parents understand the Four Concepts About Death and discuss the ways young children may demonstrate feelings associated with grief such as sadness and worries, including through their behaviors. Parents and educators can work together to develop suggestions for providing support to the children (Schonfeld, 2019a).

Family involvement is usually greater in preschool settings. Parents are often involved as regular volunteers.

College and Trade School: A Challenging Transition

When students move from high school to college or trade school, they find themselves around new people in new settings, typically with greater academic demands. Many attend schools some distance from their family homes, leaving behind friends, family, and familiar places. They may find themselves in dorm or apartment living situations where they have little privacy.

As discussed in Chapter 8, these shifts can be isolating and challenging. Most students hope to make new friends in their school. They look for ways to express shared experiences with new acquaintances. Discussing a recent death, or openly expressing grief, seems more likely to emphasize differentness and separation. As one student put it, "I didn't want to talk about my mom's death and just be a big downer with all of my new friends."

In addition, grieving students may continue to feel unsettled emotionally. This might lead some to appear more distracted and distant. Others might seem desperate for intimate personal relationships. These reactions can reduce their social appeal, making it challenging to build new friendships. Some students may compensate for difficult feelings by becoming overinvolved in school social activities, using substances to elevate their mood, or seeking closeness through sexual relationships. As a result, academic performance may suffer. It can be difficult for these young adults to establish and maintain healthy new relationships.

Especially when students are attending a school or college far from where their family lives, the usual resources for comfort are absent. Friends from high school are more difficult to reach. Students may want to avoid distressing their parents by revealing the extent of their grief. They may believe that since they are now adults, they should be independent enough not to rely on their parents for support. Some students may feel guilty for abandoning the family, especially when they hear about the emotional pain or hardships their family is still enduring.

College food is also unfamiliar. "Cafeteria food is the opposite of comfort food," one student explained. "I have no appetite. I'm not hungry when I look at it. I can't eat it." The comfort food cooked at home is not available. Neither is their familiar bed, the contemplative and special place in their backyard or local park, accustomed pastimes with friends, or other touchstones that might offer solace and comfort if they were nearer to home.

Students may not be familiar with resources on their campus, such as health services, counseling, or peer-to-peer support programs. They may not be accustomed to assuming responsibility for accessing these services on their own initiative—these might be the sort of efforts previously carried out by engaged parents or a high school guidance counselor. This is one of the reasons it is especially useful to announce and promote these services both at new student orientations and in an ongoing way throughout each term. It would also be helpful to provide training on grief for staff and volunteers.

Students may not be familiar with resources on their campus, such as health services, counseling, or peer-to-peer support programs.

When a Death Occurs in a College: Notifying Students

Colleges and trade schools are distinctly different from K–12 settings. Some students may be residential. Some may be part of the school community for multiple years, others for only a few weeks or months. Often there are multiple campus sites in different locations around the city, county, or even state. Large colleges host tens of thousands of students—they are, essentially, medium-size cities.

It is not unusual for a college this size to experience several deaths over the course of an academic year. How should the college handle notification for students and staff? In most cases, it will not be necessary, or even practical, to notify all students in small class discussions as we suggest within K–12 settings—students will have many classes and activities scheduled at a variety of different times. Instead, college counseling centers can usually focus on the students and staff who had some personal connection with the deceased. As explained later, this focus would be broadened in the event of a highly visible death, such as one associated with murder or involving a high-profile athlete whose death is covered in public media.

Here are some guidelines:

- **Check with the family to see what their wishes are.** The family may know campus friends of the deceased who would want to be notified.

The family may also have particular wishes about announcing the death or putting together a memorial for friends to share their feelings. As with K–12 schools, if the college elects to plan a memorial activity, we encourage they follow the family's wishes except when doing so might glamorize a death or involve being dishonest with students about what has happened.

- **Determine the "circle of influence."** Identify staff and students who are personally affected by this death. This might include students in the same classes or dormitory, teammates in sports, members of a sorority or fraternity, or participants in a club where the deceased was a member. Plan to reach out to these individuals to personally notify them about the death. (Expect that many students will likely have learned of the death already through social media.)

  It may be useful to provide a prepared announcement for instructors in small classes attended by a student who has died. Although this would probably not apply to every class as it would in a high school, it is appropriate to acknowledge the loss in settings where the deceased student was known personally by classmates.

- **Determine the "circle of coverage."** Some deaths take place rather quietly. Others receive a great deal of attention in local or national media. We call this the "circle of coverage." When the circle of coverage becomes larger, more people will come into the circle of influence. Even if the deceased is not someone students or staff knew, for example, they will be distressed to hear that a classmate was murdered on campus or killed by a drunk driver.

  These experiences can create anxiety for students and staff. They can also evoke reminders of earlier losses—suddenly a student is feeling incredibly sad and angry about a fifth-grade classmate killed by a drunk driver. Students who have been functioning well may find themselves overwhelmed with feelings of homesickness for the first time since arriving at college.

  Broader notification efforts will need to be organized when the circle of coverage is large. This might include such steps as a prepared announcement read by course instructors including information about where students can reach out for support. Activities coordinators and staff in the athletics department are often well connected with many students and can be helpful resources in sharing information and providing support. The college might publish an article in the campus newspaper, send a text announcement to all students, or post an announcement on the campus web site. Notices in dorms and common areas can also be effective in reaching many students.

- **Provide information on counseling services and other support staff.** Student mental health and health services should receive basic information about the death so they are prepared to support students who may be experiencing grief. A highly publicized death may be especially difficult for students with preexisting mental health conditions. It may be helpful to refer students to programs in the community that offer bereavement support groups if resources on campus are limited. Because many of these programs focus on child and family member bereavement, it would be important to check first to see what services they can offer to college students. Campus ministry programs can be a good resource for students who are faith based. Resident assistants (RAs) or other housing staff would benefit from information and a basic review of ways to provide support and help interested students access additional services.

Student mental health and health services should receive basic information about the death so they are prepared to support students who may be experiencing grief.

- **Host commemorative events when appropriate.** See Chapter 13 for more detailed information on commemoration and memorialization.

- **Offer a standard announcement about the death through the campus newspaper, web site, text or social media communication, or other vehicles.** A simple obituary can honor the deceased, recognize the loss, and reach those in the circle of influence who might otherwise have missed the announcement.

Home Schools

If children who are home schooled lose a parent, they may have also lost their teacher. If their sibling dies, they may also be grieving one of their closest classmates.

Many home school students participate in home school groups where they work with different teachers, join together for field trips, or are part of special study projects or academic competitions. Even in these more expanded settings, however, the circle is a small one.

The essential point for home school students is that any death in their network is likely to be felt deeply, often reflecting multiple roles that have been fulfilled by the person who died. There may also be substantive changes in educational relationships. If a parent/teacher dies, children lose a huge portion of their known world. A new teacher, or perhaps attendance at public school, will be part of their future.

In the face of all these changes, ongoing conversation and support will be vitally important. The process will be most effective when parents and instructors are familiar with material covered earlier in this book, such as understanding how children experience grief, knowing how to invite conversations with children, and being able to speak frankly and honestly, using words such as "died" and "dead" rather than euphemisms about death.

For home school students, any death in their network is likely to be felt deeply, often reflecting multiple roles that have been fulfilled by the person who died.

Online-Only Schools

Schools that provide only a virtual or online learning experience pose challenges in helping grieving students cope with the death of a family member or friend. These schools also face unique challenges in responding to the death of a student or staff member within the program. However, the same strategies we have described throughout the book will also work well in these settings. In fact, some students may feel more comfortable receiving this support virtually than in person—their peers won't necessarily need to know about the support, and students can respond to an educator's queries when they feel most prepared to do so.

Students participating in online programs may live in a variety of local and distant locations. College students may have selected this form of instruction because they have other responsibilities (e.g., work, parenting). Some college and K–12 students choose online instruction because of health issues, whereas others may have mental or behavioral health concerns that make an online-only school preferable (e.g., anxiety that makes classroom attendance difficult, behavioral problems that prompted a search for an alternative teaching modality).

Assessment of the emotional adjustment of online students after a death of a family member or friend can be difficult. This will be easier when the student has already established a personal relationship with a teacher and when the teacher is comfortable and willing to make the effort to reach out to offer support. We have mentioned previously that grieving students often feel isolated. This is even more of a risk when children only attend school online. The role of a trusted adult such as the online instructor becomes even more important.

In these settings, programs and instructors may be less likely to realize that a student has experienced a significant loss. It is important to inquire about absences. Consider bereavement as a possible cause of new or worsening academic challenges or delays in homework submission.

Convey to students proactively that you want to know if they have any personal or family issues that may be affecting their ability to participate in the educational program. Emphasize your wish to support them in optimal learning and let them know you will help them with academic supports and accommodations. Online learning platforms may be particularly suited to some accommodations, such as delaying testing or due dates, changing the topic of a learning activity that might be distressing, or simplifying a project.

Remember that conveying concern about how a student is adjusting to the death of a family member or friend and offering to provide academic accommodations and learning supports are appropriate roles for educators. This is not the same thing as providing mental health services. Educators who take these sorts of steps do not need to worry about in- or out-of-state mental health licensing. They will not be exceeding professional limits.

If an educator has concerns or questions about a student's mental health, it is appropriate to recommend the student speak to a local pediatrician or mental health provider. Ask students who they have in their lives as potential supports. For example, if they have anxiety, they are likely to have a mental health provider already involved in their care. Some students may have a faith-based organization that can provide some support. With K–12 students, it will also be helpful to reach out to a parent (see Chapter 6).

Effective and meaningful support for grieving students *can* be provided in a virtual setting. Over the past few years, we have seen a robust growth in online education for individuals of all ages. Telehealth for mental health has also become much more common. During the COVID-19 pandemic, our entire nation put social media and electronic resources to work to connect emotionally and share information and support. As educators and students grow ever more experienced with online education and social interactions, support in these modalities will be increasingly easier to offer and more comfortable to receive.

Charter Schools

Staffing at charter schools is not consistent from one school to another. Many charter schools do not offer student counseling services, for example. Although these services may be available at a local public school, it may not be possible for charter school students to use them.

It's a good idea for charter schools to look for other ways to infuse support for grieving students into their programs. This might involve doing professional development work with coaches, offering training to all staff on ways to support grieving students, and providing resources to mentor teachers so they are able to share their skills with others. The Coalition to Support Grieving Students web site (www.grievingstudents.org) offers a wide range of free materials that can provide information and training for educators.

Charter schools should also be familiar with resources in the community that might be able to support bereaved students, as well as crisis response services available through the public school system.

Private and Boarding Schools

Private and boarding schools are hugely variable. Some are small and community focused. Students usually have a good sense of connection with one another, and families are actively involved in classes and extracurricular activities. Others operate almost like colleges, with students attending classes across a range of facilities and studying fairly independently.

The primary emphasis of some schools can be quite concentrated. For example, the NCSCB was contacted by a small private boarding school for elite athletes, including those hoping to compete in the Olympics. One of their students had died suddenly. "We need help," they told us. We were preparing to talk to them about how to discuss the death with their students and what kind of support to offer. We were not expecting their main concern—"The students are upset and they're not staying focused. But we have a meet in two days, and we have to get them competition-ready."

This again emphasizes the need to have many staff at such a school trained and prepared to be grief sensitive. These young students were far from their families and their usual supports. It is no surprise they were feeling distracted. Although the rigorous focus on competition may be one of the expected elements of this type of setting, students' needs for clear information and chances to discuss their feelings are as great as they would be in any other school. The opportunity to participate in such discussions helps students focus more effectively on other elements in their life, whether that be an upcoming test or a sports competition.

Because the emphases of different private schools are so broad, the challenges each school faces in addressing grief will be different. In some schools, there is a sense among school leadership that families prioritize privacy and would feel that any inquiry into emotional issues or mental health would be intrusive—even to the extent of believing offers of support to a student after the death of a family member may be poorly received. In reality, most grieving families appreciate offers of support and assistance. They find the lack of outreach in a school isolating, adding further to their children's difficulties in adjusting to the death of a family member or friend. The recommendations in Chapter 6 on working with families will be helpful in preparing to reach out to and engage with families.

Because the emphases of different private schools are so broad, the challenges each school faces in addressing grief will be different.

NCSCB worked with another private school where a student had died from alcohol poisoning. Students clearly needed support to understand and work through what had happened. Instructors and other staff did not feel prepared for the task. Initially, the school had no counselor on staff. They hired someone part time, expecting that counselor to help with the school's recovery after the death. The counselor was able to facilitate a bereavement group, offer individual support for students who wished it, and provide focused support with students considered to be at increased risk because of the death. The counselor was also available to talk with parents who wanted guidance on how to best support their child. Ultimately, the school recognized the great value of this work and increased the position to full time. They began to proactively address students who were struggling with emotional, social, or mental health issues.

Community-Based Organizations

Any community-based organization (CBO) working with children and teens will be working with grieving children. Despite the many different areas of focus and emphasis in CBOs, the same general principles that work in school settings will work with an organization's child and youth participants. In fact, these organizations know that some children have closer relationships with staff or volunteers in their after-school program, summer camp, sports team, or church group than they do with their teachers or other school staff.

This makes support from CBOs crucial for many grieving children. Organizations can make a difference by training staff and volunteers about issues related to grief. CBOs also provide another setting where programs engaging parents and children together may be especially helpful.

YES, THIS IS YOUR WORK

In Chapter 1, we asked the question, "Isn't this someone else's job?" We reviewed reasons schools and educators are key resources for grieving children. Although we have focused the information and guidelines in this book on public K–12 schools, these principles hold sound across any setting where children are being educated, cared for, and protected.

Key Concepts

- **Educators in a wide range of settings can provide vital support to grieving children, adolescents, and young adults.** The general principles described throughout this book can be applied in many settings beyond public K–12 schools.
- **Colleges and trade schools will need to adapt some of the steps for informing students about a death and providing support.** It is important to consider the "circle of influence" and the "circle of coverage" when making decisions about who to notify, what information to share, and how to offer support.
- **CBOs can also provide crucial support for grieving children.** Some children have closer relationships with staff and volunteers at CBOs than they do with educators in their school.

12

Serious Illness: When Death Is a Concern

Recent decades have seen many advances that help children with serious medical conditions live longer, more functional lives. Schools now integrate students with disabilities and serious medical issues into general education classrooms. Shorter hospitalizations and more assistive technology allow children who are medically fragile to live at home and attend school. Technologies also make it possible for children with very serious illnesses to attend regular classrooms. Students at a terminal stage of illness might be in the classroom until very close to the time of death.

As a result, educators today are more likely than ever before to have students with serious conditions in their classrooms. Children with conditions that are quite complicated are sometimes able to participate in regular classrooms or alternate between home or hospital schooling and the classroom. While in the hospital, some children may also participate using live webcams or other technologies that help them stay involved in class activities.

Educators have unique opportunities to offer guidance and support in these circumstances in several areas. They can offer support to 1) the child with a serious illness, 2) other students and their families, 3) the family of the child with the illness, and 4) other educators and school staff. It is also important for educators working with children who are seriously ill to receive support for their own reactions and feelings (see Chapter 14).

Educators today are more likely than ever before to have students with serious medical conditions in their classrooms.

Educators often have concerns about talking to a child who is seriously ill. They may be anxious that they will not know what to say or that they will say something that makes the situation more difficult. They might worry that talking with these children about their illness will make them frightened or sad. These are understandable concerns; however, once again, many of the guidelines already described for grieving children also work in these instances. It is not the goal to take away children's sadness or to find the "right" answers to all of their questions. Rather, the goal is to listen to their concerns and accept their expression of emotions. Offering this kind of support is the best way to help children find their own coping techniques.

Educators have a unique role in the lives of these children. As emphasized throughout this book, educators are trusted sources of information, and therefore, children can ask them questions. An educator's goal is to help children learn. Children can engage with educators in ways that affirm that they are living actively, have important tasks to pursue, have something to contribute to their class, and are making plans for the future—even if it is the near future. Children do not usually feel the same obligations to protect educators that they feel about family members. They are less concerned that educators cannot cope with their questions or concerns about illness, disability, or death.

All of these qualities contribute to the possibility of open and forthright communication between educators and students who are seriously ill. This is immensely valuable to the children and one of the greatest gifts an educator can offer.

Terminology About Children Who Are Ill

Many different terms are used to describe the circumstances of children with serious illnesses. These are the terms used in this book. Several of these might apply to the same child.

- **Life-changing condition.** A serious medical condition that changes the day-to-day activities of a child over a long period of time. This includes medical conditions that don't necessarily have a significant risk of causing death or shortening an individual's life span. Children with life-changing conditions might need to take medications or participate in treatments, and they might have physical limitations or be unable to participate in some of the usual activities of childhood. Examples include diabetes, sickle cell disease, cancer, and severe asthma.

- **Potentially life-limiting condition.** A serious illness or medical condition that, on average, has the potential to significantly shorten the individual's life span, such as cystic fibrosis or Duchenne muscular dystrophy.

- **Serious illness.** An illness that poses a significant threat to a child's life or well-being. It may result in disability. It is usually chronic (ongoing), but it may develop from an acute condition as well.

- **Terminal illness.** A disease or condition that is expected to result in death. In general, this term is avoided even with very serious illnesses until death is imminent. This allows people with such conditions to focus on life and the future, just as others do, for as long as possible.

In this chapter, *serious illness* is used to encompass all of these situations. When *terminal illness* is used, it is in reference to a child expected to die within a matter of weeks or months at most, which is likely at some point during the current school year.

CHILDREN WHO ARE SERIOUSLY ILL

Many medical conditions can change children's lives in profound ways. Any time children have physical limitations or chronic symptoms, need regular medications or treatments, and require regular medical monitoring of their condition, they may have a life-changing condition. Some of these conditions are life threatening—children may or may not recover, and they have a risk of dying as a result of the condition. Some are chronic illnesses that can be well managed over time or result in disabilities that affect daily functioning. Some are conditions that are likely to be terminal, but the time frame is uncertain— perhaps this year, perhaps in 20 years. Some are conditions that are expected to be terminal in the short term—children who have them are expected to die within weeks or months.

Although many of the guidelines in this chapter are useful for children with any type of life-changing medical condition, the focus is primarily on children in the following two groups:

1. Children with serious acute medical problems that are potentially life threatening. Even if these children are *likely* to be cured, there is a genuine possibility that they will not be cured and may die as a result of the condition. This would include many forms of childhood cancer.

2. Children who are expected to die within a matter of weeks or months— likely at some point during the current school year.

PHYSICAL SYMPTOMS OF CHILDREN WHO ARE SERIOUSLY ILL

Children who are seriously ill can have a wide range of symptoms. Some symptoms are mild, whereas others are quite severe. Some children may look sick, whereas others may appear as energetic and healthy as other students. Sometimes children experience more discomfort from the treatments than from the illness itself.

Some children may be diagnosed with a condition that could be life limiting, but they demonstrate only a few signs of acute illness or disability. Some will focus more on the immediate experiences of medications or illness— fatigue, stomachaches, weight loss—without being especially concerned about whether their condition will end in death. Especially for younger children, the limitations in their life in the present may be more compelling than concerns about greater limitations, or death, in the future.

Some children may have serious and potentially life-limiting conditions but may show no outward signs of them. These children may nonetheless worry privately about the possibility of their own death. When discussing the needs or concerns of one student with a serious illness in a class, remember that there may be other students who have similar issues who are not identified.

When discussing the needs or concerns of one student with a serious illness in a class, remember that there may be other students who have similar issues who are not identified.

Something No One Knows

Kevin, an 8-year-old boy, became tearful when his classroom was talking about the death of a classmate's sibling, but he was otherwise silent during the discussion. Afterward, his teacher spoke to him privately and asked whether there was anything special that was troubling him.

Kevin confided that a couple of years before, he had suffered from a bleeding episode in his brain. There had been no permanent damage, but he knew that the malformation that led to the bleed was too deep in his brain to be removed safely. As a result, he was always at risk of another bleeding episode, and any bleed could cause a stroke or be fatal.

Kevin's teacher had been completely unaware of this situation. Although he had realized that some of his students might be affected by the classroom discussion in ways he had not anticipated, this experience reinforced how important it was to speak sensitively about such matters to every class.

COMMON CONCERNS OF CHILDREN WHO ARE TERMINALLY ILL

Even children who are terminally ill should be allowed, even encouraged, to continue to have hope and go on with their lives. An important goal is to help these children optimize the quality of life remaining to them (Schonfeld, 2012).

Sometimes, the most extraordinary experience children with a serious or terminal illness can have is one of normalcy. They want to feel—for a month, a week, a day, or even a few moments—just like the other children in the classroom. This means that important routines should be continued with as little disruption as possible. Because school and learning are the main work in children's lives, children who are seriously or terminally ill should be allowed to attend school when possible and continue schoolwork when they are in the hospital. Membership in clubs or groups may be able to continue. Chores in the home or the classroom are appropriate when children are physically capable of completing them.

Sometimes the most extraordinary experience children with a serious or terminal illness can have is one of normalcy.

I Want to Be in Class

Tracy, a 6-year-old girl, had a recurrent brain tumor. It was inoperable and did not respond to chemotherapy. Her condition was expected to be fatal, and as the cancer progressed, she had increasing physical problems. She lost her hair during chemotherapy. Steroid medications had caused bloating. Her eyes became crossed as the tumor increased in size. She walked with increasing difficulty.

Some of the parents were not comfortable with Tracy remaining in class. They worried that her increasing disfigurement and disability would frighten their children. Some felt she was taking too much of the teacher's attention and that other students were not getting their fair share. Several worried that her impending death would be too difficult for the class. They suggested it would be best for both the class and Tracy to continue her schooling at home.

Tracy enjoyed school and her friends, and she told her mother repeatedly, "I want to be in class." She was bright and interested in learning. She was able to continue most of her schoolwork, although she occasionally needed help with writing and was not able to walk without assistance. She liked being around the other children. Tracy's mother effectively advocated that she should be allowed to continue in school. She attended class until shortly before she died at home one weekend.

Her classmates continued to see her as their friend and an active member of the class until the time of her death. They learned to respect the contributions each person could make irrespective of health or disability. After Tracy's death, the class was proud that they stood by their friend, especially when she was most in need. They were also grateful that they had been able to learn from her and benefit from her friendship.

HOW CHILDREN WHO ARE TERMINALLY ILL UNDERSTAND DEATH

As discussed in Chapter 2, children have different levels of understanding about death. Children who are terminally ill (Schonfeld, 2019b) might struggle with the Four Concepts About Death just as other children do. Even if they have been told little about their medical condition, most of these children usually appreciate the seriousness of their illness and develop a precocious understanding of death (Clunies-Ross & Lansdown, 1988; Glazer, Pao, & Schonfeld, 2017; Greenham & Lohmann, 1982; Spinetta, 1974). They often have a sophisticated appreciation of their own mortality. They realize that their time is limited and that their situation has a powerful impact on their family and others in their lives. They may have a range of complex feelings about their circumstances, including sadness, fear, resignation, or anger.

Sometimes, families or health care providers are not forthcoming with children who are seriously or terminally ill about their health status. Understandably, they wish to protect children from distress, fear, and sadness. However, it is not helpful to mislead children in these situations. In almost every case, it is appropriate, and even kind, to inform children about their health status.

Educators may find themselves in a difficult situation if parents have decided to mislead their child about a life-threatening condition. When an educator is asked by parents to be dishonest or withholding in the face of a student's serious illness, a parent meeting would be appropriate. Educators in this situation should seek the assistance of a school mental health professional or consultant. (Working with families is discussed later in this chapter.)

Once children who are terminally ill understand the basic concepts about death and realize that they are likely to die soon, some will choose to talk openly about it. Others will choose to avoid the discussion. Either course is acceptable.

Acknowledging Death Openly

Children who openly acknowledge their impending death may ask surprisingly direct questions. "What will dying feel like?" "How will you remember me?" "Who will get my bicycle?" This level of frankness sometimes makes adults uncomfortable. Parents, health care providers, friends, and neighbors may all find it difficult to speak so directly about death with children. Children are sensitive to others' discomfort, and children who are terminally ill often feel they must protect their parents or others from the sadness that their impending death causes. They may join parents in a mutual pretense that they are unaware of the seriousness of their situation. They may talk about the things they will do when they get better, just to help everyone else feel more at ease.

This conspiracy of silence has a cost for children who are terminally ill. They may become emotionally isolated from others because they cannot fully express the complex feelings they are having. They cannot utilize services designed specifically for children who are terminally ill because that would break the pretense. They cannot openly express their wishes about making the most of the time that remains to them.

Dying is a difficult, confusing, often painful, and sometimes frightening process. Children who are going through this deserve as much emotional support and honesty as possible. Educators who can handle the direct comments and questions of a child who is terminally ill can be a powerful resource for support, especially if others have been unable to provide this.

Denying or Avoiding Death

Some children choose not to discuss their impending death directly. Once they have been clearly informed, it is rarely necessary or appropriate to confront children with the fact that they are likely to die. Instead, parents, health care providers, and educators can offer indirect outlets for expression. For example, children might express thoughts, feelings, or questions through play, art, or writing. They might respond to a story they read, a television show or movie they watched, or a video game they played. They might get quite excited about a popular song or other piece of music that expresses some of the feelings they are having.

If educators and other adults make these outlets available, children will use them when they are ready. They will express their thoughts and feelings directly or indirectly. They may seek different types of support from different people. All of this is good—it helps children continue to explore and examine this powerful experience in their lives, as well as work to make sense of it.

QUESTIONS AND FEELINGS

Children who are terminally ill have questions and strong feelings about their situation. Many of these are the same kinds of questions and feelings that adults who are facing death have. Often, the greatest concern is about the *process* of dying, rather than death itself. Although each child and situation are different, the following are some of the common issues that emerge for children who are terminally ill:

- **Pain.** Concerns about pain are often powerful for anyone with a serious illness. Children who are terminally ill often experience significant pain from medical procedures or as a result of their condition. They recognize that their symptoms are worsening as their condition progresses. Their pain may increase over time. Children may also experience periods of increasing anxiety as they face upcoming medical procedures that they expect to be painful. Reassurance that pain will be managed actively and effectively, both as their illness progresses and at the time of death, is an important message from family and health care providers.

- **The future.** Some children will have questions about the future and in particular about what the world (e.g., their family, their classroom) will be like after they have died. Other children are uncomfortable talking about the future, and they avoid mentioning a time when they will not be alive.

- **Abandonment.** Children may worry that they will be separated from family as their condition worsens. They may be concerned about hospital stays that isolate them from friends, pets, and sometimes, family members. Some children may attempt to hide symptoms or force themselves to appear more energetic so that they seem more "normal" to their families.

- **Spiritual matters.** Some children have questions about religion, spirituality, and the afterlife. This may be the case whether their family is religious. They may find spiritual practices and beliefs comforting. They may also ask questions about God, including how God could let this illness occur.

- **Concerns about time.** Children may become frustrated at having a sense of limited time available to them, and they may be anxious or angry about wasting time.

- **Creating distance.** Some children act in ways that create distance with others. They may be angry or withdrawn. This might also be a reaction to their fear of abandonment. They create the distance first, before someone else can leave them.

- **Control.** As an illness progresses, children who are terminally ill increasingly lose control over how they feel physically and what they are able to do. They may begin to act more controlling in other ways as this occurs.

- **Sadness.** Children feel grief about their own death and about leaving behind the people and things they love. They grieve the future they will not live to see. They feel sad about the things they can no longer do because of their illness.

- **Regression.** Some children who are terminally ill regress in their behaviors and begin acting like younger children.

- **Emotional outbursts.** Children often experience and express anger, sadness, frustration, and fear.

- **Acts of generosity and compassion.** Children who are terminally ill may also be inspired to act in generous and compassionate ways. They may reassure a family member or friend that they are okay. They may make special gifts for people to remember them by. They may create beautiful thank-you cards for people who have given them support. They may say things that help others recognize and appreciate the preciousness of life.

Educators might see any of these behaviors in school. In most cases, they will not be especially disruptive; however, when necessary, educators can set limits with students who are acting inappropriately around other students. It is also important to use these opportunities to reach out to children who are terminally ill and invite them to talk about their feelings or thoughts. A sympathetic, patient listener can be a great help to children in these circumstances and can often calm troublesome behaviors. If problem behaviors persist, it would be appropriate to make a referral to school mental health services or speak with the students' health care team to see what kinds of psychosocial support are being offered.

Guilt and Shame

Children and adolescents may use magical thinking to explain the cause of their illness. They may assume that their illness is the result of some wrongdoing—that they are being punished for something they did or did not do, or even something they only thought or felt. Older children or adolescents may also hear popular theories about the causes of illness and attribute their condition to such things as dietary choices, negative attitudes, or an inability to believe in their power to heal themselves. These beliefs can cause feelings of guilt— "If I could *really* believe, I could heal myself."

Children may also feel shame about having a serious illness because it represents an extreme example of being out of control. Symptoms and responses to medication may also result in shame—vomiting, diarrhea, gas, fatigue, bloating, changes in weight, hair loss, and so forth. Children need to be reassured frequently that they are not responsible for their illness. Physical changes and symptoms can be acknowledged as unpleasant but also normalized as a typical part of the process of having the condition or going through a treatment.

Children may also feel shame about having a serious illness because it represents an extreme example of being out of control.

Search for Meaning

Similar to adults, children and adolescents who are terminally ill may also engage in a search for meaning. What is the purpose of their lives? What gives their lives value if they are not able to accomplish their long-term goals and dreams? What is the value of a life lived so briefly?

These are questions all of us must answer for ourselves. Children with a religious background may find assistance with their questions through spiritual beliefs. For people of all ages, a life well lived often means being able to help others. Educators and others working with children who are terminally ill can affirm their questions about life and meaning by offering to listen. They can encourage continued thought about the issues and affirm positive things that the child offers to others. This could be something abstract, such as hope, inspiration, or an example of courage. It might be a personality feature, such as being able to make others laugh or think or commit to doing what is right. It might also be something concrete, such as a poem shared with others, a drawing of a favorite tree, or a thoughtful letter.

Children may also want to complete a particular activity or project. This can give them a feeling of accomplishment and the comforting sense that they have created something of enduring value that will outlive them. Educators and classmates may find it especially gratifying to assist these children in achieving such goals.

OTHER STUDENTS

When a student is coping with a terminal illness, classmates are also affected. Many of the common grief reactions that are described in earlier chapters might arise for classmates of a child who is seriously or terminally ill. These include sadness, grief, anxiety, hopelessness, and confusion. Peers might also feel a sense of loss about no longer being able to count on the world being a safe, predictable place.

One of the best ways teachers can support students generally is by pursuing some of the preparatory learning activities that are described in this book. If students have already been learning about death and grief in the normal course of their schoolwork through lessons and teachable moments, they will be much better prepared to understand and cope with a classmate who is terminally ill. The school might identify a school mental health professional or educator known for being approachable on sensitive topics, such as death and grief, to be an ongoing resource for students dealing with this situation. But the goal of supporting students when a peer or staff member is seriously or even terminally ill is not to explicitly prepare them for the death but rather to help them understand that the individual is seriously ill, what that means for that person and the students in the class, and how students can be of practical assistance.

Educators can also take specific steps when a student in their classroom is seriously ill. First, it is appropriate to check with the student's family to understand their wishes. Are they comfortable with the rest of the class knowing about their child's condition? How much may be disclosed? How much may be disclosed to students' families?

Ideally, families will agree that openness is the best policy, both for their child and for the other children in the school. Educators may want to talk to families about the rationale for open communication on the subject. It creates a more natural and supportive setting for their child—one where classmates can comfortably offer support and their child can ask clearly for what he or she needs.

It is also important to check directly with the students who are seriously ill. How much information are they comfortable sharing at the classroom level? How would they like their classmates to learn of the situation? Do they want their teacher to discuss this with the class? Would they like to explain the situation themselves? Would they like one of their health care providers to come talk to the class? Would they be interested in a sort of question–answer session in which they can talk about their health condition and answer people's questions?

Some children who are terminally ill want a high level of involvement in telling their classmates. Some find it difficult because they are shy, do not feel well, or do not want to answer personal questions. The goal is to find an approach that works for each child and gives classmates sufficient background about the situation.

This raises the issue of what *is* sufficient information for the class. In general, students benefit by understanding something about the underlying condition, its treatment, and the side effects of treatment. A discussion of the possible side effects of treatment could include both observable effects, such as weight gain or fatigue, and those that are not so obvious, such as learning difficulties, confusion, irritability, pain that can lead the child to express frustration, and so forth. The complexity of this information should be adapted to match children's developmental level and understanding. Risk of transmission is also a concern for many students who may believe that cancer can be passed from person to person (Chin et al., 1998) or that HIV may be passed through usual classroom activities (Schonfeld et al., 1993). Educators might also address the kind of support people with serious illness like to receive. Of course, the student who is ill can provide a helpful response to this question in particular.

The primary focus of these discussions should not be on death. It should be on the ways someone coping with a serious illness experiences his or her life. Nonetheless, children may at times ask directly or indirectly about the seriousness of the student's condition. The class can be told that the child's condition is serious, unlike many of the illnesses most children get that resolve quickly, with or without treatment. If it is consistent with the wishes of the student who is ill and his or her family, the class can be told that the medical team is doing everything possible to treat the condition but that, generally, this condition is not curable. These conversations can obviously be very sensitive. Educators should generally involve medical and/or mental health professionals in the classroom discussion.

The primary focus of discussions should be on the ways someone coping with a serious illness experiences his or her life.

It is also helpful to let the parents of other students know about these matters. Their children may have emotional responses to their classmate's illness, and they are likely to bring home questions and concerns. It would be helpful to provide parents basic facts about the affected student's condition, information about how the class learned about the situation, and guidance for talking with their children.

Parents should understand that this *is* a serious illness, different from most other illnesses that children experience. This can help them reassure their own children that they are not at significant risk for this or other serious illness. If treatment for the illness will have effects on the child that will be noticed by peers, it will be helpful for parents to understand what those might be. It can also be helpful to give parents guidelines for talking about contagion so they can reassure their children that they will not catch this illness. Educators may also want to refer parents to a reliable and informative online source of health information for children, such as the web site of the American Academy of Pediatrics (https://www.aap.org).

Some of these suggestions will be different for older students. Most high school students do not have a single class but, instead, switch classes throughout the day. The school can work with affected students and their families to find an approach that works. For example, a teen with a serious illness might ask that one or two classes deal with the matter more intensively. Or the teen might prefer to write a short statement that is read by the teacher in each class. Again, the goal is to explore different possibilities and find a solution that respects the student's wishes while providing appropriate support for all students.

Information for Parents of All Students

Information that may be helpful for parents of all students in the class includes:

- The name of the illness or condition

- The fact that the illness is serious and different from most other illnesses children experience

- Ways to reassure children who may be anxious about contracting the condition themselves

- Treatment approaches and possible observable side effects

- Misconceptions their children may have (e.g., about contagion)

- A reliable resource for further information for parents (e.g., web site, voluntary organization)

- Reassurance of the commitment of the class and the school to continue to provide an excellent education for all of the students in the class

My Teacher Would Be Perfect at This!

Seven-year-old Miles had been experiencing some general weakness in his legs. His parents watched him struggle at times, and his teacher noticed this, too. He could run but not quite as quickly as the other students. He could play outdoor games and activities, but he became tired quickly. Sometimes his physical education class was difficult for him.

Miles's parents arranged a medical evaluation, and he was diagnosed with Duchenne muscular dystrophy (DMD). This is a progressive disorder that leads, over time, to severe muscular disability. Many children with DMD require a wheelchair by adolescence. Their life span is considerably shortened, although new treatments are now allowing many to live longer.

Miles's parents told the boy about his diagnosis so that he could understand more about his symptoms and the reason for all the medical appointments and tests. They also spoke with his teacher about his condition and helped her plan appropriate classroom accommodations for their son.

Miles's classmates had also noticed his difficulties. They sometimes teased him for the slow pace of his running or for tiring out quickly. When he started a course of steroid treatments, he gained weight, and some children teased him about being fat. When teams were chosen for games, he was always one of the last chosen.

Miles talked to one of his doctors about these matters and decided that he would like his classmates to understand his condition. His mother had offered to come and talk to his class, but this idea embarrassed him. No one else's mother had come to the class to talk about her child. Miles didn't want his mother doing this.

The doctor suggested the boy could talk to the class himself. Miles didn't really feel that he knew enough about the condition because he was still learning about it. He was also quite shy, so standing up in front of the class sounded like a terrible idea to him.

The doctor then suggested that his mother give the background information to his teacher so that his teacher could talk to the class. Miles immediately brightened. "My teacher would be perfect at this!" he said enthusiastically. He turned to his mother in the middle of his clinic visit and said, "Can you call her right away?"

Teachers and School Staff

Educators and other school staff sometimes face serious illnesses as well. Many of these same principles of support will apply. Some educators will take a leave during their illness, whereas others may continue working. For those who continue working, it may be appropriate to provide information to students and parents should the effects of the illness become noticeable—treatment side effects or increased absences, for example. As with students who are ill, the focus can be on providing helpful information about the situation and the wish of the educator to continue to participate in a productive, meaningful life within the school community. Discussions might also review how the educator and school have made plans to provide continuity in students' educational activities should the educator need additional time off.

Our Librarian Is Sick

An actively engaged and well-liked librarian at an elementary school was diagnosed with stage IV cancer. The diagnosis was devastating, of course, but one of her greatest worries was how to prepare the students.

"What can I say?" she asked NCSCB. "I want to let my students know what is happening and answer their questions honestly—I'm going to have to take a leave, and I don't want them to feel abandoned or confused about why I'm gone. But I also don't want to burden them with the anticipation of my death."

We discussed some different possibilities with her. The approach she chose was to talk with students about the fact that she was seriously ill with cancer. She was able to spend a little bit of time in each classroom sharing this information. Because she knew that many children do not understand cancer well, she provided background information—that cancer is not like other illnesses, it is not contagious, and no one would "catch it" from her.

More than once, she was asked, "Are you going to die from this?" It was a blunt question, but she had prepared an answer.

"With the kind of cancer I have, it is not possible to say what will happen. What I can tell you is that I am alive today and doing everything I can to stay healthy. I am grateful every morning when I wake up and see the new day, and I hope all of you can feel that kind of happiness and gratitude in your lives, too."

This dedicated, compassionate educator was able to offer her students important information in a way that answered their questions, expressed her respect for them, and allowed them to enrich their own lives.

THE FAMILY OF A STUDENT WHO IS TERMINALLY ILL

As is true with families of grieving students, families of students who are terminally ill may turn to a trusted educator for support and guidance. Educators may want to initiate contact if they have not heard from a child's parents. As essential as it is for parents and educators to talk, parents are often too overwhelmed at these times to initiate contact themselves. Educators can offer suggestions that help a family cope with their feelings while providing the best possible support for their child. They can help parents identify resources for advice and support in the community or connect them with a mental health professional in the school who can provide specific recommendations.

About Siblings

The needs of siblings of a child who is seriously ill are often neglected. Parents, after all, have limited reserves of energy, time, and money. Their emotional resources are often stretched to the limit as their child's condition worsens. Educators checking in with families can ask about siblings. Educators who have the sibling of a child with a terminal illness in their class may find their involvement with the sibling to be critical to the child's academic success and emotional adjustment. The following are some suggestions of guidance to families:

- **A little attention can go a long way.** Many siblings understand the demands that parents are facing. Even a few moments of one-to-one attention can make a difference in the quality of their day. An occasional short walk together, a grocery store run, or an errand together can offer parents opportunities to stay connected to their other children.

- **Siblings should be informed about the ill child's health status and treatment plans.** Sometimes siblings are overlooked, especially when they are young. Parents may feel siblings would not understand what is happening or may simply feel they do not have the ability or time to explain it. This can leave siblings with the kind of anxiety that thrives around secrecy. What the child imagines might be happening is almost always worse than what is true.

  Siblings should understand that their brother or sister has a very serious illness. Once children who are terminally ill understand the seriousness of their condition, their siblings should be informed in an age-appropriate fashion as well. Siblings should also be given an opportunity to participate in the care of the ill child. Young children may be given simple tasks, such as bringing in cards from the mail and opening them, watering plants in the room, or bringing toys to a child in bed.

  It is important not to overload siblings with unreasonable chores or responsibilities, especially older children and adolescents. Continued involvement in activities outside the family—such as peer groups, sports teams, and after-school activities—is a valuable source of support for siblings, especially because support at home may be limited.

- **Siblings respond to these situations with the same range of emotions that adults do.** Siblings may be angry at the ill child for receiving all of the attention or for abandoning them. They may feel guilty about being healthy and surviving, or they may believe that they are responsible for the illness in some way. They may feel hopeless, sad, or confused about what to do to support their sibling.

- **School support is important.** Siblings' teachers should be informed of the family situation. School staff can make an extra effort to reach out to siblings of children who are terminally or seriously ill. Educators of siblings can also play a critical role in giving them support at a time when their families may have limited resources, time, and energy. Educators can watch for any signs of troubled behavior, and if a sibling has significant changes in academic or social behavior, a referral for counseling would be appropriate. Families may feel more reassured if they know that school staff are expressing special interest in the siblings.

  Some hospitals, clinics, hospice programs, disease-specific support groups or organizations, and schools provide programs or family support groups that are open to siblings of children with chronic or serious medical problems. School mental health or medical staff such as the school nurse, family pediatrician, or other health care provider may know of these resources.

Working with a student who is terminally ill is one of the most stressful personal and professional experiences an educator can face. It is important for educators to seek out resources for support. Strategies that educators can use for their own support are described in Chapter 14.

Key Concepts

- **Medical advances have made it possible for children with serious medical conditions to live longer and participate in school more fully.** It is not unusual for students at a terminal stage of illness to be in the classroom until very close to the time of death.

- **Educators can take certain steps to provide support to such students and their families.** These include communicating honestly, helping the child have positive interactions with classmates, and working with the child and family to determine what information should be shared with classmates and their families.

- **There are also steps educators can take to support the classmates of children who are seriously or terminally ill.** These include helping students understand more about the illness and its treatment, as well as how to receive support for oneself and provide support to others.

13

Memorialization and Commemoration

It is natural for people to want to remember, honor, and reflect on those who have died. We do these things through funerals, events that commemorate the deceased, the placements of memorial markers, and similar rituals.

When a member of the school community dies, there is also a need to publicly acknowledge the death. However, considerations in school settings are somewhat different from those in private ones. The choices schools make will have an impact on a large number of students and staff in the present *and* in the future. They also have an impact on the family and friends of the person who died.

Taking the time to develop appropriate general policies *before* a death occurs allows schools to make the best possible decisions for their setting and community. A number of guidelines will help these activities provide meaningful and positive support for students, staff, and families. When this kind of careful planning does not occur, it is far more likely that a commemoration or memorial will ultimately cause unintended negative consequences.

You can find a number of sample policies focusing on the issues addressed in this chapter at the web site for the Coalition to Support Grieving Students (https://grievingstudents.org/).

> **Taking the time to develop appropriate general policies before a death occurs allows schools to make the best possible decisions for their setting and community.**

The authors would like to acknowledge Thomas Demaria, Ph.D., for his assistance in reviewing and providing input for this chapter.

GOALS OF MEMORIALIZATION AND COMMEMORATION

Death can be confusing to survivors. Why did it happen? What is the purpose of life if this is all it comes to? Why is grief so painful? One of the reasons we develop memorials and commemorative events is to provide a framework in which survivors can begin to find answers to these questions. Typically, after the intense emotions of the initial grieving period, survivors search for meaning and purpose in the life of those who died. We remember something special they did, a contribution they made, or a way our life was changed because we knew them. We may be reminded by their death that life is precious—a gift to be appreciated every day. We may make our own commitments to do more to help others, be true to ourselves, reach our goals, or appreciate our lives.

Children can find helpful support through involvement in different phases of the commemorative process (see Schonfeld, 2002). Initially, commemorative activities or events help children accept the reality of the loss. They also provide an opportunity for them to express and cope with difficult feelings that might otherwise seem overwhelming to confront alone. They can draw on the support of a caring community—their peers, teachers, and school- or community-based counseling staff. They can learn from others who are also facing these challenging feelings, and everyone can share techniques for coping. Subsequent commemorative activities can give children language for making meaning and for further discussion with their parents or other family members.

Commemorative activities in school settings following the initial bereavement period do not need to be elaborate. Often, a brief and simple activity is all that is needed. This might be a short class discussion about the ways that students want to remember the life or contributions of the person who died. When schools do plan a more structured or lasting memorial, the process will be most helpful if the following guidelines are kept in mind.

Give Students a Voice

It is vital that students have a role in planning how to commemorate a classmate, teacher, or other member of the school community who has died. What event is planned is actually far less important than *how* it is planned. When children take the lead, they can suggest activities that are relevant to their circumstances and developmental needs. They will think of activities that have meaning to them—and these sometimes are not the same things that have meaning to adults. Children have many creative and unique ideas, and they often think of things adults do not.

It is more productive for children to remember someone in a way that they have chosen and that has meaning for them than it is to walk mechanically through a ritual someone else has selected. By choosing an activity or a ceremony that speaks to them, children are putting effective ways to cope with their grief directly into practice. They and their classmates are modeling coping together. They are learning about positive ways to deal with painful emotions such as grief that will serve them in their future lives.

It is vital that students have a role in planning how to commemorate a classmate, teacher, or other member of the school community who has died.

Children are also taking some measure of control in a situation that might otherwise leave them feeling quite powerless. They may not have been able to prevent the death. They may not be able to stop their own feelings of sadness. However, choosing what they want most to remember and how they want to express that remembrance is an important way for them to experience greater self-determination. Going through this process can help them increase their confidence that they can master some of the difficult feelings that accompany grief.

Another important reason for involving children in planning a commemorative activity is that when this is not done, students often prematurely come up with their own means of memorialization. Under some circumstances, these informal memorials can pose problems (see "Spontaneous Memorials" later in this chapter).

Planting Flowers

After the death of a fourth-grade student, the school organized a memorial assembly for her classmates and others who had known her. The principal and several teachers spoke to the group about their classmate. The adults remembered what a kind child she had been and how much she had enjoyed helping others. They reminded the students of how much she had enjoyed nature and gardens.

At the end of the assembly, the principal told the students that they were all going to go outside and plant flowers in the garden as a special way to remember their classmate. The children formed a line and each was given a small flower to plant. They went outside and found the flower bed prepared and ready. The teachers helped them put the flowers into the soil. The students stood back and watched as one of the gardeners carefully watered the newly planted flowers. Then they returned to their class.

The principal and teachers found the planting of the flowers quite emotional. The students, however, were not as moved by the activity. This wasn't the thing that they remembered most about their classmate. They weren't entirely sure what the flowers had to do with their friend's death. During the assembly, they hadn't been able to express their feelings or hear from one another about how they were coping with the loss. Although they politely went through the motions of planting their flowers, the activity did not give them a greater sense of control or a deeper understanding of their own feelings.

Although the flower planting was clearly a useful symbol for the adults involved in this memorial, it was of little help for the students themselves. They would have been better served by an activity they had chosen that allowed them to acknowledge and express their own feelings.

Help Students Plan a Positive Activity

Teachers, school mental health staff, or other school staff can help children develop an activity that makes sense for students. In the initial period after a death, a helpful way to start is engaging the children in a discussion that explores their feelings and how they are coping. They can then talk about ways these can both be expressed in the activity. Teachers and school administrators often worry that such discussions, or the commemorative activities themselves, will upset students. Of course, it is the death of someone they know and care about that is the true source of distress, not these conversations about it. Having the conversation also allows educators to observe what students are feeling and thinking. It is better for these things to be out in the open, where children can receive support, than for children to feel they need to keep their feelings hidden.

These conversations work best when staff facilitate open-ended discussions with students. Asking questions and listening to answers provides much useful information. It is important to avoid the temptation to tell students how they should be feeling about the death. Although adults can offer suggestions, especially to initiate the conversation for younger children, the children themselves should suggest their own ideas regarding the approach they believe will best express their feelings and facilitate remembrance. Educators can offer sufficient guidance so students do not feel burdened by a sense of responsibility for the design and implementation of the activity.

Some open-ended questions that educators can ask to start the conversation may include the following:

- **What do you remember about the person who died?** This question provides a wide-open palette for children to remember and remind each other of the things that were important to them. In a fully open discussion, students might include both positive and negative qualities about the person or some unpleasant memories about the person's illness.

- **What do you want to remember about the person?** This allows children to filter through their memories and focus on those that are positive.

- **What are some ways we could take time to observe or mark these remembrances?** Let students suggest a range of ideas. Some may be completely impractical, whereas others may be movingly poignant. Often, students come up with ideas that are both pragmatic and simple—a 10-minute remembrance in which students can say a few words if they wish, or a picture that the group makes for the family of the person who died.

Once several ideas are on the table, students can work with their teacher or other staff to select those that seem best in their situation. This gives students the opportunity to express their ideas and feelings in the group, come to a shared understanding about the commemorative activity, and collectively identify a meaningful and helpful way to commemorate the person who died. When students can participate in planning and carrying out their own ideas, the results are likely to have greater relevance for them. The following story is a good example.

What Shall We Do With His Desk?

Two schools experienced similar tragedies. In each case, a child found a gun, played with it, and accidentally discharged it. In both instances, a second-grade student was killed. In each classroom, the surviving students were confused and troubled about what to do with the desk of the student who died.

No one wanted to sit at it. No one wanted it removed because that would feel like they were forgetting their classmate. No one wanted it sitting there empty because every time they came into their classroom, they all looked right at the empty desk and remembered the tragic circumstances of their classmate's death.

Clearly, something needed to be done to symbolize each class's grief, sense of remembrance, and commitment to move forward. But what would it be?

In each case, the students themselves came up with a solution, but each class came up with a different idea. Both of these ideas worked well for their particular class.

In the first class, the students all talked about what they wanted to remember about the student who had died. They decided they wanted to honor his strengths. He had been a good reader who loved books and encouraged other students to read. They chose to move his desk to a corner in the back of the classroom and place a selection of books on the desk. Students with free time could sit at the desk. They could read a book of their own or choose one from those placed on the desk. They could remember their classmate while they improved their skills at reading—something they all knew he would appreciate.

In the second class, the students decided to clear all of the desks in the room of personal possessions. They stacked all of their books, papers, and pencils on their chairs. The custodians came into the class that night and scrubbed all of the desks clean. Then the custodian rearranged them so no desk was in the same place it had originally been.

The next day, students went back to their chairs and saw before them a freshly scrubbed, thoroughly cleaned desk. The desk of the student who had died was among them, but no one knew exactly where. They liked knowing his desk was still part of the classroom. As they filled their "new" desks with their possessions, all of the students had a sense that they were making a fresh start.

When choosing how to commemorate a student who died, students and educators can consider some of the hallmarks of a positive commemorative activity. These may include some of the following:

- **The activity makes sense to students.** The commemorative activities speak to their interests, needs, and memories of the deceased. Participants have an opportunity to feel their grief, try to make sense of what has happened, and feel hopeful about the future.

- **An opportunity is provided for students to share coping techniques with their peers.** Some part of the planning, the commemoration, or the discussion afterward includes students sharing feelings that they have had in response to the death and how they are coping with these feelings.

- **Students' emotional lives are respected.** A wide range of emotions is a normal part of grief. Students should understand that it is okay to have strong feelings—or to not have them. Students can be encouraged to talk about the things they are thinking and feeling before, during, or after the commemoration. Support should be available to students who wish to talk with a school mental health professional about their responses, either in the period immediately after the death or many months into the future.

- **There is a focus on helping students learn to manage and cope with their feelings about this and other losses.** From these experiences, students understand that when people have strong feelings related to grief or other issues, they can take steps to receive support.

- **The function and purpose of the school is kept at the forefront—learning, education, and promoting well-being and health.** Informed schools understand that the death of a student or staff member will have a profound effect on some members of the school community. Such schools provide support for the school as a whole as well as individual students and staff. They understand that grief can be distracting and challenging. They respect the grief process and the needs of the school community. They also keep focused on their primary functions. They return to usual routines and a focus on learning as soon as they reasonably and sensitively can.

CHALLENGES FOR SCHOOLS

Schools face a number of challenges in planning and managing commemorative activities and formal memorializations. These are the sorts of issues that are best dealt with proactively, before a death occurs. For example:

- **Some events might glamorize risky or self-destructive behaviors.** If a student has died by suicide, other vulnerable students may find the attention of memorialization appealing. A student who feels isolated or depressed might think, "I'd like to be remembered this way," or, "I wonder if the people who have ignored me would feel as sad if I died." Students may have similar thoughts about a fellow student who was a victim of a gang-related killing. Attention given to the death might inadvertently glamorize gang violence or play a role in provoking retaliation.

  Memorials for a student who died while engaging in other risky behaviors might also make these activities more tempting. This could include such things as a drug overdose, drag racing, a game of chicken, or climbing to the top of a local landmark. Formal memorialization in this context may contribute to the desire of peers to create a narrative casting the death in a more heroic fashion, rather than seeing it as a consequence of a poor decision or impaired thinking.

- **Students may be confused about what is expected.** If students did not know the deceased well, they may be uncertain about how much to say, what they are supposed to feel, and whether they are obligated to participate in a ceremony. If they choose not to participate, they may become the focus of criticism or even bullying by peers. If they *did* know the person who died well, they may feel that some aspects of a broadly drawn memorial trivialize the death and that people who did not care much for the person in life seem to be using the death as a way to draw attention to themselves. Students who did not get along with the deceased may feel it is inauthentic to participate in a remembrance but feel pressured to do so.

- **Precedents are set.** When a student is remembered in an official school capacity, a precedent is set. If a school puts great effort and resources into memorializing a popular student who dies tragically in a car crash, what steps will it take a year later when a lesser-known student dies? If something less is done, what message is given to that student's family and friends or to other quiet, less well-known students in the school?

  Furthermore, what is done about students who die while engaging in risky or illegal activities? What about a student who dies by suicide? Situations quickly become complicated if all memorializations are not generally similar in scope.

- **Markers, plaques, or other memorials often send mixed messages.** Some memorialization approaches are more likely to disturb students than console them. For example, if many students in a community have died by violence and a school memorializes them by planting a tree in a special "peace grove" each time a student dies, what do students see in these trees? Are they constantly reminded that they live in a neighborhood of extreme violence and that many of their classmates are not living to adulthood? Instead of helping them cope with their grief and move forward in their lives, the trees may feel more like a body count. Students might wonder when their own trees will be planted.

- **Memorials may be vandalized, damaged accidently, or fall into disrepair.** This can be painful to the family of the deceased, and it can also communicate a sense of disrespect for the deceased or what they represent.

GUIDELINES FOR RECOGNIZING AND REMEMBERING

Some schools have established policies for recognizing and remembering students or staff who have died. Policies can help schools encourage the planning of appropriate commemorative activities—those that benefit students and staff and help them cope with their grief. When policies or guidelines are in place, they can also help schools avoid some of the common difficulties with memorialization just described.

Memorial and Funeral Services

Chapter 3 discusses some of the reasons it is helpful for children to attend the funerals of friends and family members. When a death touches an entire school, however, the question of how to plan for student and staff attendance becomes more complicated.

Schools should check with the family of the deceased to see if they have any wishes about students or staff attending the service. If many people in the school knew the deceased, students and staff may be able to participate in visitation outside of school hours. Ideally, the service itself would also be scheduled for a time when school is not in session. This helps minimize disruption of the school's schedule. It also makes it easier for students to attend with their families, which is generally the best choice for children and teens attending funerals or memorial services.

If the service is during school hours, schools may want to set a policy about student absences. For example, students who have permission from their parents may be excused to attend. Substitutes can be arranged for teachers and other school staff who wish to attend. It might also be helpful to have school mental health staff present at a memorial or funeral service that is likely to be attended by many students as a show of support and to offer comfort. It will also be helpful to have them available at the school after the service.

Attendance at services should be completely voluntary. Sometimes, students feel pressured to attend services by peers, even if it is not what they want to do. Requiring parental permission to attend may allow reluctant students to communicate to peers that this was a decision guided by their parents' wishes. If regular classes can go forward as scheduled, they should. Students who have missed class activities to attend a funeral may need some extra help catching up on assignments or going over the content of missed classwork.

Attendance at services should be completely voluntary.

Funerals and Memorials on Campus

Sometimes, families ask to hold a funeral or memorial on the school grounds. We recommend against this in public school settings. Allowing one family to arrange a funeral on campus can set a precedent for a practice that would not be constructive in all situations. For example, it might not be productive to host the funeral of a student who died by suicide or while committing a crime. It is also problematic if a school becomes the de facto "funeral home of last resort" for large events or for families who cannot afford the cost of a funeral home. These events can also be disturbing to students and create uncomfortable associations with the site in the school where the service was held.

Religious schools may set different policies—for example, memorial services or funerals might appropriately be arranged at an on-campus chapel.

It is still important for students to understand that attendance is voluntary and that their decision about attending the service is a personal one. Whether they do or do not attend, their choice does not reflect negatively on their faith or their relationship with the deceased.

One of the greatest benefits of setting up these types of policies *before* decisions need to be made is that they allow administrators to respond fairly and consistently in highly charged, emotional situations. Decisions do not appear arbitrary to families. Administrators and other educators can emphasize that these policies are in place in service of schools' primary commitment, which is the education and well-being of their students.

A Simple Memorial, Here at the School

The family of a high school student was devastated when he was hit by a car and killed while crossing a street near the school. Because he was well-liked and had many friends at the school, the family requested the opportunity to host a funeral service for their son on campus. The superintendent, feeling this loss deeply herself, offered to assist in any way possible. The service was set up in the school's gymnasium. The family arranged to have their son's casket on site for the event, and although attendance was optional, many students and staff participated in the service.

In the days after the service, some students expressed discomfort being in the gym. It was difficult for them to set aside thoughts of this tragic death and the suffering of their classmate. Some didn't want to go into the gym at all. Others complained about being distracted from their school work. The superintendent reached out to a school bereavement specialist for guidance.

This was the first time she heard the recommendation that memorial services not be held on campus. Because of the reactions within her own district after the on-campus funeral, she could see the wisdom of this advice. As she implemented a plan to provide support for students at the school in question, she also worked with the school board to draw up a policy prohibiting on-campus memorials in the future.

A few weeks later, another student death occurred in the district. The family of that student also requested an on-campus event and was hurt and angry to hear that district policy now prohibited such events. Their understandable response complicated the ability of the school to provide support to that family and to the younger siblings of the deceased who were also students in the district. This is a good example of the benefits of having policies in place before they are needed.

Spontaneous Memorials

Informal memorials often quickly "spring up" after the death of a student or teacher. People might place flowers, notes, photos, books, stuffed animals, and other sentimental items somewhere on the school grounds. The memorials might also involve written messages on walls, along walkways, or on lockers.

There is not necessarily anything wrong with informal memorials on school property. In fact, it is helpful to have a memorial close by, where it can be monitored (discussed later in this chapter). Students and staff may find them helpful in the initial expression of their grief. However, it is important for schools to place limits, as appropriate, and quickly determine how long such a memorial is left in place. Usually a few days to a week is appropriate.

The school should clearly communicate the plan to students (e.g., "The memorial will be removed on Friday afternoon."). Describe what contributions are acceptable, such as letters, notes, and photos, but clarify that permanent marking of school property is not allowed. Often, students place significant emotional value on items left at a memorial. Let students know that a thoughtful and sensitive plan will be enacted that will preserve the sentiments expressed in these items. Students can be assured, for example, that photographs will be taken of the items before they are removed, and these images will be shared with the family of the deceased. (We recommend using photos because bereaved families may find that the sorting and storage of actual memorial materials is an additional burden on them during a time of great loss.) Students should be invited to check with administrators or school mental health staff if they have any questions or concerns about the memorial.

Sometimes the content at informal memorials can be a problem. They should be monitored regularly in case something inappropriate is placed at the site (e.g., a bottle of beer, a suggestive photograph). They should also be checked to ensure that students do not post harmful messages. For example, after a student has died by suicide, someone might write a message that says, "You made the right decision." If someone died in a gang-related incident, a message might say, "I'll find the person who did this and make sure he joins you." In other cases, students may contribute messages that are negative or critical about the person who died. They might say, "You were a jerk," or "This couldn't have happened to a better person. I'm glad you're gone." These are obviously hurtful and inappropriate and need to be removed.

Monitoring of spontaneous memorials that appear in the community rather than on school property can be challenging. The location of the memorial is often near the place where the student died. It can be difficult for school personnel to regularly access the site to check for inappropriate materials or messaging or supervise student activities there. It is not unusual to see evidence of substantial substance use in some of these spots—community memorials are often littered with empty bottles of alcohol or drug paraphernalia. The setting may also incite other risk-taking behavior, especially if the location is dangerous, such as near the railroad tracks where a student died by suicide. Having students linger in a secluded area while sad and abusing substances is particularly worrisome when in close proximity to a lethal means of suicide. Coordination with local law enforcement may be helpful. (See Chapter 10 for more detailed information about responding to a death by suicide.)

Providing alternative commemorative opportunities for students and engaging them early on in planning the response efforts may help minimize interest in informal memorials. Students may benefit from creative writing projects addressing their feelings about such things as the person who died, personal losses they have experienced themselves, or how to remember people we care for who have died. Art projects or other creative endeavors may also help students express their thoughts and feelings.

Guidelines for Spontaneous Memorials

Some guidelines that schools have found helpful include the following:

- Set a reasonable length for the memorials to be in place, usually a few days to a week. Communicate the plan to students.

- Ensure that objects placed at the memorial do not interfere with access to lockers, classrooms, stairs, walkways, or emergency exits. Work with students to identify an alternate site if necessary. Usual safety standards should be maintained.

- If necessary, move a memorial to a new location, away from areas where students and staff need to pass or congregate each day. This allows students and staff to actively decide whether to visit or avoid the area.

- Let students know that content will be monitored and inappropriate objects or messages, even if they are well-intended, will be removed.

- Invite students to check with administrators or school mental health staff if they have any questions about or responses to the memorial.

- Monitor the memorial and student reactions regularly throughout the day. Remind students that visiting the site may be helpful for some, but not all, students.

- Discourage the development of personal commemorative items (e.g., wrist bands, shirts) and messaging (e.g., "Never Forget"). It is difficult for schools to limit how long these items can be displayed because they are the personal property of students. Although initially these gestures can be a way children and families express their grief, they can become problematic in the long term. Over time, the words and symbols may trigger and distract students who feel ready to focus on their studies. Students may feel pressure from peers to continue to wear these items even when they are ready to set them aside.

  When students do appear wearing these kinds of commemorative items, schools can suggest limits on how long it is appropriate to bring them to school. Do so with sensitivity to the meaning the items carry for students, and express the limits as a way of being supportive of their peers and building a stronger school community moving forward.

I Must Find a New Shirt!

A high school experienced the death of a popular student. His friends created a commemorative T-shirt emblazoned with a slogan he had often used. They were pleased and gratified when students throughout the school purchased the shirts and began to wear them daily. The shirt quickly became a symbol of belonging to the popular clique of students—or of the aspiration to be a part of that group.

One morning, a student's mother called the school leadership, frantic. "I washed my daughter's commemorative shirt and it was destroyed in the laundry! She cannot attend class until I'm able to locate another one for her."

After this, the principal spoke with some of the deceased student's close friends. She explained the reasons wearing the shirts could create problems for their classmates and talked with them about other ways they might continue remembering and honoring their friend. Each day after that, fewer students wore the shirts until they rarely appeared on the campus.

Using Virtual Memorials to Remember Those Who Have Died

It is common these days for virtual memorials to appear on Facebook or other social media platforms or on a newspaper's obituary page. Sometimes, families or friends want to keep the page of a deceased student active so messages and remembrances can be posted at the time of death and on into the future. These can be effective ways to deliver condolences, receive support, and remain connected to the deceased. They can also facilitate continued connections to the family of the student who died.

As mentioned in Chapter 5, educators can offer advice and guidance for these situations that is consistent with other social media education—be thoughtful about what you post, be thoughtful about what you read. Avoid posting comments that are negative or hurtful. Take a break if reading comments becomes overwhelming; it isn't necessary to read every post. If you are being harassed in some way, seek support from an appropriate adult. If negative comments are having an emotional impact on you, find someone to talk to.

Timing of Commemorative Activities at School

Although there is no "right" framework of time for personal bereavement, the overall goal for the school is to recognize feelings about the death, remember the deceased, *and* move forward in a sensitive way with their main function: the education of children.

In the immediate aftermath of a death, the focus should be on notifying students and staff and providing them with opportunities to receive emotional support. It is important to give the school community a certain amount of time and space in which to notice and understand their emotions and thoughts about the death. Deaths of members of the school community are major events. Their impact takes time to emerge.

Activities to memorialize someone who has died can begin too quickly. Steps such as raising money for a scholarship fund to honor a teacher who died are sometimes begun within hours, or even minutes, of the death being announced. When this happens, energy is diverted from the immediate emotional experiences that students and staff are having. People often get the sense that emotional closure is expected rapidly. This discourages children and adults from experiencing their emotions fully. Students, staff, parents, or the community in general may feel the school is rushing to "close the chapter" on grieving.

We know of school districts that have a policy that no building, room, or other area on campus can be named after someone who has died until at least a year after the death. This provides ample time for people to move beyond the immediate period of acute grief. After a year, they will be better able to consider a variety of factors in planning an appropriate recognition.

Commemorative activities or reminders that go on too long can also be a problem for students and staff. Feelings of sadness or confusion may be prolonged instead of being allowed to gradually decrease in intensity. Students or staff may believe they are expected to continue to express the loss in an immediate and powerful way, even if this is not authentically what they are feeling.

It can be helpful to think of this process in three phases. The initial focus is on expressing feelings and coping with the loss. In the second phase, commemorative activities can shift attention to remembering the person who died. In the third, the focus can be on legacy and meaning-making, with activities addressing what can be learned from the experience of loss and how to apply these lessons in the future.

Sometimes, conflicts arise about the type or length of a memorial effort. The loss is felt most profoundly by the family of a student who died or the student's closest friends. They might wish for a constant reminder, such as a marker, photos, or a semi-permanent installation of flowers or candles, often because they worry that students and staff might otherwise forget someone so central to the family's lives. Other students or staff might feel distracted by persistent reminders of an event that was traumatic or that did not affect them as deeply. Even students who were close to the deceased may be confused by a protracted memorial process. When these efforts are sustained for a long time, they may give children the impression that they must continue to hold on to their grief as a way to maintain their memory of the person who died.

This is not the message that should be given to children or the model that should be provided. This is why, in school settings, it is important to establish mechanisms by which different members of the school community can express their needs and views on how to best meet these needs and, as a community, reach a respectful compromise. This might include students and their families, administrators, teachers, school mental health staff, and other school staff. Staff can also determine the wishes of the family of the deceased and communicate these to the school community.

When schools listen to this varied input, they can mediate and guide decisions to align with best practices. This promotes the adjustment of the majority of students and the primary mission of school, which is teaching and learning. In situations where the desires of family members of the deceased differ from the needs of students, administrators must ensure that the primary focus remains on the surviving students and staff.

This is one of the reasons the Coalition to Support Grieving Students (https://grievingstudents.org/) was created—to build a consensus among professional organizations about best practices in these situations. It is difficult for any school to satisfy all of the different wishes and perspectives when a member of the school community has died or a school has experienced a crisis. This process of gathering different views and working toward informed choices supports school leadership in making decisions that are sometimes difficult.

Our Boy's Favorite Toy

Gilbert, a student in the kindergarten class, died suddenly, shortly before the winter holidays. He was an only child, and his parents, who had filled their lives with his interests and activities, were devastated by his death.

The children in his class were told of the death, as were other students in the school. The kindergarten teacher and one of the school counselors worked closely with the children and their families during this time to make sure the students understood what had happened and felt comfortable expressing their feelings about it. They all seemed to be managing well.

When the school presented its annual holiday concert, the kindergarten class sang a beautiful winter song. Gilbert's parents came to see the concert and brought along their son's favorite toy—a small plush bunny with floppy ears. They chose their seats in the auditorium and sat the bunny on the seat between them.

All of the families around them noticed, and some were moved to tears. A few spoke to the parents after the event and said how glad they were to see them there. Many of the children in Gilbert's class were saddened when they saw the boy's parents and his favorite toy. A few cried. A couple of the children said they felt bad having the concert because now they were remembering their classmate. Their teacher reassured them that the concert was a good thing to do and did not in any way take away from their feelings about their classmate.

In February, the kindergarten class had a special event for President's Day. Students told stories about Abraham Lincoln and George Washington and sang patriotic songs. Then they had apples and punch. Some of the parents attended. Gilbert's parents appeared, once more bringing their son's bunny and giving it a seat. Again, some of the children were upset. Should they be celebrating President's Day? Was it right to have a party? The teacher overheard two of the students talking about the toys their parents would bring if they died.

At the end of the year, the class was planning its graduation. By this time, the teacher was uncomfortable with what she called "the bunny situation." She saw that it was distressing the children and thought this ongoing reminder of Gilbert's death was not helpful. A few of her students' parents had also raised the issue. She asked the principal to speak with Gilbert's parents.

The principal did not agree. "These parents have lost their child. These simple events obviously offer them some degree of comfort. Can't we just give this to them? They have lost so much."

The parents came to kindergarten graduation, and the bunny came along.

This pattern continued as the children grew older. The bunny came to winter and spring concerts, school fairs, and other special events. As the years went by, Gilbert's former classmates were reminded of him each time they achieved something themselves. New students came into the school who had not known Gilbert. "What's with the bunny?" they would ask. "Oh, you'll get used to him," other students would answer.

In a sense, however, the students did not really "get used to" the bunny. It continued to be a reminder to them that they had moved forward while the boy the bunny represented stayed frozen in time. The parents showed them an immobile state of grief—unable to make true meaning in their lives without their son's presence. These children were burdened unfairly, compelled to continue carrying grief for this child they had known only briefly and long ago. The parents may have believed the bunny helped keep the memory of their child alive. In fact, for many of the classmates, it had become a reminder not of Gilbert's life, but only of his death. It was not a healthy way to model and practice bereavement.

The bunny situation ended after sixth-grade graduation. At that point, the children moved on to a larger school. The principal had never quite been able to tell the parents that the bunny had become a disturbing reminder, not an honorable remembrance, of their son. If the school had established a different process for making decisions, this situation could have been resolved early on before it became a problem for the students. For example, the school crisis team, which usually includes mental health staff, teachers, and administrators, could have worked through the situation with the principal. Together, they would most likely have found a better solution to this difficult and delicate situation.

A Way to Remember Them All

A school experienced a tragic shooting in which three students were killed. Almost immediately, people began to talk about a memorial to the victims. A small work group came up with the idea of creating a sculpture garden for the town green that would include full-size, lifelike sculptures of each of the students who died. A parent of one of the victims designed the project. The mayor and town council quickly approved the plan.

In this town, every public building surrounded the town green. Students passed by it on their way to school. Families went along the pathways on their way to the library. The police department and courthouse faced the green.

The problem with this heartfelt and sincere plan is that it was developed very quickly, with few people offering input. There were no opportunities to imagine and consider other ideas. As citizens began to hear about it, some voiced concern. One student said, "I will see these sculptures every day on my way to school. They won't remind me of my classmates. They will remind me of their murder."

Fortunately, the group that developed the memorial was willing to reconsider their plan. More people became involved in the process. Ultimately, the town decided to design and install playgrounds in three different locations throughout the town. The playgrounds would recognize those who had died by creating a physical place where other children were allowed to simply play and be children.

COMMEMORATION AFTER A SCHOOLWIDE CRISIS

When an incident involves multiple deaths or otherwise profoundly affects an entire school, plans are often made for commemoration at the 1-year mark. As with any other school-focused memorial or commemoration, it is important to involve students in the planning. Students need an opportunity to identify what will be useful for them. Educators can play an essential role in encouraging student voices and offering support and guidance. (See Chapter 9 for more suggestions about responding to a schoolwide crisis.)

Schools that have experienced these events often find it useful to offer a range of choices for students. Depending on the situation, families and community members may be invited to participate. Some options might focus on self-care (yoga, mindfulness). Others might invite reflection and conversation (writing workshop, small-group discussions) or positive social exchanges (noncompetitive outdoor games, a guided nature walk, a group breakfast).

Service-oriented activities also resonate well with students and communities around the country. These usually require more planning than other events. However, service learning has been shown to support social and emotional learning as well as academic performance. Allowing students to provide service to others can be both empowering and healing.

Guidelines for Commemorations Marking a Schoolwide Crisis

- Involve students in planning the events.

- Offer a range of options when possible.

- Avoid language about the "anniversary" of the incident, which suggests celebration. Instead, you might use language such as "1-year mark," "commemoration," "remembrance," or "observance."

- Emphasize that participation in these events is voluntary. No one is required to attend.

- It is not necessary to plan the commemoration on the actual anniversary date of the incident. A nearby date is also acceptable. In regions with severe winter weather, it might be more practical to mark the event in the spring in order to offer a broader range of outdoor or community-based service activities.

- In some situations, it may be appropriate to plan commemorative events at 2- or 3-year marks as well.

In one high school that suffered a shooting with multiple injuries and deaths, a day of remembrance was planned at the 1-year mark. Students were required to check in at the school in the morning to register their attendance. They could then select one of several monitored activities on campus. Free breakfast and lunch were offered, and school mental health staff were available for small-group or individual conversations.

After lunch, students could choose to participate in a special half-day of service in the community. They could attend in groups or with their families (the school did not want students to be alone at this time). Students had identified a number of projects or charities that aligned with the interests of each victim. The school had arranged service opportunities at these organizations.

Students who participated in these activities were encouraged to choose a focus that had meaning for them personally. They were reminded that by going to any of these events, they were honoring all of the victims. That evening, there was also a communitywide event at a local park.

Examples of Commemorative Activities Schools Have Used

- Beach cleanup

- Musical performance by students

- Serving meals to first responders who assisted during the crisis

- Mindfulness activities

- Yoga workshops

- Helping at an animal shelter

- Reclaiming a vacant lot

- Drawing cards for hospitalized children, military service members, residents of nursing homes, etc.

- Art projects

- Going to a nearby elementary school to read a story to younger students

---

MONITORING EXPRESSIONS OF GRIEF

Sometimes students wish to write letters or draw pictures to send to the family of the deceased. Before such activities, talk with students about what might be most helpful to the family. Sometimes, students believe that the family would like to know how emotionally upset they are. They may want to provide suggestions about how the family can cope with their loss. Help students understand that most grieving families appreciate specific memories about their child. They will welcome stories about the ways their child was valued by his or her peers. This can help guide what students draw or write. (Because writing or drawing pictures can be a useful way for students to express and process their personal feelings, it is also acceptable to do these activities for that reason alone, without necessarily sharing them with the family.)

Consider when it will be best to deliver the letters or pictures. In the immediate aftermath of a death, a family may not have the ability or desire to see them. Schools can check with the family to choose a time that works best for them.

It is also essential that any of these materials be reviewed before they are sent out to make sure they are appropriate and will not be disturbing to the family. It is also possible that some students will express troublesome thoughts, such as feelings of despair and hopelessness or thoughts of suicide.

It is not usually helpful for educators or school administrators to interpret students' drawings or writing—these assessments take specialized experience and training. However, if they observe content that raises concerns, it would be prudent to ask a mental health professional in the school to review the materials and, if indicated, speak with the student who produced them. It is not unusual for a death to bring up painful memories or thoughts, and written or drawn expressions of grief can be an outlet that brings these forward.

We recommend against activities that solicit anonymous statements, such as posting large pieces of paper or using social media sites where students can write out their thoughts and comments about the deceased without identifying themselves. Some students have written disturbing comments in such activities—threatening suicide or harm to others, for example—and school staff cannot identify these students to intervene. In some instances, especially after posts have been up for a few days, critical or negative comments about the deceased appear. This is damaging for everyone in the school. Such posts should be removed immediately.

Affirming a Range of Responses

When someone in the school community dies, students and staff will have a range of responses. Some individuals will have a closer relationship to or stronger identification with the person who died. Some will have other problems in their lives that have been creating a burden. They may be especially vulnerable to powerful feelings of anxiety or sadness when they learn of the death. Some may have little emotional response at all, perhaps only a cordial concern for the surviving family members or a passing sadness that someone has died.

It is important to affirm this full range of expressions when talking to students about their feelings. Just as we cannot predict with certainty who in a group of students may be deeply affected by a death, we cannot know the students for whom the death will have little impact.

Children should not feel pressured or coerced into showing their grief. It is not necessary to refer them to a mental health professional if they have not shed tears after the death of someone close. The goal, after all, is to support students in having *authentic* feelings and thoughts and to give them guidance to move along in the process at a pace that is appropriate for them. If children believe there is a particular way they are supposed to act or something they are supposed to do, they will not have an opportunity to truly learn about grief, loss, or managing their own emotions.

Just as we cannot predict with certainty who may be deeply affected by a death, we cannot know the students for whom the death will have little impact.

Am I Supposed to Go to the Funeral?

Cheyenne, a middle school student, was saddened to learn one Monday morning that the mother of one of her classmates had died over the weekend. She didn't know the girl well, but she had no trouble imagining that this was an extremely painful experience.

The girl's friends wanted to find ways to support her. "The funeral is tomorrow," they told Cheyenne. "We're all wearing purple that day as a sign of our support. And we need to get permission from our parents to leave school early to go to the funeral. Don't forget!"

Cheyenne was confused. She had great sympathy for the girl, but she wasn't a close friend. She had never met the mother. She didn't know the family.

She also didn't have anything purple to wear—she never liked the color. Was she supposed to go buy something to wear the next day? Was she supposed to get permission from her parents to go to the funeral of someone she didn't know? She hadn't been to a funeral before, and it seemed odd and sort of dishonest to her to contemplate going to this one.

Many of Cheyenne's friends were planning to attend the funeral. What would they think of her, she wondered, if she showed up in another color? What if she skipped the funeral? Would they think she was stuck up? Would she be left out of social events in the future if she didn't participate?

Cheyenne liked her English teacher a lot. After class, Cheyenne asked her what she thought she should do. Her teacher assured her that she did not need to attend the funeral and that she should only take steps that felt honest and authentic to her. She encouraged Cheyenne to talk to her parents about her concerns.

Cheyenne did talk to her parents, and, with their help, they came up with a solution. First, she let her friends know that she wasn't going to attend the funeral, and she explained why. They were disappointed but accepted her explanation. Then she asked her mother to help her choose an outfit for school. They found one that felt both comfortable and true for Cheyenne—a simple dark blue T-shirt and slacks. She attended classes as usual and wished her friends well as they departed for the funeral service.

When the girl whose mother died returned to school a week later, Cheyenne approached her and said, "I was sorry to hear about your mother's death." The girl smiled and thanked her.

COMMEMORATION AT TIME OF GRADUATION

When it is time for students to graduate, how can schools best remember a student or educator who has died? What is appropriate? What is helpful?

The overarching principle for a graduation ceremony is that it exists to celebrate the achievements of the class cohort. It may also be a time when memories arise of loved ones who have died—for example, a student wishes his father, who died several years ago, could see him graduate. If a student within the cohort has died, this will also be on the minds of students and staff. When thinking about commemorative actions, it is important to acknowledge these kinds of feelings while keeping the focus on the achievement of graduation. This is not the setting for deep tributes to someone who has died.

Guiding Principles for Commemoration at Time of Graduation

1. This is an occasion for students, families, and the school community to celebrate the achievements of the class cohort and accomplishments of individual students as they embark on the next stage of their academic or vocational development.

2. Milestones such as graduation are times when memories of those who have died arise.

3. Commemoration of students or staff who have died may help people continue to process their loss. It can also reassure family members that their loved ones are remembered.

4. Some students and staff may not be emotionally ready to process their loss. Others may choose to focus their attention on celebration rather than grief. This full range of needs must be respected.

We suggest the following policies for these situations:

-   **Reading of names during graduation ceremonies.** Reading the names of students in the graduating class or others in the school community who died during the time the cohort was in the school may help those participating in the ceremony honor the memory of people they cared about. Inform participants beforehand that this will happen (e.g., through an announcement to students and a note in the program).

-   **If family members of those who died are interested in participating as observers, welcome them.** Let family members know if and how their loved one will be recognized (e.g., in a reading of names).

-   **Award posthumous diplomas to qualified students.** Students who completed sufficient credits to graduate prior to their death may qualify for a diploma. It can be presented to someone the family chooses (family member, coach, teacher) at the graduation ceremony.

Again, inform participants beforehand this will be happening, present the diploma in the same manner as other student diplomas, and note that the diploma is posthumously awarded (perhaps in a footnote in the program). This award should not overshadow the accomplishments of other students.

- **Photographs of deceased students or staff can be included in the yearbook.** The yearbook might include a page with photos and names of all students and staff who have died during the period the cohort was attending the school, but a tribute section or page honoring a single individual is usually best avoided. Photos of school activities that include someone who has died may be included. Photos taken at family events or by friends outside of the school are not part of the collective experience of the class and are therefore usually less appropriate.

HANDLING REMINDERS OF SORROWFUL OR TRAUMATIC EVENTS

The goal of memorialization is for students to remember the person who died and what they wish to learn as a result of their relationship with the deceased. This is not the same as remembering the details of the death itself.

Sometimes, planned memorial events heighten sad or distressing reminders of the person or of frightening, sudden, or violent events that led to the death. This can underscore fearful feelings or worries about safety.

When a school, community, or nationwide crisis occurs, students and educators alike may experience a resurgence of feelings associated with the event around the time of the 1-year mark. The tendency to reference major violent crisis events by their dates (which became especially prevalent after "9-11" was used widely to reference the World Trade Center attacks in 2001) may increase the extent of such anniversary reactions. Students may notice other markers as well—graduation, special events, the 2-year mark, and so forth. Coverage in public and social media at these times may include photos, video, or sound recordings that can serve as painful or even traumatic reminders.

When possible, it is best to minimize explicit, detailed reminders of the traumatic event. For example, a moment of reflection during morning announcements a year later to remember a classmate who died on the playground may be helpful. However, scheduling a moment of silence to occur during a special gathering on the playground near the site of the death and at the same time of day the incident occurred has a greater risk of triggering memories of the traumatic event itself.

SUPPORT FOR THE FAMILY

In addition to commemoration or memorialization, it is also helpful for schools to think through the types of contacts they will have with the family of a student or staff member who has died. For example, schools will want to arrange a time for the return of the deceased's personal effects to parents or family members. They can check with the family to see when they feel emotionally ready to receive these items.

After a student has died, let classmates know that their belongings are going to be returned to the family. The materials can be gathered together, typically outside of regular school hours, and made available at the office so that the parents do not have to go through the emotional challenge of cleaning out their child's desk or locker; a representative of the school may offer to bring the child's belongings to the family's home. This exchange may take place after school hours to protect both the family and the students. We recommend that a member of the school crisis response team or school mental health staff be available as well to provide support to the family.

In most cases, the family should also be removed from the school mailing list as appropriate (e.g., if no siblings are in the school), so they do not inadvertently receive routine mailings. However, some families may wish to receive ongoing information so they can follow the progression of their child's friends and classmates.

In some cases, families blame the school or school staff for their child's death. Staff who make contact on behalf of the school with a family should be chosen carefully for their ability to offer compassion and understanding while not commenting on the cause or responsibility for the death. Staff should be informed of any previous contact with the family that suggests these types of issues may arise. Even without any advance warning, it is useful to recognize that anger and blame are common expressions in grief. Be prepared for the possibility of negative reactions.

On the other hand, schools that prohibit all contact of staff with the family after a death may only reinforce the family's perception that the school is uncaring. It also deprives family members of the support that might otherwise come from continued contact with people who knew their child well and were important in their child's—and the parents'—lives. The social life of parents often revolves around their child's life, and school is a large part of this.

MOVING FORWARD AS A COMMUNITY

One of the overarching goals of all of these commemorative efforts is to keep the school on track doing what schools do—caring for children's well-being and supporting teaching and learning. Each situation is different, and the goal of policies related to commemoration is not to establish hard-and-fast rules that are rigidly applied but to come up with a process that involves the input of interested parties with appropriate expertise—administrators, school mental health staff, students, teachers, and other educators.

Sometimes, it may be appropriate to make an exception to a policy. This is something that must be considered on a case-by-case basis. There are no absolute guidelines. For example, we agree with the notion that schools should generally not be renamed after a deceased student or staff member immediately following their death. However, we know of a private school that made the decision to rename their school after a school administrator, who was also the school's founder, following his death. This idea was embraced by students, staff, and parents alike.

Ultimately, the way each person is remembered by friends, teachers, peers, or colleagues depends on the particular situation. This includes who the person was, what caused the death, and how those who grieve feel they want to express their feelings and cope. It involves the ways they want to offer support to the family and the rest of the school community. It is important that memorialization in different situations is equitable and fair. This does not mean it must always be the same.

It is also helpful to remember that school communities that come together to support each other and commemorate one of their members who has died are often brought closer together by the experience. The death of a student or staff member can be transformative for students, their families, staff, and the school community as a whole. Educators who understand the importance of giving children appropriate guidance and assistance at such times are in an ideal position to support such possibilities. The best outcome of the transformation is the support of growth and resiliency through which students and staff alike know themselves a little more deeply than they did before.

Key Concepts

- **Commemoration and memorialization help provide a context in which survivors can begin to make sense of a death.** They may find meaning and purpose in the life of the person who died.

- **Commemoration and memorialization can be helpful to children and are appropriate in school settings when a death has affected a classroom or school.** Simple activities are often all that is needed.

- **It is vital that students have a role in planning how to commemorate a classmate, teacher, or other member of the school community who has died.** Children can suggest activities that are relevant to their circumstances.

- **Educators and schools can take steps to ensure that students plan a positive activity that makes sense to them.** These include asking questions, engaging them in discussion, exploring feelings, and helping them find direction.

- **Policies about commemoration and memorialization can help schools plan appropriate activities that are most likely to benefit students and staff.**

14

Taking Care of Yourself

When educators and schools take the steps outlined in this book, they help bereaved students in some of the most important ways possible. They can offer families advice and support that help them cope with their own grief while supporting their children. Through guidance and teaching, educators can also help all students develop a deeper understanding about death, loss, compassion, and how to be supportive of a grieving friend. They can model for students the ways in which to reach out to others in time of need. They can help establish a sense of community where students care about one another and express this in words and actions.

Educators can realize benefits, as well. Most educators go into their profession because they want to help children learn and grow. There are few better ways to do this than to help students cope with one of the most difficult challenges of their lives. It is gratifying to reach students by understanding their needs and helping them better understand themselves.

There are few better ways to help children learn and grow than to help students cope with one of the most difficult challenges of their lives.

Educators who make these efforts often find they can connect with their students in a qualitatively different manner. They impact students' lives in powerful and meaningful ways, helping them realize that adults around them can and do care. Quite often, just a small amount of effort, which may be associated with a bit of initial discomfort on the educator's part, can have a significant positive impact on students. Ultimately, this can be very uplifting for educators. It is quite gratifying to realize that a small amount of work can play a role in helping children manage these difficult situations and minimize the time in which they feel isolated, confused, and distressed.

However, many educators feel somewhat unprepared or apprehensive about addressing topics such as death. Some are afraid that if they reach out to a grieving student, they will do the wrong thing or start something they will not know how to complete. Sometimes, educators may be so moved by a particular student's or family's situation that they find they want to extend themselves a bit further. This can be difficult to manage, given educators' already busy days.

Another possible difficulty, which was mentioned previously, is that once students know they can approach a teacher or other staff member on difficult matters, they may want to talk about other challenges in their lives. Such educators may receive more requests from both students and colleagues to respond to children's needs about bereavement, difficult family situations, conflicts with friends, or a wide range of other matters. When too many of these requests are focused on one individual, that educator is likely to feel overburdened by the demands.

One of the best solutions to all of these issues is to train educators broadly in how to support grieving students. Talking with children about grief should not be the special province of one or two individuals, but something that many educators feel prepared to do. Training helps educators build skills, ensures that schools have many staff prepared to help grieving students, and strengthens the emotional support that allows educators to do this work well. Educators can also think carefully about how confident they feel doing this work, as well as how much they are able to offer in terms of practical matters such as time and emotional energy (see "Preparation: Ready to Help Students" later in this chapter).

Talking with children about grief should not be the special province of one or two individuals, but something that many educators feel prepared to do.

I Care and Want to Help

Paul, a 7-year-old student, was participating in a study about ways children understand death and experience loss. He had given a response to an interviewer named Laura that raised concerns. She spoke with the head of the study, who worked at the school as a consultant. This individual followed up by requesting a private meeting with Paul. The teacher released the student from class to speak with the consultant. Paul came in and said hello. He recognized the man because he had talked to Paul's class earlier about death and grief.

The consultant said, "I was concerned about something you said when you spoke to Laura last week. It made us wonder if something was bothering you, and if there was anything we could do to help."

Paul looked surprised, and then he started to cry. Yes, he was troubled. His father was abusing cocaine. It was getting worse every day. He wanted someone to make sure his father would be okay and that he would not die. He worried about this all the time.

When the consultant spoke to the principal about Paul's concerns, it became clear that this wasn't the same Paul who had given the troubling response to Laura. A substitute teacher who didn't know the students' last names had sent the wrong boy. Yet, this student, essentially chosen at random, was simply told someone cared and wanted to help. He revealed some deeply troubling concerns in his life.

Every day, children carry to school feelings related to big problems. They deal with homelessness, parental substance abuse, community violence, bullying in school, and a host of other issues. Educators identified as trustworthy resources for support may discover many challenging things about their students.

Educators do not need to solve all these problems; however, having resources on hand that can provide some assistance is helpful. Educators should involve school mental health professionals for children with more significant concerns. If children do not receive support for their concerns, it will be difficult for them to concentrate on their work and make true progress at school.

COMMON REACTIONS FOR EDUCATORS

Educators identify a number of personal challenges when dealing with bereaved students. The following section outlines some of the most common issues, as well as suggestions for addressing these concerns.

Triggers for Personal Grief

Few educators have not been touched in some way by grief and loss. Most have experienced the death of a friend or family member. Any time people are exposed to others' grief, it can act as a trigger for their own past experiences. This is one reason people cry at movies or manage to "keep it together" at a funeral until they see someone else crying. It is not surprising that talking with students about the death of someone they loved could trigger an educator's grief.

These triggers can be even more powerful if the death affecting a student is in some way similar to an important loss the educator has also experienced. Educators who lost a parent while young may feel a student's loss of a parent quite deeply. Someone whose father died of cancer may feel more deeply affected by a student whose father also died from cancer.

_____

Any time people are exposed to others' grief, it can act as a trigger for their own past experiences.

_____

Remembering Her Brother's Murder

A high school teacher found herself deeply disturbed after the shooting death of a student at her school. More than a month later, she was still having trouble sleeping; she felt distracted, jumpy, and sad. She was sometimes overcome by powerful urges to cry in the middle of a class and felt uncharacteristically irritable with her students. The intensity of her feelings puzzled her because she was not present at the time of the shooting and had not known the student who was killed.

A consultant came and spoke to the staff about the impact of grief on students and staff. He mentioned triggers for personal grief. It suddenly occurred to the teacher that the student died on the anniversary of her own brother's death—he had been murdered many years prior. She had not made the connection until that moment. Understanding this helped her feel much better; she no longer felt as distressed and was finally able to get a good night's sleep.

Having to explain death to children requires that educators put into words things many of us may find hard to acknowledge—their family member or friend is dead and will never be back. Once someone we love dies, we will never see that person again. It is quite likely that we will miss the person for the rest of our lives. This reminds educators of people they have lost and the reality that they, too, will continue to miss those people.

Concern About the Support Grieving Students Receive From Their Families

We probably all have a picture in our mind of the "perfect" supportive setting for children and families to cope with grief. However, what educators see in reality is often less than perfect. Some families do not have the resources that many of us take for granted—caring friends, extended family, or a faith community. We might come up with a dozen good suggestions for providing support to a grieving student, none of which are practical for a particular family at that point in time. At these incredibly stressful moments, good parents may not be at their best. Parents who are already challenged by mental illness, substance abuse, health issues, or other matters may be even less able to support their children.

Resentment and Guilt

Many demands are placed on educators. There are few other professions that ask for as much with so little recognition. If this is the baseline for educators, and then they are asked to do even more for bereaved students, feelings of resentment might understandably emerge. Resentment is most likely to occur when educators feel they are expected to do something they have not been prepared for, are not supported in, or do not have the time to do. They may feel that they are just being given more work to do, asked to spend more time, or expected to learn more skills—and that the work is emotionally challenging in the bargain.

Guilt is another uncomfortable but understandable reaction that educators sometimes have. They might feel guilty because they are resentful about the extra work and effort it takes to support grieving students (e.g., "How can I feel resentful when my student is suffering so much more than I am?"). They might feel guilty because they do not feel that they are spending enough time with a bereaved student. They might feel guilty because a bereaved student is coping with a level of suffering and loss they have never even imagined in their own lives.

Resentment is most likely to occur when educators feel they are expected to do something they have not been prepared for, are not supported in, or do not have the time to do.

RECEIVING AND GIVING SUPPORT

One of the things educators are asked to do with bereaved students is to encourage them to seek support from friends and adults they trust. Talking about the complex experiences of grief and loss is one of the best ways for children to work through their feelings and come to a meaningful personal understanding of a death.

This same strategy works for adults who are supporting bereaved children. Educators, parents, health care providers, and mental health professionals all benefit from the opportunity to discuss their own responses to children's losses. It is important to identify friends, colleagues, and professionals who can listen well. It is also helpful to consciously plan personal strategies for such things as managing personal triggers, concerns about students' families, feelings of resentment, or the stress, sadness, or other states that can interfere with work and personal life. The following are some suggestions:

- **Remember that grief is difficult.** These are painful feelings to experience and to witness. When grieving children—or adults—are asked to talk about the things they are feeling, they usually look distressed. They may become upset. They may cry or express anger or hopelessness. It is difficult to feel as if someone has been helped if he or she is obviously upset. If the person seems more distressed during or after the talk than prior to it, the educator might feel as if reaching out was unsuccessful. Yet, this very expression of painful feelings is what people most need to be able to do when they are grieving.

  People often offer this kind of support at the point when the distress is greatest. If they do not have further discussions with the bereaved person, especially conversations about feelings, they may not see the signs of movement and recovery. This is an excellent reason to follow up with students even a year or two later. Educators will feel gratified and reassured when they see children doing better.

- **Talk with others.** Among family, friends, and colleagues, several people might be able to lend an ear. Simply telling the story (while respecting privacy issues) can sometimes lift the burden of sadness, discomfort, or concern. Even when educators know rationally that they have been helpful to a student, that the reactions they are having are common, and that they have offered the type and amount of support that is appropriate, it can help to hear someone they trust affirm this.

It is also useful to look for something positive to share. Was an educator struck by a surprising bit of wisdom from a student? Was the educator gratified to know that a student trusted him or her? Was the educator pleased to realize that he or she knew how to respond to a student's comments or questions? Adding a positive observation makes the sharing easier on the listener. More important, it helps bring greater balance to the situation.

- **Talk with professionals.** There are times when the support of family, friends, and colleagues is not the right match for one's concerns, or it is simply not enough support. This is usually the case when discomfort, guilt, resentment, personal mourning, or other troublesome feelings persist, become especially strong, or interfere in some way with personal or work life. Talking with a mental health professional is also an important step when educators are unsure about what to do for a grieving student, a family, or a class coping in some way with death. Professional help might come in the form of an employee assistance program, a mental health or bereavement specialist who acts as a consultant to the school or district, or a private therapist.

- **Build skills in stress management.** Education can be a stressful profession, and having strategies for personal management of stress makes sense for all educators. These skills can be particularly helpful for educators when they offer support to bereaved students and come in a wide range of approaches. Some may work better than others. People have used simple exercises, such as deep breathing or muscle relaxation. Some find that regular physical activity and a healthy diet help them manage stress, feel better in general, and sleep better. Daily meditation, walks in nature, time with pets, and music are other approaches that are successful for some individuals.

  Courses and self-help books are also available to teach stress management exercises and skills. It is a good idea to identify several different approaches that work. Some can be used proactively (e.g., daily exercise), and others can be used when experiencing a particularly stressful day or moment. If one strategy does not work well in a given situation, another one might work better. Often, the approaches that work for managing stress are also good strategies for coping with other powerful feelings, such as sadness, frustration, anger, or anxiety.

- **Remember, you may be grieving as well.** It is difficult to experience the death of a student or colleague. Your own grief may affect feelings about your work, your students, and the future.

- **Give support to others.** Other members of the school staff may also be helping bereaved students. Listening to them describe some of their own challenges is a generous and compassionate act, and it can be helpful personally. This may be an opportunity to learn from the modeling of others—perhaps a colleague uses an approach with students that other educators have not thought of or tried. Often, someone else's experience provides a chance to work through a difficult situation vicariously. Thinking over what might be done in the same situation helps build skills in problem solving or provides a good way to answer a confusing question from a student.

  Finally, the simple act of helping others—in this case, by listening to their concerns—helps reinforce the positives in one's own life. People who have opportunities to connect with others and offer support generally experience greater overall satisfaction in their lives.

- **Seek consultation.** Educators are much more likely to find it stressful to support a grieving student when they lack confidence in their skills in this area or are unsure of how to deal with the particular situation. Teachers should not hesitate to seek the advice of their school's mental health professional or another staff member who is particularly experienced in this area. They could also seek the help of a consultant outside the school. Receiving additional training helps build skills and confidence. In addition, reading this book, we hope, is an important step in that direction.

SPECIAL CHALLENGES FOR LEADERS

Sometimes a death deeply affects an entire school, district, or community—because the deceased was especially well known and liked, or the death was particularly troubling, or a crisis incident such as a school shooting has occurred, or the media has become involved for some reason and is driving the conversation. Anyone who holds a leadership position in a school will be carrying unique responsibilities and burdens in these instances. Distinct challenges confront principals, superintendents, school boards, public information officers, chairs of school crisis response teams, directors of mental health services or related departments, or other leaders who stand before students, staff, parents, or the broader community.

Common Experiences for Leaders After a School Crisis

- **You will doubt your decisions.** A natural tendency of a good school leader is to take decisive action that protects students, supports staff, and keeps the focus on the school's primary purpose of education. No matter what steps a leader chooses in this kind of situation, however, things will not work out to everyone's satisfaction.

People will be upset, they will react with anger, and they will criticize your choices—often vocally and publicly, possibly amplified through social media at a local, state, or national level. You can't make everything okay. Not surprisingly, even very effective leaders begin to doubt their ability to make good decisions when literally every decision falls under intense, critical scrutiny.

- **You will have feelings about what has happened.** Someone has died. Leaders feel this loss. They see staff and students expressing grief, sadness, anger, and other emotions. This may accentuate leaders' own feelings about the death or bring up earlier losses. Yet many school leaders are uncomfortable sharing deeply personal or difficult feelings with their staff.

   You may find it difficult to accept emotional support from people you supervise. Some leaders share greater decision-making responsibility with their leadership team during these moments. This can create a sense of shared accountability for decisions. It can help create natural avenues for mutual emotional support as well. You may also find it helpful to seek support from a consultant or professional outside the school system. It is just as important for you to seek advice and to talk about your feelings as it is for your students and staff to do so.

- **Control issues may emerge.** It is not unusual for things to begin to feel out of control in these situations. Powerful feelings continue to materialize. There may be troubling revelations or accusations about the cause of the death(s) from family members or the community. There may be a disturbing series of social media posts or a negative story in the media. Some leaders respond to such moments by trying to exert more control.

   Stay thoughtful and aware of the ways your own control issues appear at these times. Most of these situations call for reflective consideration. An overexertion of control is unlikely to be productive.

- **Conflicts and disagreements will arise.** Some will be unique to your situation. Others will be more common across different circumstances. Examples include:

   ○ *Security.* If the incident involved a threat to students, some will appreciate the presence of extra security measures or ask for even more. Others will complain that the additional measures are unnecessary and make them feel less safe. Parents and staff may question whether it is safe enough to return to school after an infectious disease outbreak or pandemic, whereas others may argue that certain risks are unavoidable or even acceptable.

   ○ *Time lines.* How long should grieving take? When should the school focus as much again on academics and learning and less on recovery? The time frame will be too long for some and too short for others.

- ○ *Commemoration and memorialization.* As we discussed in Chapter 13, there can be many disagreements about how to commemorate a crisis incident or memorialize students who died.

- ○ *Use of donated funds.* After a crisis, community members and businesses often wish to make donations to help out. Expect many different opinions about the best way to put these funds to use.

- **There may be calls for your removal, or that of other leaders.** After a tragedy, it is natural for people to wonder if there was some way it could have been prevented. This is why school leadership carefully examine crisis events to identify steps to ensure greater safety in the future. The steps schools take, however, will not be satisfactory to some in the community. Parents may find it difficult to send their children back to school if they feel nothing substantial has changed or that the changes made are insufficient. Grief may be channeled into anger and blame. If no one in leadership is responsible for the crisis, then there is nothing that will clearly prevent it from happening again. Many parents will find this unacceptable.

  As a school leader, you may become the focus of this blame and outrage. You may be described as someone who has erred or demonstrated incompetence. There may be calls for your removal. These are further reasons to consider a shared decision-making process and the support of an outside consultant.

- **Colleagues may be more difficult to work with than usual.** The reactions people have when they are experiencing crisis, grief, loss, fear, uncertainty, and confusion will be varied. Some will step up to be more present, helpful, and committed. Some will become more irritable, inflexible, or intolerant. Most will probably be a bit of both.

  You may be struggling with colleagues who are less predictable and more difficult to work with. This is a time for much patience and understanding (and another good reason to consider sharing your own frustrations with an outside consultant).

- **You will still need to integrate new people into your system.** How many new staff come into your school or system each year? These educators are likely to know about the events that have occurred and come with an intent to help. However, it can be difficult for staff present at the time of a crisis to fully accept or feel comfortable with new people who have not shared the same experiences.

  Bring particular attention to onboarding processes for new staff. This might include such steps as an orientation that provides full information about what happened and how the school is taking steps to recover; assignment of newcomers to mentors who will actively welcome them; and professional development for all staff that addresses, among other topics, the impact of crisis and loss on professionals and how it can alter team dynamics and school climate.

- **All of your other work will continue.** The work of leadership cannot come to a full stop to focus on the recovery of the school. School administrators who are putting great amounts of time and effort into responding to a crisis will still need to put great amounts of time and effort into all the other tasks of leading a school or district.

  You might be given some leeway on deadlines for reports, policies, or new hires, but these are usually temporary. We ask students to talk about their feelings after a death or a school crisis because doing so helps them cope with what has happened and become prepared to focus again on learning. You can gain similar benefits when you are able to share your thoughts and feelings through this process—you will be better able to stay on top of general tasks as they continue to develop rather than fall behind.

- **You will need to schedule time off.** Yes, the work continues. And it will never be done. Leaders need sleep, time with their families, and time to eat a nourishing meal. They need time to read a good novel or look at the stars or listen to their favorite music.

  These may be the most difficult times for you to focus on self-care. We have seen leaders who are literally working 20-hour days, 7 days a week, sometimes for months after a crisis event. You will not make your best decisions or live your best possible life if you do not build in time to rest and restore.

PREPARATION: READY TO HELP STUDENTS

The NCSCB strongly endorses ongoing training for educators on issues of grief and bereavement. Training provides information, builds skills, and establishes norms about what educators can and should do to support grieving children. One of the greatest benefits is that schools or districts that organize such trainings are making a clear administrative pronouncement that this type of support for students is appropriate, expected, and supported.

Trainings also allow a broader sharing of responsibility for the support of bereaved students. When more educators understand and gain these skills, they can act with greater confidence. Students receive better support, and individual educators are less likely to feel overwhelmed or resentful because they are carrying an unfair share of this work.

Because every grieving student's situation is unique, and because some students' situations are complicated, the NCSCB also encourages schools to establish an ongoing relationship with another professional who can provide consultation regarding issues that affect students who are grieving. This might be a school nurse or a health or mental health professional within the school district or in the community who is familiar with child development, mental health, and bereavement. Many communities have children's bereavement centers and programs with staff who specialize in bereavement among children and adolescents. Some have mental health, crisis, or bereavement programs affiliated with local medical or educational institutions.

Ideally, a consultant could help deliver staff trainings on children and grief. In addition to helping teachers and other staff learn about supporting bereaved students, this provides an opportunity to meet the consultant and make a connection. This will make it easier for educators to contact the consultant at a future time with questions about specific situations they are facing.

TAKING CARE OF YOURSELF

Here is a simple truth about supporting children who are grieving: *If you are talking to children who have lost a family member or friend or talking to students generally about death and grief, you will find yourself examining your own feelings about death.*

Students, through their own natural curiosity about the world, will offer all kinds of interesting ideas and questions. Because students can be quite sensitive to the feelings that accompany grief, educators may see powerful expressions of emotion. Educators will have reactions to students' comments, experiences, and feelings.

If you are talking to children who have lost a family member or friend or talking to students generally about death and grief, you will find yourself examining your own feelings about death.

Educators' own life experiences will become part of this process. If they have lost loved ones in the past, they will probably revisit some of that grief. If educators have unresolved emotional issues with someone in their life who has died—a mother they did not get to say goodbye to, a brother who died after a painful family argument—those issues may well emerge again.

If someone in an educator's life is dying, educators may feel their own anticipatory grief more keenly when talking with a bereaved student. As mentioned earlier, these are times when an educator may have less to offer the grieving student and when it will be important to find others to step in.

Even if educators have never known well anyone who died, they will come face-to-face with feelings and ideas about death. They might wonder if, when they do have this experience, they will cope as well as their students. They might struggle with how unfair it is that a child has to go through such a profound loss. They might feel anxious about the perfectly healthy loved ones in their own lives, because talking with children about death involves the recognition that life is fragile and uncertain—we and the people we love will also die one day.

Here, we think, is another truth about supporting grieving students: *You will be rewarded for doing it.* When we reflect on our conversations with children about death and grief, we find ourselves examining some of the most essential issues of our humanity. What is life? What is it about? What is it for? Why do people suffer? What is my purpose?

These connections with students allow educators to find meaning in their work and enrich their personal lives. If we never think about losing the people we care about, we may not be able to value our relationships as deeply. If we are overwhelmed by fears that those we love will die, we will find it difficult to enjoy the time we have in their company. However, when we find we are able to cope with these apprehensions, our acknowledgment that death is inevitable for everyone can actually enhance our lives.

Great literature, drama, movies, and art usually focus on issues of loss for good reasons. We are drawn into that experience for a period of time and then released, often with a deeper understanding of our own lives. Sharing in the experience of grief with children often has a similar effect.

This *is* emotional work. Taking steps to take care of oneself and support one's colleagues is an essential component of the work. By doing so, educators will be able to offer the most useful support to their students. They will also get the most out of the process—personally and professionally.

Key Concepts

- **Educators benefit from offering general advice and guidance about death to all students and support to grieving students.** They impact their students' lives in powerful and meaningful ways, and this is very uplifting for most educators.

- **Educators may also feel apprehensive about taking these steps.** Educators may feel unprepared to address matters related to death and grief, worry that they will say the wrong thing, or feel overextended and unable to offer the extra effort.

- **Educators have a range of common reactions to these efforts.** These include such things as experiencing grief triggers, worrying about the support students will get from their families, or being uncomfortable talking about death.

- **It is important for educators to think about and plan ways to receive support from others when they are supporting bereaved students.** Talking with friends and colleagues about the complex experiences of grief and loss can help educators manage many of the challenges of these efforts.

- **Witnessing the grief of a child can be an unsettling experience.** It is important to have friends and other adults with whom to talk to about these things.

- **School leadership will face particular challenges in self-care after a student or staff death or other school crisis.** It is helpful for administrators to understand these challenges and develop personal skills and leadership strategies to address them effectively.

- **Educators who talk with students about death and grief often find themselves examining their own feelings about death.** This can be both difficult and gratifying.

Afterword

SUPPORT FOR THE PRESENT AND THE FUTURE

Educators know they can play an influential role in the lives of their students. Most go into the profession because they, too, were inspired and supported by educators when they were young. They care about the welfare of children, and they believe in the power of education to transform lives and societies.

The death of a family member or friend is a common experience that most children will have before they complete their schooling. When educators step in to help children cope, it can be a powerful intervention. On balance, it is an excellent investment of time and effort. Often, adding just a few extra moments to an already existing lesson or responding to an unplanned teachable moment gives students a chance to understand more about common reactions to grief or the Four Concepts About Death—general advice and guidance that will serve them well at whatever point they might face the death of someone they know. When a death does occur in a student's life, it usually takes only a little bit of time for an educator to relay his or her concern to the student. These brief interventions can be enormously meaningful. They may be some of the most important and enduring lessons any educator will provide.

We think the following stories from educators who have taken such steps say it best.

I teach sixth-grade science. A student in one of my classes lost her mother to illness. I wasn't sure how to be a support for her but decided to go to the funeral and hoped that would be helpful.

Her family's culture was different from my own, so there were things going on at the graveside and the service that weren't familiar to me. I felt some awkwardness personally, but I just kept being there, being respectful, thinking about my student, wishing her the best. After the service, I went up to speak to her. She turned around and just hugged me, and really held on! We stood there holding each other for a couple of minutes. I kept saying things like, "This must be so hard for you," and "You're going to be okay. I know it's really hard."

I'm so glad I made that effort to be there and to speak to her. I knew it made a big difference to her, so I felt better about myself as a teacher and, frankly, as a human being. It was the right thing to do. And she continued to be very connected to me and to the class through the rest of the year.

One of my students lost her brother tragically in a car accident. He was very young. I didn't know the family personally, but I did go to the wake. My student seemed appreciative that I attended.

I hugged her at the wake and told her I was sorry. She was out of school the rest of the week but returned the following Monday. I just let her know she could take her time making up the work she missed. She didn't really need the extra time. She had kept up with everything.

After this, she seemed as if she was trying to show everyone she was fine. She smiled more than I had seen her smile all year. I checked in with her occasionally and let her know she could talk with me if she wanted to. But she never did.

I hope she felt supported by the things I said and did. It's a little hard to know for sure, but I'm still glad I reached out to her.

I had a student last year whose father died. She was having a hard time coping with this loss. Her mother never allowed her to express her emotions about this. She kept insisting her daughter just "get over it."

Fortunately, our district social worker had set up a support group for bereaved students. She's someone who has a counseling degree, and she has been a wonderful resource for our students. I referred my student to the group. The meetings occurred once a week during the school day. This made quite a difference for the girl. It was important for her to have some place where she could experience and make sense of her grief, and the group made that possible for her.

I teach in our school's special education program. I have an eighth grader who has a reading disability but otherwise learns easily. She's good with people; a little street smart; and a vivacious, outgoing girl. Both teachers and students have always liked her.

Early this year, something changed dramatically. She was angry, she acted out, her classroom performance went way down. No one could figure out what had happened—she just took a dive. I pulled her from class one day and said, "What's going on here? You're not the same person."

She told me that her "granny" had lung cancer and was going to die. This was clearly very upsetting to my student, but just having the opportunity to talk about it seemed to make things a little better. I let her know we could talk again any time she wanted. Soon after this, her family arranged for her to move in with the grandmother to help with her care.

Then this girl had another backslide. She was angry again. She didn't pay attention in class. She got into a yelling fight with another girl.

So, I talked to her again. She said she couldn't sleep. Every night when she went to bed, she worried that she was going to wake up in the morning and find her grandmother dead. I called in the mother for a family talk. I told her, "You know, this is a lot of responsibility to put on a 14-year-old." Her mom agreed, and so she moved in with the grandmother, too.

That really seemed to settle things down. The grandmother passed away a couple of weeks ago. I was supposed to go away that weekend, but I felt like I needed to be at the funeral, and I'm glad I was able to go.

The girl is making a good recovery. She's back in school, keeping up with her work, getting along with her classmates. When I checked in with her, she said, "I never knew that teachers cared." That was a pretty powerful line for me to hear.

I think if I had not talked to her, she would have continued to have problems and probably would have left our school. And really, all I did was tell her it was okay for her to feel sad and scared about this—anyone would in this situation. My own father died of lung cancer, so I felt like I understood a lot of what she was going through. I believe the whole experience was healing for both me and my student.

In the work we have done through the National Center for School Crisis and Bereavement, we have been repeatedly impressed with the power of educators' concerns for their grieving students. We welcome you into this community of educators who have made the effort to serve this critical role for their students. We are sure your students will be better off because of it.

References

Adams, D., & Deveau, E. (1987). When a brother or sister is dying of cancer: The vulnerability of the adolescent sibling. *Death Studies, 11*(4), 279–295.

Cain, A. C., & LaFreniere, L. S. (2015). The taunting of parentally bereaved children: An exploratory study. *Death Studies, 39*(1–5), 219–225.

Chin, D., Schonfeld, D., O'Hare, L., Mayne, S., Salovey, P., Showalter, D., & Cicchetti, D. V. (1998). Elementary school-age children's developmental understanding of the causes of cancer. *Journal of Developmental & Behavioral Pediatrics, 19*(6), 397–403.

Clunies-Ross, C., & Lansdown, R. (1988). Concepts of death, illness and isolation found in children with leukaemia. *Child: Care, Health and Development, 14*(6), 373–386.

Emswiler, M., & Emswiler, J. (2000). *Guiding your child through grief.* Bantam Books.

Ewalt, P., & Perkins, L. (1979). The real experience of death among adolescents: An empirical study. *Social Casework, 60*(2), 547–551.

Glazer, J., Pao, M., & Schonfeld, D. J. (2017). Life-threatening illness, palliative care, and bereavement. In A. Martin, M. Bloch, & F. Volkmar (Eds.), *Lewis' child and adolescent psychiatry: A comprehensive textbook* (5th ed., pp. 946–956). Wolters Kluwer.

Greenham, D., & Lohmann, R. (1982). Children facing death: Recurring patterns of adaptation. *Health & Social Work, 7*(2), 89–94.

Hoven, C., Duarte, C., Lucas, C., Wu, P., Mandell, D., Goodwin, R., Cohen, M., Balaban, V., Woodruff, B. A., Bin, F., Musa, G. J., Mei, L., Cantor, P. A., Aber, J. L., Cohen, P., & Susser, E. (2005). Psychopathology among New York City public school children 6 months after September 11. *Archives of General Psychiatry, 62*(5), 545–552.

Krell, R., & Rabkin, L. (1979). The effects of sibling death on the surviving child: A family perspective. *Family Process, 18*(4), 471–477.

Leash, R. (1994). *Death notification: A practical guide to the process.* Upper Access.

National Center for School Crisis and Bereavement. (2020). *Guidelines for responding to a death by suicide.* National Center for School Crisis and Bereavement. https://www.schoolcrisiscenter.org/resources/guide-responding-suicide/

National Center for School Crisis and Bereavement. (2020). *Guidelines for responding to the death of a student or school staff.* National Center for School Crisis and Bereavement. https://www.schoolcrisiscenter.org/resources/guide-responding-death/

Osterweis, M., Solomon, F., & Green, M. (Eds.). (1984). *Bereavement: Reactions, consequences, and care.* National Academies Press.

Rando, T. (1993). *Treatment of complicated mourning.* Research Press.

Schonfeld, D. J. (1993). Talking with children about death. *Journal of Pediatric Health Care, 7*(6), 269–274.

Schonfeld, D. J. (1996). Talking with elementary school-age children about AIDS and death: Principles and guidelines for school nurses. *Journal of School Nursing, 12*(1), 26–32.

Schonfeld, D. J. (2002). Almost one year later: Looking back and looking ahead. *Journal of Developmental & Behavioral Pediatrics, 23*(4), 1–3.

Schonfeld, D. J. (2005). Helping children deal with terrorism. In L. Osborn, T. DeWitt, L. First, & J. Zenel (Eds.), *Pediatrics* (pp. 1600–1602). Elsevier Mosby.

Schonfeld, D. J. (2007). Coping with the death of a student or staff member. *ERCMExpress, 3*(2), 1–12.

Schonfeld, D. J. (2012). Providing support for families experiencing the death of a child. In S. Kreitler, M. W. Ben-Arush, & A. Martin (Eds.), *Pediatric psycho-oncology: Psychosocial aspects and clinical interventions* (2nd ed., pp. 223–230). John Wiley & Sons, Ltd.

Schonfeld, D. J. (2019a). Helping young children grieve and understand death. *Young Children, 74*(2).

Schonfeld, D. J. (2019b). Death during childhood. In M. Augustyn, B. Zuckerman, & E. Caronna (Eds.), *Zuckerman Parker handbook of developmental and behavioral pediatrics: A handbook for primary care* (4th ed., pp. 198–202). Lippincott Williams & Wilkins.

Schonfeld, D. J., & Demaria, T. (2018). Supporting grieving students in the aftermath of a school crisis. In E. Bui (Ed.), *Clinical handbook of bereavement and grief reactions* (pp. 217–240). Springer.

Schonfeld, D. J., & Demaria, T. (2020a). Supporting children after school shootings. *Pediatric Clinics of North America, 67*(2), 397–411.

Schonfeld, D. J., & Demaria, T. (2020b). Supporting grieving students. In E. Rossen (Ed.), *Supporting and educating traumatized students: A guide for school-based professionals* (2nd ed., pp. 209–231). Oxford University Press.

Schonfeld, D. J., Demaria, T. (2016). Supporting the grieving child and family. *Pediatrics, 183*(3), e20162147.

Schonfeld, D., Johnson, S., Perrin, E., O'Hare, L., & Cicchetti, D. (1993). Understanding of acquired immunodeficiency syndrome by elementary school children—A developmental survey. *Pediatrics, 92*(3), 389–395.

Schonfeld, D., & Kappelman, M. (1990). The impact of school-based education on the young child's understanding of death. *Journal of Development & Behavioral Pediatrics, 11*(5), 247–252.

Schonfeld, D., Kline, M., & Members of the Crisis Intervention Committee. (1994). School-based crisis intervention: An organizational model. *Crisis Intervention and Time-Limited Treatment, 1*(2), 155–166.

Schonfeld, D., Lichtenstein, R., Kline, M., & Speese-Linehan, D. (2002). *How to prepare for and respond to a crisis* (2nd ed.). ASCD.

Schonfeld, D., & Newgass, S. (2003, September). *School crisis response initiative.* OVC Bulletin. U.S. Department of Justice, Office of Justice Programs (NCJ 197832). https://www.ovc.gov /publications/bulletins/schoolcrisis/ncj197832.pdf

Schonfeld, D., & Quackenbush, M. (2019). *After a loved one dies: How children grieve and how parents and other adults can support them.* New York Life Foundation.

Schonfeld, D., Quackenbush, M., & Demaria, T. (2015). Grief across cultures: Awareness for schools. *NASN School Nurse, 30*(6), 350–352.

Schonfeld, D., & Smilansky, S. (1989). A cross-cultural comparison of Israeli and American children's death concepts. *Death Studies, 13*(6), 593–604.

Smilansky, S. (1987). *On death: Helping children understand and cope.* Peter Lang Publishing.

Speece, M., & Brent, S. (1984). Children's understanding of death: A review of three components of a death concept. *Child Development, 55*(5) 1671–1686.

Spinetta, J. (1974). The dying child's awareness of death: A review. *Psychological Bulletin, 81*(4), 256–260.

Index